Theaters of the Everyday

Theaters of the Everyday

Aesthetic Democracy on the American Stage

Jacob Gallagher-Ross

NORTHWESTERN UNIVERSITY PRESS
EVANSTON, ILLINOIS

Northwestern University Press
www.nupress.northwestern.edu

Printed in the United States of America

10 9 8 7 6 5 4 3 2 1

Library of Congress Cataloging-in-Publication Data

Names: Gallagher-Ross, Jacob, author.
Title: Theaters of the everyday : aesthetic democracy on the American stage / Jacob Gallagher-Ross.
Description: Evanston, Illinois : Northwestern University Press, 2018. | Includes bibliographical references and index.
Identifiers: LCCN 2017043917 | ISBN 9780810136663 (pbk. : alk. paper) | ISBN 9780810136670 (cloth : alk. paper) | ISBN 9780810136687 (ebook)
Subjects: LCSH: Theater—United States—History—20th century. | American drama—20th century—History and criticism.
Classification: LCC PN2266 .G26 2018 | DDC 792.09730904—dc23 LC record available at https://lccn.loc.gov/2017043917

CONTENTS

Acknowledgments *vii*

Introduction
Re-enchanting the World *3*

Chapter 1
Brightness Is Seeing in a New Way: Thornton Wilder's Everyday Departures *37*

Chapter 2
Mediating the Method *75*

Chapter 3
As in Heavenly Raiment: Stuart Sherman's Ecstatic Quotidian *105*

Chapter 4
Dancing to the Cosmic Murmur: Nature Theater of Oklahoma's Poetics of the Everyday *147*

Coda
Ghosts in the Machine: Noise, Presence, and the Archival Everyday *193*

Notes *205*

Bibliography *221*

Index *229*

ACKNOWLEDGMENTS

I would never have begun this project, much less completed it, without the steady guidance, unfailing support, and luminous example of Marc Robinson. He shepherded the early research that led to this book with his perfectly judged editorial suggestions, large and small, his generously given ideas, and his unflagging faith. And he has continued to offer essential support and guidance since. His beautiful scholarship sets the standard to which I aspire. The only way I can think to repay him is to strive to be as good a mentor to my students as he has been to me.

It was thanks to Tom Sellar that I first saw Nature Theater of Oklahoma, the smallest of many gifts over years of fruitful collaboration. His graceful prose and editorial acumen have shaped the way I write or edit anything, be it an email, a review, an essay, or a book chapter. The influence of my other teachers at the Yale School of Drama—Elinor Fuchs, Catherine Sheehy, Jim Leverett, James Magruder, Gordon Rogoff, and Paul Walsh—is everywhere in these pages. Simple thanks don't adequately evoke the transformative years I spent in their classrooms learning to read, write, and see all over again.

I've been lucky in my editors over the years. Jessica Lustig, Angela Ashman, Jane Kim, Tom Finkel, and especially Brian Parks, my former editors at the *Village Voice*, provided an ongoing master class in style while I worked on this manuscript. (Michael Schulman was equally exacting and equally edifying to write for at another publication I'm not supposed to name in print.)

I'm grateful to my superb editors at Northwestern University Press, first Mike Levine, and now Gianna Mosser, for their careful attention and indispensable insights, and to the entire NUP team, especially Nathan MacBrien and JD Wilson. My thanks also to the two anonymous peer reviewers whose generous, thoughtful, and helpful reports have improved this book in all kinds of ways.

Jonathan Kalb read early drafts of two of these chapters, and I benefited tremendously from his astute comments. At several key points along the way, John Muse gave crucial advice, suggestions, and book recommendations. Alan Ackerman asked germinal questions. Joe Roach provided wise guidance. I'm indebted to Paige McGinley for her good counsel and good example over the years about teaching, writing, and much else besides. Martin Harries and Keri Walsh have been vital interlocutors. Robert Blacker and Des McAnuff gave me the life-changing chance to work for three seasons as a dramaturge at the Stratford Shakespeare Festival, the scene of my boyhood theatergoing, while I was in the early stages of conceiving this book, and I even, in one felicitous year, worked on Thornton Wilder's *The Matchmaker* while I was starting to write about his early plays.

Much of the work on this book occurred while I was teaching at the University at Buffalo. I'm especially grateful to Robert Knopf for essential advice and support, and to Lindsay Brandon Hunter, Tero Karppi, Eero Laine, and Ariel Nereson for their friendship and camaraderie. Sarah Bay-Cheng is in a category of her own. I count myself extremely fortunate to have had her as a mentor at the beginning of my academic career, and now as a friend. She's perennially provocative, and perennially inspiring. Her advice and example have influenced me incalculably.

I finished this book in my new academic home at the University of Toronto, and I'm grateful to the marvelous colleagues who have made me feel so welcome here, especially Nancy Copeland, Alexandra Gillespie, Holger Syme, VK Preston, T. Nikki Cesare, Scott Richmond, Antje Budde, and Tamara Trojanowska. Special shoutout to the carpool: Liza Blake, Melissa Gniadek, Danny Wright, and honorary member Terry Robinson.

Kelly Copper and Pavol Liska of Nature Theater of Oklahoma have been extraordinarily generous with their time and ideas, both during our initial interview and in correspondence since. Tappan Wilder kindly read a draft version of my Thornton Wilder chapter and bolstered me with his insights and enthusiasm. I'm grateful to Mark Bradford, the executor of the Stuart Sherman estate, for his support of this project, and for his permission to quote from previously unpublished writings. Thanks are due to the terrific librarians and archivists at the Fales Library at New York University, the Beinecke Library at Yale, and to Electronic Arts Intermix for graciously accommodating my many requests to view their holdings.

Writing workshops at the Mellon Summer School for Theater and Performance Research at Harvard University, under the expert leadership of Katherine Biers, provided many useful suggestions that remained operative through years of revision. My thanks to the Mellon class of 2011 for their insights and their camaraderie, and to Martin Puchner for convening an extraordinary assembly of thinkers. I presented early versions of portions of these chapters at the Cage: Credo centenary conference at the University of Toronto, the Intimate Mediations and Avant-Gardes working groups at the American Comparative Literature Association conference, the Risking Encounter, Virtuosity, Postdrama, and Transmedia working groups at the American Society for Theater Research conference, the Rethinking Realist Acting symposium at Fordham, the Performance Studies Working Group at Yale, the University at Buffalo Humanities Institute, and the Mediations of Authorship in Postdramatic Mediaturgies conference at the Vrije Universiteit Brussel. I'm grateful to these groups' various participants and organizers for the chance to rehearse my ideas in public, and with such helpful colleagues.

I'm lucky to be growing up in the profession with a cohort of young theater and performance scholars I deeply admire. I'm indebted to Julia Jarcho, Chris Grobe, Matt Cornish, Julia Fawcett, Christine Mok, Kate Bredeson, Drew Friedman, Joe Cermatori, Shane Boyle, Jen Buckley, and Ariel Watson for many transformative conversations over the years—and I look forward to many more to come.

The editors of *Theatre Survey*, *PAJ*, and *TheatreForum* gave me welcome opportunities to publish early versions of sections of this book, and offered many helpful suggestions for revision. I'm particularly grateful to Harvey Young at *Theatre Survey*, and to Nicholas Ridout, for their editorial acuity, guidance, and insight.

As I revised, I've been fortunate to draw on the editorial assistance and insights of brilliant scholars and friends whose ideas immeasurably improved this book. Larry Switzky has often asked the right questions at the right time. The amazing Shonni Enelow, ever incisive, ever inspiring, gave me crucial suggestions—many times over—for both my introduction and my Method acting chapter.

Miriam Felton-Dansky has been my invaluable friend, first reader, colleague, editorial collaborator, and strategic ally for more than a decade now, since we were both fledgling critics in our first semester of graduate school. She read every word of this book, most of them more than once, and every chapter, page, paragraph, and sentence is better for it.

A book takes a long time to write, and requires much sustenance. My friends outside academia—especially Joshua Sadlier-Brown, Benjamin Critton, and Mitch Smolkin—helped me keep the hardships of writing in perspective. This book is dedicated to my family: to my wonderful parents, Kathleen Gallagher-Ross and Arthur L. Ross, who kept me afloat in all these years of writing with their inexhaustible reserves of pride and love; and to my beloved sister, Anna, and beloved brother, Daniel, who likewise nourish me with their humor, care, and love. It is also dedicated to Gwyneth Muller, who entered my life while I was researching the last chapter of this book, and has brightened my everydays since. Through these years of change, some tribulation, and much joy, across distances, and now across a border, the shining thread that joins us has held fast, its light undimmed.

Theaters of the Everyday

Introduction

✦

Re-enchanting the World

The Little Things We Hardly Notice in Space and Time

"Choose the least important day in your life . . . It will be important enough."[1] This is the knowing counsel given by the ghost of Mrs. Gibbs to Emily Webb, herself recently deceased, as she is about to make her brief, wrenching return to the world of the living in the third act of Thornton Wilder's play *Our Town*. When Emily does return, she finds the humble phenomena she previously took for granted, the texture of an unimportant day, staged before her in a theater of revived experience. At once a spectator and an actor in the resurrected drama of her own past, Emily watches milk being delivered and breakfast prepared, listens to chat about the weather, and observes the matter-of-fact affection of daily family life. An audience to all the quotidian things she never really saw before, she finally notices the fragile beauty of the everyday life she couldn't apprehend while living it. Her impossible second look provides the clarifying insight of a first principle: "Do human beings ever realize life while they live it?—every, every minute?" Emily asks.[2]

This book presents the work of four American theater artists and groups for whom Mrs. Gibbs's injunction is both an artistic philosophy and a moral perspective, and to whom Emily's question is a haunting challenge. To them, the least important day, with its discarded words, fleeting sights, cast-off gestures, and forgettable objects, is more than important enough. By deliberately choosing such mundane subject matter, they dedicate their theater to transforming spectators' conceptions of what constitutes importance, both on and offstage. Thornton Wilder's theater unveils the constant motion roiling beneath the seeming stasis of everyday life. Lee Strasberg's acting methodology and the performances of the Method disciple Marlon Brando pay acute attention to the grain of authenticity in everyday speech, and attempt to teach spectators to listen that way, too. Stuart Sherman's miniatures reveal the mutual interpenetration of language and sensation in day-to-day life, unraveling audiences' perceptual assumptions. Nature Theater of Oklahoma's everyday epics reframe streams of casual thought to reveal the hidden narrative structures of consciousness, staging redemptive transformations that uncover the artistic forms latent in ordinary experience.

Each of these theaters of the everyday formulates unique aesthetic solutions to a common problem: how to truly see the ordinary world around us, to pay homage to the worlds of experience that arrive and disappear in every sensate moment. Each of these theaters of the everyday finds a wealth of artistic inspiration in phenomena seemingly beneath notice. In all of these theaters, the everyday is both a source of formal innovation and a central thematic preoccupation. My book endeavors to describe this theatrical poetics.

The everyday is at once an obvious and an elusive idea. Everybody has one, but its essence is predicated on not noticing it. Maurice Blanchot, observing that "the everyday belongs to insignificance," defines it as "what we never see for a first time, but only see again."[3] Fernand Braudel suggests that the everyday consists "of the little things one hardly notices in time and space."[4] Ludwig Wittgenstein, in an untitled text fragment, imagines a theater of the everyday in which we could see the invisible progress of an ordinary life—what we see all the time, but never from "*that*" mysterious transfiguring "point of view."[5]

Emily's situation as both actor and spectator in Wilder's thought experiment illustrates a complexity that is particularly germane to the everyday. This elastic concept encloses both our daily experience of the world, and that all-too-familiar world itself. As Rita Felski puts it, "we need to recognize the doubleness of everyday life, which enfolds two distinct constellations of issues; a mundane social world and a phenomenological relationship to that world."[6] In other words, the very idea of everyday life encompasses a theatrical relation: the perceiving and the things perceived; the spectator and the spectacle.

The everyday inheres in phenomena both vanishingly tiny and as big as our lives. It ceases to be everyday the moment we notice it, but it surrounds us through every waking moment. The everyday thus includes both the material stuff that populates daily life—objects used so often as to be unremarkable, landscapes tuned away into the background because of their familiarity—and the less solid business of perception and cognition. It names the clamoring experiential surplus that exceeds memory, consciousness, and thought. It encompasses perished sensations never articulated into concepts; half-verbalized ideas that fail to achieve writing's permanence; and the offhand gestures that color speech or fill the space between habitual movements. It refers to both the drudgery of the workaday human world and the recurrent, heedless cycles of the natural one. Always disappearing, replaced by new perceptions, vanishing into routine, the everyday is as ephemeral as any theatrical performance. But the corollary to the everyday's evanescence is its concreteness and stubborn solidity. It is always there, tempering high-flown ideals or exalted abstractions with day-to-day practicalities.

In saying that the everyday belongs to insignificance, Blanchot touches on two important, intimately connected truths about both quotidian experience and its translation into artistic form. The first is that, by definition, the everyday is not significant because it is not articulate or easily articulated. If it becomes remarked-upon, noteworthy, memorable, it ceases to be everyday. The everyday is what we don't remember, and it forms the vast bulk of our sensing and thinking, a great void surrounding our paltry recollections. The second is that the everyday, by most artistic definitions, does not signify. It is not visible within the usual vocabulary of art. Most artistic ideologies, idealist or grittily realist, classical or vanguard, deliberately exclude or repress the everyday either as insufficiently transcendent, in the former case, or as a necessary backdrop to exceptional doings in the latter, fading before the violence of the plot or images. Throughout the twentieth century, the everyday was most often visible as a scandalous disturbance in art: Duchamp's ready-mades, Cage's *4' 33"*, Warhol's soup cans. As Arthur Danto has argued, this disturbance generally manifested itself as unease about the corrosive emptiness or undermining banality of such seemingly meaningless artworks. These works, for many, heralded the end of art itself as it had been previously understood.[7]

Although Duchamp, Cage, and Warhol could hardly be said to share the same conception of the everyday, the outrage that attended their works was similar, at least inasmuch as it arose from similarly vehement perceptions of a border transgressed. In such debates, the everyday appears in negative: as the not-art, the insufficiently aesthetic, the risibly banal, the raw residue of the quotidian world. And we can also identify a concomitant aesthetic imperative—or, perhaps more precisely, an anxiety. If art's borders are not vigilantly policed, the weltering chaos of life outside the precincts of the museum or concert hall—or theater—will swamp everything. But for the theater artists I present in this study, the very insignificance of the everyday is a signal source of its aesthetic potential. Because so many of its phenomena lie outside the usual territories claimed by art, the everyday remains a vital source of unexhausted ideas, unnamed experiences, and un-depicted realities. This is perhaps what Jacques Rancière meant when he memorably described the "splendor of the insignificant."[8]

If the everyday disturbs conventional understandings of what subject matter belongs within the realm of art, broadly considered, it is perhaps even more disruptive of theatrical norms, where the age-old preference for action remains an article of faith. According to most received ideas, theater and the everyday couldn't be more antithetical. The mere notion of "drama," in both its casual and canonical definitions, implies doings transcending the ordinary. All the way back to Aristotle, the theater has usually been theorized as the home of the rough exception, not the humdrum rule: violent climaxes, explosive feelings, moral dilemmas, crisis, testing, incident, eruption, the final argument, the terrible choice, the decisive breaking point, and so on. This holds true of the acknowledged canon of American realist drama as well as the melodramatic theater it superseded. It is equally true of many avant-garde experiments designed to flout the conventions of these established forms.

Despite efforts to democratize the settings and demographics of drama throughout the twentieth century, theater's age-old bias toward the exceptional event held firm. Nothing could be less quotidian than the brutal life-or-death choices faced by Willy Loman (no matter how "common" his surroundings), the harrowing ordeals of Blanche DuBois, the inebriated confessions and reckonings of the Tyrone family. "I believe that the common man is as apt a subject for tragedy in its highest sense as kings were," writes Arthur Miller in *Tragedy and the Common Man*, which is perhaps the best-known encomium to the ordinary in American dramatic theory.[9] Although he dispensed with tragedy's class hierarchies, Miller preserved its traditional formula of a flawed protagonist struggling against an immutable universe:

> There are among us today, as there always have been, those who act against the scheme of things that degrades them, and in the process of action, everything we have accepted out of fear or insensitivity or ignorance is shaken before us and examined, and from this total onslaught by an individual against the seemingly stable cosmos surrounding us—from this total examination of the "unchangeable" environment—comes the terror and the fear that is classically associated with tragedy.[10]

To take a more avant-garde example, one tendency among theater collectives of the 1960s like the Living Theatre was to magnify everyday conflicts—"I'm not allowed to travel without a passport!"; "I'm not allowed to smoke marijuana!"—into revolutionary flashpoints, attempting to achieve Paradise Now! or the permanent blurring of art and life. And many contemporary efforts to render the durational qualities of everyday experience into theatrical form still maintain drama's bias toward what Fredric Jameson has called a "marked time brutally differentiating itself from ordinary existence": the momentousness of a decisive episode separating undifferentiated experiences from meaningful ones.[11] Annie Baker's recent play *The Flick* (2013), for example, which scandalized some audience members—prompting walkouts—with its dilatory silences, stuttering dialogue, and glacial plot development, all hallmarks of its devotion to everydayness, nevertheless revolves around a classic love triangle and stages a key juncture in its floundering characters' lives.[12]

But if we look at the everyday with fresh eyes, as the artists in this study all, in individual ways, strive to do, we find other theatrical attractions. Theater, the quintessential art form of disappearance, is particularly apt at capturing the fugitive nature of everyday experience. Its concentrated situation of perceiving spectators regarding material bodies and objects makes it a sensitive instrument for retuning perceptions of fleeting ephemera we might not notice outside the focusing frame of the theater. Inside the auditorium we notice more, and we notice our noticing. These qualities make the theater a threshold zone poised between the experiential surfeit of everyday life and the composed objecthood of more stable forms of art. The four American theater artists and groups presented in this study take up this potential of the theater as a perceptual laboratory, attempting to create artworks that enable Blanchot's impossible first glimpse of the everyday: to catch it as it escapes. They strive to stage Wittgenstein's *that* point of view.

The artists I examine do not seek to dignify the commonplace by democratizing conventional theatrical structures. Instead, they have invented new theatrical forms and aesthetics to focus spectators' attention on the perishable or habitually invisible aspects of everyday experience, the material objects that populate it, the evanescent words and thoughts people use to make sensible shapes of reality's unmanageable surfeit—even as those shapes disappear into contingent memory or simple oblivion. By thinking about the everyday in this way, I am deliberately tracing an alternative narrative of American theater, one that passionately refutes American realism's representational hegemony over the quotidian. To adapt a phrase from Peter Schjeldahl, I am interested in the artists who, rather than seeking to possess reality by creating fictional microcosms, instead allowed themselves to be possessed by it,[13] making inquiries into elusive matters of perception, memory, day-to-day creativity, and the wavering borderline between art and life. In choosing my case studies, I gravitated to artists for whom form and content merged in long-term artistic investigations of the everyday. Each of these chapters considers artists who spent years, or even decades, staging the ordinary across large bodies of work; sometimes, as in Stuart Sherman's case, throughout their entire creative lives. In all four of my examples, theater is conceived of as a medial site, situated between art and everyday life. It's a vehicle that carries one toward the other, in constant experiential arbitrage.

This book, then, traces a genealogy of the American theater of the everyday—an alternative tradition that is aesthetically and philosophically distinct from realism but is often obscured by it. Eschewing the high-stakes moral conflicts and tumultuous events that have remained the lifeblood of realist drama claiming roots in everyday life, these artists focus attention on the smaller but no less profound dramas of perception, experience, and affective life. For them, the everyday becomes a space in which to negotiate the competing demands of innovative form and democratic availability.

Unlike the anti-art provocations of the European avant-gardes, American artists, less subject to the weight of classical tradition, have been less interested in shocking confrontations than in dialectical exchange between the poles of "art" and "nonart," revealing unexpected philosophical and artistic terrain in the ongoing exchange between these two terms. In this way, the artists I consider here share characteristics with the tendency Lisi Schoenbach calls "pragmatic modernism."[14] They do not seek to abolish art's institutions altogether; rather, they point to the possibility of gradualist transformation in both institutions and the art forms they structure. As James Harding has recently pointed out, art's institutions played an equally foundational role in both the theory and practice of the American avant-garde as refuges from the instrumental pressures of the market and as hotbeds of intellectual ferment.[15] And so it shouldn't surprise us to discover that practitioners of the American theater of the everyday have not shared European artists' hostility to the structures and viewing practices of the theater itself. They have sought to renovate from within, rather than tear down and rebuild from scratch.

A simple commonality among the diverse artists considered here serves to illustrate this difference. None seeks to entirely abolish the distinction between spectators and actors or the basic viewing arrangements of the theater, two hallmarks of European avant-garde experiments in importing everydayness into the auditorium. In fact, it's hard to find a work of avant-garde theater—futurist or dadaist, surrealist or constructivist—that doesn't seek to dispense with this division in one way or another. But as I'll discuss a little later, the division between art and life, as formalized by the theatrical auditorium, is both more porous and less anxiety-producing for the American theater of the everyday. However, if the theater of the everyday's rhetoric is less vehement, the implications of its perceptual investigations are perhaps even more radical than the bellicose vision of the European avant-gardes.

With their practice, these artists formulated a definition of theatrical aesthetics that is intimately concerned with the materiality of perception, and the radical subjectivity of artistic experience. For them, every human mind is unique, and so is its encounter with an artistic object. These artists stake a claim for the aesthetic vitality of the humdrum, the mundane, the habitually ignored aspects of quotidian speech, movement, affective life, and indeed, consciousness. All these artists share an interest in tapping new aesthetic veins, making art from thoughts, affective states, or perceptual data that are usually considered too abject, inarticulate, amorphous, or ephemeral to find their way into art's delineated forms—reminding spectators of how much of our daily experience goes unnoticed, unseen, or unremembered. They find a place onstage for ignoble objects, orphaned speech, abandoned gestures, and the fleeting feelings that never find a place in more conventional art's rationalized pictures of emotion. They promulgate the democratic idea that art is an experiential category, not an inherent quality.

This makes the theater of the everyday an essential element of the much larger, and still unfinished, project of democratizing the American theater, of creating space for unheard voices, elided narratives, and most broadly, for difference—of perspective, experience, aesthetic priority, and aesthetic material. Artists seeking to make room for marginalized and elided voices in the American theater have always needed to change not only its narratives but the poetics of representation itself. To take just a few disparate examples: think of Suzan-Lori Parks's Great Hole of History, holding stories never written down and thus incapable of being inscribed in conventional narratives; or the geometric spectacles Robert Wilson built around his collaboration with the unique worldview of Christopher Knowles, who is autistic; or, very recently, the keenly poignant rites of queer mourning enacted by Trajal Harrell's fusion of classical tragedy, pop music, the drag ball, and postmodern dancing.

Artists of the everyday, likewise, seek to create space for material that has previously not made it into art at all: the humdrum aspects of daily existence, the transitory sights and sounds, the background objects and habits. But these easily overlooked quantities also insistently index foundational elements of experience, such as race, class, gender, and sexuality. Throughout this study, I attend to artists' revelatory insights—or their equally startling blind spots—about these constitutive realities. Method acting's search for the uncanny in everyday speech reinforced unexamined assumptions about race and gender, even as it transposed the sounds of immigrant voices to mainstream theaters and cinemas. Stuart Sherman's object performances unveil the queer and gendered realities obscured by the normative world of things, and map the manifold ways that ideological norms are reinscribed by everyday objects. For all the artists in this book, new ways of seeing forecast new modes of representation, and can suggest new ways of being in the world.

American theater has always found big meanings in the smallest things. Beginning with touristic plays like Benjamin Baker's *A Glance at New York* (1848) that portrayed day-to-day urban life as inassimilable clamor, a kaleidoscopic whirl surfeiting the eye, and with temperance dramas that staged the harmony of well-ordered domestic life as edenic innocence disrupted by insinuating drink, the melodramas of the nineteenth-century American theater housed transcendent implications in quotidian events. Early realists like David Belasco could allow themselves to be swept away by their scenic effects. You need only think of the protracted evocation of a moonlit night in the Sierra Mountains that opens *The Girl of the Golden West* (1905), lingering longer than any simple scene-setting, savoring the chromatic complexities, or his painstakingly perfect onstage re-creation of a Childs Restaurant—complete with cooking facilities—for *The Governors Lady* (1912) to understand that Belasco was chasing more than atmosphere. Susan Glaspell's incisive *Trifles* (1916), meanwhile, skinned back the surface of domestic life to reveal the powerful gendered biases conditioning attitudes toward household space and household objects.

In the 1920s, playwrights of the Harlem Renaissance like Zora Neale Hurston depicted ordinary African American lives in order to redress the pernicious representational politics of the American theater. Hurston's scrupulous attention to the rhythms and idioms of Southern black speech was carefully calibrated to refute the nostalgic idylls of plantation life still in widespread currency on American stages. She found authenticity—and the pervasive presence of painful histories—in the small details. This tendency was taken up and amplified by modernists like Thornton Wilder, becoming a primary engine of theatrical innovation throughout the twentieth century and into the twenty-first. It has also been a countervailing current arguing against American realism's aesthetic dominion over portrayals of everyday life. My book traces this theatrical lineage, as the everyday shifts from thematic content to formal principle. No longer satisfied with staging fictional representations of everyday objects and events, artists began to import "American things" themselves into the auditorium—ready-made gestures, found words, quotidian objects, overheard narratives.

Escaping the Iron Cage

The title of this introduction makes deliberate reference to Max Weber's famous pronouncement that modernity is characterized by the ever-increasing rationalization of daily life and with it, the progressive—and ineluctable—disenchantment of the world. Following Weber, we could even say that the notion of an "everyday" life, which is characterized by routine, habit, quotidian separation from larger cycles and schemes, and an even expanse of profane time, bifurcated between work and leisure, is a product of this process of encroaching rationalization. In Erich Auerbach's classic essay about the representation of the everyday in realist fiction, an early sketch for the project that became *Mimesis*, he makes a similar point, arguing that the everyday is characterized by relentless duration: by a sense of droning time unleavened by meaning or myth, both ephemeral and interminable. Indeed, he suggests that this temporality is partly the result of modern historical consciousness. The everyday is at once absolutely representative of the spirit of an age, profoundly meaningful, and utterly fleeting, the victim of history's remorseless forward drive, impossible to see in its full complexity.[16] In this view, the everyday is both ubiquitous and obscure. Fredric Jameson observes that the "more crucial point in Auerbach's differentiation of this 'everyday reality' from all the other traditionally named and categorized situations lies precisely in the fact that there is no name for what this one represents."[17]

But paradoxically, Weber also argues that because this pithed mundanity is the most representative product of a disenchanted world, the everyday will also be the scene of that world's attempted redemption. Writing on the cusp of the twentieth century's violent revolutions—artistic and political—he prophetically predicts that disenchantment will produce compensatory mystifications, re-sacralizations through intensified experience, in terms that describe the impetus behind both the artistic avant-gardes and the rise of political mass movements like Nazism and totalitarian Communism.

> But today there is the religious nature of "everyday life." The many gods of old, without their magic and therefore in the form of impersonal forces, rise up from their graves, strive for power over our lives and begin once more their eternal struggle among themselves. But

> what is difficult for modern man, and most difficult of all for the younger generation, is to meet the demands of such an everyday life. All hunting for "experience" stems from this weakness, for not to be able to look the destiny of time full in the face is a weakness. It is the destiny of our culture, however, that we will once more become more clearly aware of it, after our eyes have been blinded for a thousand years by the allegedly or presumably exclusive orientation towards the sublime pathos of the Christian ethic.[18]

For Weber, experience, as it will be for John Dewey, is the unit of analysis that reveals modernity's meaning problem. Without the old categories, we're left searching for new architectures to buttress a world that seems to have lost its plot, the consoling dramatic structure.

Revisiting Weber at the beginning of the twenty-first century, Jane Bennett picks up on this implicit paradox—that the everyday is both symptom of disenchantment and the scene of its possible redemption—arguing that despite the perpetual expansion of the rationalized world, there is always something left over in the abstracting of experience, something stubbornly resistant to its ordering. Like Zeno's arrow, the process never arrives at its projected target:

> Even where rationalization has achieved its widest scope, there remain aspects of experience that elude it, incalculable bits that float in and out of the iron cage, and inexplicable compulsions and convictions that make camp in the rationalized self. Nevertheless, in a disenchanting world, such bits are not let be but are treated as fugitives; they become targets of attempts to enclose them in a rational scheme. Perplexing phenomena are, for example, defined as temporal mysteries that will be resolved as science evolves—they are calculable even if we cannot yet do the math. Or, the fugitives can be referred to divine order of which they surely are a meaningful part. Finally, those pesky irrationalities can be relegated to the private realm of mysticism, or personal "values."[19]

Throughout this book, I'll argue that the theater of the everyday's recourse to the small, the accidental, the inexplicable, and the unforeseen pits it against the creeping calculability of the world. Bennett shows us another way to understand the insignificance, the smallness of the unnoticed everyday: as the grit in the austere gaze of modernity. The artists considered here seek to claim the "fugitive" aspects of experience. But they do not do so in order to enclose them within an enlarged rationality. Rather, these artists chase such experiential fugitives in order to find in their very imponderability a renewed wellspring of wonder, astonishment, and awe, the reenchantment of a secular world. Henri Lefebvre eloquently describes this mode of thinking when he points out that prolonged attention to the trivial makes it suddenly very important—and very strange.

> Once separated from its context, i.e. from how it is interpreted and from the things which reinforce it while at the same time making it bearable—once presented in all its triviality, i.e. in all that makes it trivial, suffocating, oppressive—the trivial becomes extraordinary, and the habitual becomes "mythical." In the same way, a humble plant taken from the soil and from the plants around it, seen up close, becomes something marvelous.[20]

This is the same vertiginous experience that Viktor Shklovsky famously referred to as "defamiliarization" (*ostranenie*). He argued that art should effect a redemptive departure of the everyday from the habitual, a departure that leads, in turn, to a redemptive return, through enriched attention, of the everyday to itself. Art exists, he said, "that one may recover the sensation of life; it exists to make one feel things, to make the stone *stony.*"[21]

These ideas help to clarify an essential distinction between realism and the art of the everyday. If we keep Weber and Bennett in mind, realism would seem to be the quintessential artistic style of a disenchanted world, creating calculable scale models of a quantified real. But as Fredric Jameson has argued, the realist impulse is characterized by an irresolvable conflict between narrative and experience. It ratifies the veracity of the former with vivid appeals to the latter. As such, realism is always confronting the preordained fable of the plot with the more ambivalent urgencies of what he calls "affects," feelings for which there are no ready-made names. For him, realism is a realm of named, objectified experience, but one that nevertheless contains the dialectical seed of its own dissolution.[22]

Departing from these ideas, I'll argue that the everyday is elusive territory, the territory of the not-yet named, half-articulate, felt-but-not described, seen-but-not-remarked-upon. The American theater of the everyday further radicalizes one side of Jameson's equation: The artists considered here mostly dispense with narrative in favor of concentrated attention to perception and affect. If revelatory moments of estrangement can only occur when a humble object or gesture suddenly leaps out from its accustomed, unnoticed place in our mental cabinets, we cannot remain satisfied with any such stable disposition. In this sense, the everyday remains the preserve of mystery, enchantment, and wonder because it's the realm of the unclassified, and unclassifiable—the real before it becomes an "ism." When fables do appear in the theater of the everyday, they are usually more self-reflexive, narratives about the making or watching of the artwork itself.

Nor, and this is an important distinction, do the artists discussed here seek the reenchantment of humble phenomena in the name of a valorized irrationalism or a primitivist resort to an imagined pre-civilized utopia.

The everyday does not lead them back in time or across borders. Rather, the everyday provides an occasion to acknowledge the notion, prevalent in current affect studies, that our lives, inner and outer, are not subject to our wills, and that the borders between thought and feeling, perceiver and perceived, object and subject, volition and accident are easily and habitually transgressed. If these artists seek a glimpse of the world before it is sorted into words, concepts, and percepts, they have no programmatic scheme for what such a glimpse might bring with it. Instead, their theater pragmatically recognizes that we are not completely rational creatures, and that no rational world can ever account for the strangeness of our minds. These reenchantments are clear-eyed, resolutely secular, and purposeful, not the result of unwitting ideological reification or regressive obscurantism.[23]

Jane Bennett's sense of the large meanings potentially radiated by small phenomena—the escapees from the iron cage—illuminates my understanding of the ready-made object tradition in art and theater. This tradition, I argue, extends far past the simple incorporation of everyday objects into collage or sculpture, encompassing Thornton Wilder's attempts to capture the roving glances of everyday life, Method acting's integration of mumbles and the Judson Dancers' restrained steps, Stuart Sherman's phenomenology of kitsch, and Nature Theater of Oklahoma's staging of ready-made narratives "found" in the minds of their acquaintances.

The appearance of ready-made objects in art is often considered evidence of the subversive desire to desacralize art, to skin it of its aura, and open the museum (or theater) to vertiginous ontological reevaluations. (Why should a shovel not be exhibited alongside a sculpture? Why is written poetry better than the sound of a blaring car horn?) But as Boris Groys puckishly reminds us, the ultimate ready-made was Jesus Christ, and all such re-ontologized objects participate in a tradition of messianic thinking that goes back much further than the very idea of "art" itself. In other words, what we "find" in the found object is the possibility of redemptive transformation. What Groys means is that, just as Christ was God appearing in the form of a human being, mostly indistinguishable from other human beings until his divine status was revealed, and then still a matter of perception bolstered by faith, the ready-made object is art masquerading as regular object—until, that is, the object's aesthetic nature can be revealed, by the prophet-artist.[24] Our disenchanting world preserves the possibility of such transformation in aesthetic precincts, even as its messianic implications fall away. Groys calls this a "difference beyond difference," and notes that such a recategorization allows the ready-made to transcend its usual material and historical limitations. In the museum, the object "lives longer and keeps its original form longer," looks "more 'alive' and 'real' . . . than in reality itself."[25]

I argue that a similar effect occurs when an everyday object, word, or gesture is transposed to the stage. This idea is important because the artists in this study resort to the accidental, reclaimed, abject, precisely because such profound reframings imply the possibility of other, unforeseeable transformations. Epistemic formations can be shaken by new ways of seeing. The everyday contains the seeds of its own transformation. Arthur Danto, too, points indirectly to this messianic armature beneath the radical provocations of anti-art art. The "transfiguration of the commonplace," as he calls it, is the aesthetic equivalent of the Christian idea of the salvation of the poorest, the least. For him, Duchamp's urinal raises a question that seems to demand a metaphysical answer: "why that particular urinal should sustain so impressive a promotion, while other urinals, like it in every obvious respect, should remain in an ontologically degraded category."[26] In this way, found objects, gestures, words, or stories, once de- and-re-contextualized, refute the disenchantment of the world. They refuse to sit still in the places we have assigned them. They embody the tantalizing promise of a difference beyond difference, hovering only just out of reach.

Theorizing the Everyday

This outlook separates the artists I consider here from the perspectives elaborated by much French everyday life theory. It's important to take a moment to elaborate these differences precisely because this body of thinking has been incalculably influential, providing inspiration and insights that were formative in both performance studies and broadly throughout the humanities. The best-known corpus of such theory originates with an extraordinary group of thinkers who confronted the new realities of post–World War II France with a potent mixture of penetrating suspicion and guarded optimism. It's no accident that the great flowering of French everyday life theory began in a period when suspicion of grand narratives was high, the Cold War put many kinds of promised utopias into deep freeze, and French culture seemed besieged on all sides by a creeping Americanism, colonizing daily life with commercialism and fetishized commodities. As historians and cultural theorists like Kristin Ross and Ben Highmore have in various ways pointed out,[27] France's thinkers turned inward to pore over the fabric of everyday experience during a particularly vexed time for French identity. France was simultaneously losing its colonial possessions while being colonized by American products, ideas, and lifestyles. This put Marxist thinkers like Henri Lefebvre in quite a bind; they were left to defend French habits from encroaching American ones (inseparable from modern capitalism) while also condemning them as quiescent and politically retrograde. (The Annales school of historians, Fernand Braudel prominent among them, took the long view. Retreating from human activity as the guiding principle for historical narrative, they fit the ebbs and flows of societies into larger natural cycles.)

For Lefebvre and, later, Guy Debord, faced with this conundrum, performance and theater became important theoretical tools. In Lefebvre's case, theater provided a model for cultivating a mode of sight capable of gazing, X-ray-like, past the familiar, to arrive at the deep ideological architectures of the everyday. Lefebvre begins the first volume of his magisterial *Critique of Everyday Life* with a paean to Brecht. The German theater theorist's conception of estranging reality onstage, revealing the hidden economic and political forces expressed in every social encounter, becomes the pattern by which similar germinal revelations might occur in daily life.[28]

A corresponding ambivalence about the political potential of the everyday characterized the tumult of the late 1960s, when the situationists assumed the mantle of both the historical avant-gardes and the political vanguard of the Left, merging aesthetics with politics. If redemption—historical, cultural, intellectual—would not come from grand historical forces, perhaps it could be found in daily life instead. And if totalizing theories weren't enough, perhaps art's methods could be a guide to revolt, gathering utopian energies, envisioning new futures in the present. Having lost the buoying narrative of organized revolution, the emphasis shifted to spontaneous performance in everyday life, rather than concerted action on the redemptive stage of history.

As Rita Felski points out, the project of both Lefebvre and Debord was in many respects the continuation by other means of the historical avant-gardes' war on bourgeois sensibilities. The values championed by many of the postwar everyday life theorists were indebted to those of their artistic forebears: disruption of habit, confrontation of the familiar with the strange, anti-institutional gestures, aesthetic shock as the spark for social transformation. According to this strand of everyday life theory, best represented by Lefebvre and by Debord's situationists, the everyday, as Felski eloquently puts it, "is seen to harbor inchoate impulses and unconscious desires that foreshadow an incandescent future of revolutionary upheaval."[29] When that transfiguring day arrives, the situationists declared, "everyone will become an artist in a sense which artists have never before achieved—in the sense that everyone will construct his own life."[30]

Several things about this perspective are worth highlighting. The first is teleology. This view, which finds redemptive power in the aestheticizing of the everyday, is directed toward a Marxist revolution that will permanently transmogrify society, and with it, art. Once everyone is free to unlock the inner artist, there will be no more art, in the hidebound, institutionally confined sense, since all of everyday life will be art. The artwork, in this view, is only the vicarious container for repressed energies that would be better expended fomenting revolt, or the surrogate for the spectator's own pent-up creativity. Furthermore, because all roads lead to revolution, this perspective is apodictic—in a manner that indicates a surprising paternalism latent in the French theorists' supposed championing of everyday life. The true everyday is unaware of itself, occluded by alienation, passivity, conformity, and unknowing-ness. As Felski incisively sums up:

> Thus even as theories of everyday life seem to embrace the mundane, they sweep impatiently and often imperiously over ordinary repertoires of belief and meaning. They assume a stark contrast between the political unawareness of the masses who deny or repress their alienated condition (Debord speaks of ordinary people censoring the question of their own everyday life) and the iconoclastic vision of a small embattled minority. This latter group defines its mission with a militant, quasi-messianic fervor; everyday life must be rescued, redeemed, saved from its own regressive tendencies. And like other avant-gardes, it draws on a future-oriented temporality to authorize its own project.[31]

For both Lefebvre and Debord, then, the unreconstructed everyday is a conservative force, made of history-denying repetitions and centuries of political quietude.

While Michel de Certeau, by contrast with Lefebvre and Debord, sees the everyday as a space of tactical resistance, the small subversions he theorizes still take place within a wider environment of repression, alienation, and coercion. In perhaps the most famous passage from his *Practice of Everyday Life*, he argues:

> Many practices (talking, reading, moving about, shopping, cooking, etc.) are tactical in character. And so are, more generally, many "ways of operating": victories of the "weak" over the "strong" (whether the strength be that of powerful people or the violence of things or of an imposed order, etc.), clever tricks, knowing how to get away with things, "hunter's cunning," maneuvers, polymorphic simulations, joyful discoveries, poetic as well as warlike.[32]

Allan Read makes the compelling argument that de Certeau's theory of everyday tactics is best understood as a rejoinder to Foucault's envisioning of a totalizing apparatus of power, a panopticon from which it is impossible to escape.[33] Indeed, de Certeau's gleeful enumeration of daily life's small victories over the powers that be is quickly succeeded by a grim reminder that these tactics merely "introduce an element of Brownian motion" into a system "too vast to be their own, too tightly woven for them to escape from it."[34] As Liesl Olson points out, in de Certeau's conception, "the everyday might resist the status quo but can never have any true systematic political power."[35]

De Certeau's terms, too, push toward a conception of everyday life as performance, subversive improvisations on the themes provided by social texts. But these small seditions are doomed by a fatalistic mode of theatricality. While de Certeau's virtuosic practitioners of everyday tactics may enact resistant variations, they ultimately remain bound by ideology's scripts. And, as Rita Felski's analysis again makes clear, de Certeau's "tactics" owe a large debt to avant-garde gestures. His resistant strolls and deliberately opaque dialects are subversive in their unreadability, their aleatory nature, their dada inscrutability.[36] In this light, you could even say that they bear the same relationship to prescriptive ideology that Marcel Duchamp's urinal does to classical sculpture: the exception that flouts, but also proves, the rule.

I have found the outlook of both American thinkers about the everyday and American practitioners of the theater of the everyday to be profoundly different with regard to these specific problems. In the American theater of the everyday, ordinary repertoires of belief and meaning are full of dignity and potential aesthetic power. And everyday experience is figured as an ideology-dissolving solution, rather than an ossifying encrustation. If human beings do not always notice everything they should, it's not because they lack awareness or motive, or because they are in thrall to false consciousness. They just need to be reminded, gently, to look again.

For American thinkers and artists of the everyday, neither structural social transformation nor consciousness-cleansing theory is required to transform the everyday into art. Art is there already, and spectators already possess the capacity to freely render their own experience as such. The aesthetic inheres in the everyday and requires a consummating glance, not a revolution, to be released. In other words, in the American tradition, change is gradual, and occurs over time, through many acts of perception; it works from the individual outwards, but toward no programmatic goal. And though the transformative project of the American thinkers and artists is also oriented toward the future, it does not aim at a specific target. Nor does it imagine a redemptive end point. It forecasts no pat conclusion to its transformations. In important ways, then, it is a progressive viewpoint, not a revolutionary one.

These fundamental philosophical differences have made me cautious about uncritically applying the insights of French everyday life theory to American theaters of the everyday. Many individual observations by these theorists have been immensely helpful to me in grasping the everyday's slippery qualities, and I will rely on them, and those of colleagues like Maurice Blanchot and Gaston Bachelard, at various points throughout this book. But it's important to keep in mind that these thinkers are heavily indebted to Continental traditions of avant-garde artmaking and vanguard politics that do not easily translate to my American examples. In order to clarify those differences, I'll now return to the relationship between art and everyday life, and especially the ways that relationship has been theorized with respect to artistic avant-gardes.

On the Blurring of Art and Life

Even before it became the scene for the trickling-down or covert flouting of ideology, the everyday was a limit case for twentieth-century artistic theories. In the wake of Marcel Duchamp's provocations, taken up by John Cage, and the American artists working in his wake, artists keen to trace the limits of the aesthetic, to prove that "art" was a matter of perception and experience, not auratic objecthood, began to investigate introducing everyday material into artworks. There was no better test of the democratic proposition that art is what happens in the mind of the viewer than bracketing the mundane, marginal, and habitually muted aspects of daily life and perception as, in themselves, worthy of aesthetic transfiguration.

As theorists like Peter Burger have argued,[37] the European avant-gardes sought to break down the barrier between art and life, using politically charged aesthetics to hurry along utopia: when art empties into life, this line of thinking suggests, life will be permanently transmogrified. When the walls of the museum are forced open, the fetish objects of high culture can resume their place as community touchstones; revolutionary artworks are templates for revolutions to follow. But as Toril Moi points out in her landmark study *Ibsen and the Birth of Modernism*, this habit of avant-gardist thinking is predicated on undoing an old opposition between art and everyday life that was built on idealist foundations: according to this ideology, art is the home of reality-transcending visions and moral uplift, the place where messy experience is scrubbed clean of the grime of material bodies and daily routines, purified and elevated.[38] As both Peter Szondi and Hans-Thies Lehmann have observed, building on Hegel, the fictive cosmos of "drama"—the neoclassically derived form of idealism that took hold of European theater in the eighteenth century, casting a long shadow over the nineteenth and the beginning of the twentieth—was founded on the notion that theatrical reality needed to be purified of any taint of everydayness, so as to transcend it. In fact, in this reading of Hegel, theater becomes the model of the world becoming idea, the transubstantiation of fallible, contingent materiality—actors, props—into timeless moral principles. This is what Lehmann calls the "'catharsis' of the dramatic form" by the "exclusion of the real."[39]

Moi's theory provides a salutary reminder of just how overbearing idealism's exclusions of the everyday were for European avant-gardists. It accounts for the schizophrenic moment of homeostatic compensation in which naturalism and symbolism appeared, virtually simultaneously, as twinned refusals of idealism: the former all empirical everydayness, deliberately disenchanted, the other in pursuit of revivified myths, intuiting occult realms behind everyday realities but without resort to idealism's transcendent truths.

Both of these aesthetic schools were to be influential in the American theater, but the theater of the everyday, though it can bear surface resemblance to each of these movements, differs in basic ways. The theater of the everyday's moments of transcendence insistently draw our attention back to everyday things, not into realms beyond. And its careful attention to the observable quanta of everyday experience leads it to reframe their meanings, not to pinion daily reality on the social grid created by the complementary determinisms of heredity and environment.

In the early twentieth century, the introduction of ready-made or deliberately crude materials into artworks—the raw everyday, uncooked by art—by avant-garde movements like the dadaists and futurists acquired its revolutionary force through its even more radical refutation of idealism's long-standing twinning of art and morality. They sought to forcefully reacquaint art and everyday life, which had been made strangers by idealist-derived aesthetic philosophies. The characteristic modalities of this process were correspondingly bellicose: shock, disruption, juxtaposition, surprise, confrontation, and so on. The avant-gardes attacked idealism by tearing the fabric of drama's idealized stage world. Because, in the European tradition, aesthetic values were so closely identified with both political and moral ones, the rejection of old art was also a thoroughgoing rejection of the historical past, a revolutionary act, and the necessary precursor to social revolution.

But there is also a distinctly American school of thinking about the everyday, and its relationship to art, that far predates these preoccupations. This tradition goes back to Emerson and Thoreau, continues with pragmatists like William James and John Dewey, and moves on to John Cage, the artistic pioneers of the 1960s, and beyond. And its priorities emerge in sharp relief when considered against those of European predecessors.

Underlying my argument throughout this book is a suggestion that the division between art and everyday life was never as absolute in American thought as it was in the thinking of the old world, nor was this boundary so thoroughly moralized or politicized. In fact, as recent interpreters of Emerson and Thoreau like Branka Arsic, Stanley Cavell, and George Leonard have in various ways argued, that border was far from secure as far back as the early nineteenth century. You could even say that the deliberate redrawing of the line linking art and life was a key—perhaps *the* key—characteristic of early efforts to define what a distinctively American aesthetic philosophy might look like.

Cavell points to *Walden* as an early parable of the productive blending of thinking, writing, reading, and quotidian existence. He argues that the writing of *Walden* was inextricably bound up in the picture of transcendentally simple daily life it describes: Thoreau was composing *Walden* and living Walden at the same time.[40] Leonard's fascinating *Into the Light of Things* proposes Emerson as the direct intellectual ancestor of Andy Warhol, demonstrating that the philosopher's ideas about art demote the finished object and exalt the thought that prompted it, seeing art and artistic practice as simply tools to prepare the way for an enriched perception of everyday life itself. To Emerson, the art object is the mere residue of the more important inspiration that produced it. He imagines a future in which artmaking as such will no longer be necessary because humanity will at last have learned "the immensity of the world." As Leonard explains:

> For the *time being*, art objects have a particular "office" to fill. That office, Emerson was writing in 1841, was "to educate us to the

> perception of beauty." Art is not an end, but an education . . . Man, Emerson argues, is "immersed in beauty" which he lacks the eyes to see. Habit, sheer familiarity has closed his eyes to the world's perfection; art exists to open them.[41]

This image is not unlike the consummated world of everyday creativity imagined by Guy Debord. The difference here again is teleology. Human beings can bring themselves to this awareness without the intervention of revolution. In this way, for Leonard, Andy Warhol's soup cans and Allan Kaprow's Happenings merely follow the early path cut by Emerson, as, I argue, do Thornton Wilder, Lee Strasberg, Stuart Sherman, and Nature Theater of Oklahoma.

It's against this intellectual background that John Dewey, in his 1931 William James lectures at Harvard—later published as *Art as Experience*—made his radical assertions that art is experience and experience is art. He argued that all experience contains the latent potential to become art, and that art in its conventional definitions is merely the concretized form of that potential. The aesthetic, Dewey writes, is

> no intruder in experience from without, whether by way of idle luxury or transcendent ideality . . . it is the clarified and intensified development of traits that belong to every normally complete experience. This fact I take to be the only secure basis upon which esthetic theory can build.[42]

With these limpid sentences, and others equally clarifying, Dewey bypasses centuries of European wrangling about aesthetic theory, building an alternate foundation for American artistic experimentation. Art need not be purified of the everyday to become art, because the everyday is immanently artistic, and the everyday doesn't need to be forcefully returned to art, because it never left. As Ben Highmore observes, this doesn't mean that *every* experience is aesthetic in the same way. Dewey is careful to note that much of the run of daily experience is characterized by "drift" or "slackness."[43] But this observation serves to foreground the dialectical nature of his thinking on the relationship between experience and art, a dialectic that matches the aesthetics of the everyday I consider here: between first-order experience and its consummation as art.

Dewey's championing of experience as the true measure of art presides over the perceptual investigations of the diverse theater artists I assemble in this book. It underwrites their faith in artistic experience as a transformative phenomenon, and dictates the open-ended valence of that transformation. Though Dewey's ideas weren't addressed to any one aesthetic medium, but deal with the function of art in general, they're particularly suited to the consideration of theater. Theater, more than any other art form, depends on shared experience in space and time. And the theater is a place where artists and spectators, artwork and everyday experience, meet. As such, it's a particularly apt schoolroom for the refinement of perception, the clarification and intensification of experience. Indeed, as James Harding has recently observed, for Dewey, "all artistic experience is like drama."[44] He cites the section of *Art and Experience* in which Dewey argues that aesthetic experience "requires a stage, a space, wherein to develop and time in which to unfold."[45]

As Martin Jay points out in his study of concepts of experience in American and European thought, Dewey wanted

> to overcome the gap between producer and consumer in modern life, of which the split between artistic creation and artistic appreciator was one symptom. But unlike the defenders of the elitist genius, whose . . . experiments in self-fashioning could end in destructive self-indulgence, he sought to reconcile it with the values of democratic self-realization . . . he sought to transcend the distinction between the useful and the ornamental in order to transfigure everyday life.[46]

To put it another way, Dewey was seeking a third path for artistic modernism, distinct from both the hermetic autonomy of high modernism and the ideologically tethered art-for-use of the more avowedly political avant-gardes. Dewey's ideas acquired particular urgency because of the hurried tempos and crowded experiential fields of everyday life in the modern world: "No one experience has a chance to complete itself because something else is entered upon so speedily. What is called experience is so dispersed and miscellaneous as hardly to deserve the name."[47] For Dewey, art was intended to heal the fractured perceptual fields engendered by the noisiness—the confusion, distraction, and fragmentariness—of modern life. The artists in this study take up Dewey's challenge by attempting to make experiential shards into meaningful creative material, redeeming noise for art.

"Shared experience" Dewey once wrote, "is the greatest of human goods."[48] But this doesn't mean that humans have to share the *same* experience, agree about its correct interpretations, or deduce the same meanings from it. Jay characterizes the political ethos behind Dewey's ideas as progressive, not in the limited social democratic sense the word is usually given, but in the more radical meaning of constant change, growth, and revision:

> There was, moreover, in Dewey, a belief that the fruits of experience were in the future rather than in the present. To the question "growth toward what end?" Dewey would have answered "toward more growth."[49]

As Jay goes on to argue, "such an open-ended telos could encourage skeptical responses . . . But others would see it as a wise acknowledgement that fulfilled democracy is always a project to be realized, always a condition still to come."[50]

This resolute pursuit of open-ended perceptual change, I argue, with its attendant political, social, and intellectual implications, is a particular characteristic of the American theater of the everyday. And awareness of this paradigmatic difference should inflect our understanding of American vanguardism. Too often, the American avant-garde is relegated to the status of an inferior rehearsal of an intrepid original—a Neo-Avant-Garde, as Peter Burger termed it.[51] With that assumption comes the further premise that the American avant-garde was likewise hostile to the Euro-avant-garde's particular shibboleths: the institutions of art, the classical tradition, habit, cultural continuity, and, of course, the division between audience and performers (emblematic of so many other divisions). While American artists have certainly shared the more avowedly revolutionary ambitions of the European avant-gardes on occasion, particularly in the bellicose 1960s, they have also tweaked the life-art equation in more subtle ways, using everyday life to transform art, so that art, in turn, can allow spectators to see life more clearly. Less stridently political, these experiments were also more open-ended, without a predetermined teleological end point or guiding ideology.[52]

American theaters of the everyday represent what might be called a progressive avant-garde, positing a politics of dissensus,[53] a radical democracy at once subversively inclusive (every audience member's perceptions are unique, and as artistically valid as any other spectator's and the artist's) and radically subjective (no two audience members see the same thing in the same way). These theater artists don't seek to entirely abolish the distinction between art and everyday life; rather, they see the frame of the theater as a synecdoche for the bracketing attention that transforms experience into art, a clarifying source of distinctions, a model for enriched attention, or an invaluable source of metaphors. For them, the border between art and life is a constantly shifting horizon that is nevertheless valuable *as* a horizon, a line dividing useful differences.

Because artists resorting to the everyday in form and content have often been viewed as apolitical, retreating from social struggles into comfortable myopia, part of my intention with this project is to recover such efforts as deeply, and perhaps even more lastingly, political than political art as it is conventionally conceived. Creating room for perception to perceive itself is a radical endeavor, far more so than simply taking up the cause of a particular preexisting stance. Transforming the perception of everyday life means opening up the possibility of new conceptions of the everyday—possibilities with unpredictable political valences.

Open-ended change, untrammeled by the channels of ideology, but tempered by respect for valuable institutions, is what these artists advocate with their upending approaches to the humdrum. To put the matter simply: as Michael Warner lucidly reminds us, questions of attention are also questions of value,[54] and these experiments resolutely leave the valuation of the everyday open to reinterpretation. By refusing to settle on a solid-state view of the everyday (such as realism), they hold with the utopian idea that the everyday contains the possibilities of its own transformation, a profoundly political idea behind seemingly hermetic work. Stuart Sherman's "spectacles," to choose just one example, delve into the imbrication of language and perception in creating our everyday worlds, proposing that unseating one object from its field, one word from its accustomed place in a sentence or a paragraph, one visual rhyme from its usual pattern, can bring reality crashing down, to be replaced by unknown new possibilities, identities, and meanings.

This is a different definition of representational democracy than that to which we are accustomed. These artists share an ethos of fervent egalitarianism, becoming fiercer as the decades pass, in their conceptions of what can or should be represented in a piece of theater, what can or should be considered part of the rarefied vocabulary of "art." In *Pullman Car Hiawatha*, one of Thornton Wilder's early plays, objects and humans, landscapes and proverbs all vie for equal place onstage. Lee Strasberg's incorporation of the orphan sounds of speech into the lucid world of theatrical dialogue was the perceptual counterpart to his effort to include the sound of immigrant voices on America's mainstream stages. Sometimes, as the furious debates surrounding the advent of Method acting will illustrate, the consequences of this deliberate disavowal of representational hierarchies could be profoundly discomfiting, seeming to prefer the insignificant to the significant, the inarticulate to the meaningful, the unimportant to the important, nonsense to sense.

But the impulse underlying these radical revaluations is also democratic in the vital sense that these artists make use of material common to everyone to make their art. Some experience of quotidian existence, an understanding of everydayness, is native to all. In this sense, the theater of the everyday aspires to the ideal of a culture held in common. It avers that, to borrow a phrase from Raymond Williams, culture is ordinary. Here is a paradox unique to the theater of the everyday. Taking a cue from Dewey, it unites modernist difficulty with vernacular appeal, formal innovation with plainspoken gregariousness, familiarity with strangeness. An ethos of deriving artistic innovation from recognizably everyday materials is part of these artists' common belief that the meaning of our surroundings remains in flux. For them, the modernist aesthetic imperative to "make it new" has a redoubled meaning: to remake art with everyday life, and by creating new artistic shapes, to renew perceptions of everyday life.

These twinned injunctions force us to recalibrate our expectations of artistic resistance, so central to theories of modernism and the avant-gardes. Some of these plays and performances may not initially appear formally daring, but become so upon contemplation. Thornton Wilder's seemingly colloquial scenes clad profound perceptual investigations. Nature Theater of Oklahoma takes mundane chat as a cue to examine the deep narrative structures of consciousness itself. Conversely, works that may appear forbiddingly dense or impossibly abstract on first viewing prove to deal with the most elemental, common conundrums of everyday perception and experience. Stuart Sherman's spectacles dig deeply into the manifold ways that we find the tangible objects of the everyday world reflected in our words and thoughts, and our words and thoughts mirrored in the material world outside. For all of these artists, art is not a rarefied autonomous realm, nor do they see the necessity of protecting art from the incursions of everyday life.

Always Beginning Again

As will already be clear, these theaters of the everyday passionately refute the notion that there is or ever could be a normative American everyday that should (or could) be represented on stage. Far from it. For the most part—Method acting is a complex case—these are theaters that acknowledge the irreducible particularity of everyday experience, and attempt to make such subjectivity an intrinsic part of theatrical experience, too. Tapping into the everyday is an essential part of their idiosyncratic self-identification as American artists producing recognizably American art. But these theatrical exceptionalisms are all very far removed from a stable nationalism susceptible to chauvinistic declarations, or even easy articulation.

The theater of the everyday begins from estrangement, and its practitioners have mostly been, in various ways, outsiders. Sometimes, that outlook is afforded by an immigrant's perspective (Lee Strasberg, Nature Theater's Pavol Liska); at other times, by the vantage point of queerness (Thornton Wilder, Stuart Sherman). In the latter cases, neither artist explicitly thematized queerness or queer identity in most of his pieces. In keeping with his straitened time, Wilder was fiercely private, with some surprising exceptions; Sherman only began to make more avowedly queer work very late in his career, as I'll discuss. But I argue that queerness is everywhere in their art, providing a sense of critical distance that inflects their representation of everyday realities as contingent, mutable, subjective. Without intruding too much on these artists' jealously guarded privacy, I think we can infer that queerness informs the radically democratic vision of representation that underlies both artists' work, with its attendant project of renovating perception toward more inclusive visions.

In considering the career of John Cage, another artist who made few public declarations about his sexual identity but who nonetheless created a profoundly queer aesthetic, Jonathan Katz argues that Cage resorted to noise, to deliberately nonaesthetic sounds, in his compositions because "what makes a noise a noise is precisely its freedom from any preordained conceptual or ideological system."[55] This statement could apply equally well to the theatrical experiments of Wilder and Sherman, both artists who resisted making any kind of public disclosure of their sexual identities, but who made work embodying a queer aesthetic of the everyday and espousing a radical democracy of artistic representation and artistic means. Katz argues that noise contains the germ of future meanings. New ideas, new bodies, new definitions can coalesce around sounds that have no place in the reified regimes of art, or of normative reality. Noise, in both this ideology-unraveling sense, and that developed by media theorists, will be a foundational concept throughout this book. The idea provides an inflection point at which to trace the shifting boundaries between art and life, sense and nonsense, importance and unimportance.

Wilder and Sherman achieved a similar effect by scrambling representational norms. Wilder argued that material objects, natural features, offhand sites, and forgettable events demanded to be staged alongside human figures and more recognizably dramatic predicaments. Sherman's object performances aim to redistribute the sensible by hand and eye, working from first principles and material substrates, to imagine other ways of making sense, other modes of seeing, other potential configurations for the multitude of human-made and human-manipulated objects that populates our daily lives—the stage from which our thoughts and perceptions arise.

This allies their aesthetics of the everyday with the notion of queer futurity developed by Jose Esteban Muñoz, one that resists cosseting definitions, instead preferring constant revision and reimagining. Muñoz argues that we need "to step out of the rigid conceptualization that is a straight present" in order to arrive at "something fuller, vaster, more sensual, and brighter."[56] ("Brightness," Wilder once wrote, "is seeing in a new way.") This kind of stepping-out is precisely what lies behind the theaters of Wilder and Sherman. By liquefying received representations of reality, they allow for a departure into different conceptions of time, space, and perception, creating a transitive interval during which we might catch a glimpse of other possible worlds.

All four of these artists share a sense of America as a vision to be realized, rather than an achieved ideal. In his magisterial study *The Rites of Assent*, Sacvan Bercovitch traces the ideological transformations of the Puritan notion of the errand in the wilderness, of America as a stage for the working out of God's plan. He argues that what remained of this founding myth by the time it spliced with capitalism, American exceptionalism, and other potent cultural ingredients was the pervasive idea of America as a culture in perpetual motion, even as the projected destinations differed. He talks about the power of consensus in American life. Both the culture's reactionaries and its radicals make their criticisms based on the nation's fulfillment of, or failure to live up to, the promise of its democratic ideals and mission.[57]

One side of this idea of consensus, of course, is dangerous reactionary passivity. But its obverse, pursued by the theatrical experiments I describe here, is radical and progressive, in Dewey's sense of the word. If America is something made and revised by Americans, an idea-in-progress created by the matching of many diverse ideas and lives, then by estranging the familiar, making art that compels us to continually reappraise what we see and how we see it, the artists in this book are also reminding us that America is a destination we have not yet reached. To these artists, "America" is a vehicle-in-motion, a thought in quicksilver transit, a project-in-conception, an evolving timbre of speech and meaning. It's a contract made and remade by the collective perceptions and acts of Americans. It's no accident that images of speed and movement abound in these artists' work, whether it's Wilder's sense of the tragic velocity of experience ("We go so fast," Emily says); the Method's fanatical determination to record the sound of authenticity as it whispers by; Stuart Sherman's relentless attempts to match the pace of performance to the pace of thought; or Nature Theater of Oklahoma's harvesting of streams of ordinary talk, otherwise destined to disappear.

Graphing the syncopated movements of temporality germane to participatory reenactments of the American Civil War, Rebecca Schneider arrives at a revelatory insight about American historical consciousness and its relationship to performance. Defying the lockstep march of historical movement as understood in its Enlightenment sense—forward, ever forward—American history is always doubling back, making traumatic returns, resurrecting ghosts, or leaping forward into imagined futures before the present has a chance to catch up.[58] This syncopation is characteristic of everyday experience as well. So much of ordinary perception and cognition disappears, only perhaps to suddenly return. In both its self-conception, as a nation perpetually new, and in its perennial propensity for ideological erasures of the past, America is always beginning again. And so too do we all, every day of our waking lives.

The Unconscious of Everyday Life

Throughout this book, I examine the germinal role of technologies of reproduction in reshaping definitions of the everyday, and in making its perishable phenomena available as artistic material and objects of artistic investigation.[59] The incidentals of gesture and speech—the ums and ahs, the inadvertent fidgeting—were never really visible until film and audio recording preserved them, revealing, in Walter Benjamin's memorable formulation, the "unconscious" of daily life, the nonsignifying superfluities customarily edited by perception.[60] The interference produced by these media themselves can also be added to this list: the hiss of the tape recorder, the jump of a rogue frame, the deterioration of film stock producing livid shapes.

This material, dubbed "noise" in media theory, the signals emitted by the medium, existing apart from the message, became a primary source of inspiration for theater artists, providing new and smaller "unimportant things" to seize upon and transfigure into art.[61] From Method acting's studied cultivation of streetwise reality to Nature Theater of Oklahoma's technologically enabled transcriptions of offhand speech, with stuttering and dangling clauses intact, these artists elevate the "noise" of speech and gesture to equivalent status with their meanings.

But I am not simply arguing, alongside Friedrich Kittler, that "media determine our situation,"[62] or upholding an easy equation of modernism with technological innovation. Rather, my argument is that new modes of thought and perception suggested by technologies, as both means and metaphor, grafted themselves onto older ideas about the importance of finding larger meanings in habitually invisible or abject phenomena.

William James, the philosophical middle term between Emerson and Dewey, for example, was forever seeking a mode of perception, what he once called "radical empiricism," that would enable him to see "the flux of life which furnishes the material to our later reflection with its conceptual categories."[63] (Dewey's sense of experience, too, relies on its potential as a solvent to previously fixed ideas.) James describes the elusive goal of achieving "pure" experience in terms that anticipate, in very different ways, Thornton Wilder's attempt to stage "pure" description; Lee Strasberg's discovery of the uncanny grain of truth in the unbiased ear of the tape recorder; Stuart Sherman's attempts to see the primordial perceptual field that exists before the interference of language, shape, color, or other ways of sieving experience into preordained categories; and Nature Theater of Oklahoma's fervent belief that we miss too much beauty because everyday talk goes by so fast and we can't hear all of it.

James writes, yearningly:

> Only new-born babes, or men in semi-coma from sleep, drugs, illnesses or blows, may be assumed to have an experience pure in the literal sense of a *that* which is not yet any *what*, tho' ready to be all sorts of whats; full both of oneness and of manyness, but in respects that don't appear . . .[64]

All the artists I discuss in this book are interested in staging the interval of experience in which a "that" is not yet a "what," though ready to be any number of "whats"; for them, the possibility of converting experiential givens into new and perhaps unforeseeable shapes is the very essence of the theatrical enterprise.

For some of these artists—Lee Strasberg, Nature Theater of Oklahoma, Stuart Sherman—the unfiltered hearing of the tape recorder or the unblinkered seeing of the camera became models of this sort of unfiltered attention, aids to registering the fleeting gestures or sounds that perception usually tunes out. Thornton Wilder pursued this mode of sight without the direct intervention of recording technology, but with results that contemporary critics compared to stop-motion photography. And his characters often achieve their startling insights in collaboration with modern technology: while glancing out the window of a speeding car, for example, or riding an overnight train.

The harvesting of these quotidian data from such apparatuses became a source of direct inspiration. Media and philosophy fed on each other to create artistic programs devoted to claiming the humble and offhand for art, in the service of new, "purer" modes of experience that could lead to new ways of seeing the world. (There is, of course, a profound irony in using secondhand experience to access a more primary way of seeing the world, but for all these artists, it's a productive one.) This line of thinking leads to a usefully expanded definition of what Philip Auslander has dubbed "mediatized" performance, investigating the deep penetration of technologies of mediation into theatrical performance, far beyond the obvious presence of onstage screens and microphones.[65]

The opposed concepts of noise and music—marking the shifting borders between art and nonart, the perceived and the unperceived—have therefore been a useful way to talk about the radical import of these artists' ambitions to retune perception so as to find significance in the insignificant and sense in nonsense, to make the invisible visible.[66] For these artists, noise can be a democratic sound. Selecting sounds does not mean excluding them (as music does). As we'll see in my chapter about Method acting in particular, the noisiness of new art could be frightening, representing the negation of received artistic standards and the cultural norms they upheld. But for the artists of the theater of the everyday, noisiness can also be joyful. The true sound of democracy is a chorus of difference, not a choir of conformity.

Discussing Kafka's fiction, Jane Bennett points out that such investigations inevitably lead us to reassign narrative hierarchies, reversing the priority of figure and ground, accidental and purposive:

> It seems, then, that Kafka crafts his story from the bits of experience ordinarily discarded as irrelevant to such story. Instead of recounting those events that contribute to the reader's narrative preoccupation, Kafka names contemporaneous events that constitute other stories. *The Trial* is less a photograph of Joseph K.'s trial than its negative: "background" objects are vivid, while one strains to discern the slightest trace of the "foreground." These acts fall into the shadow of your rushing indignant body. You note them—they are within the purview of your experience—but you pass them by. But if you were to gather up these dark, discarded scraps and peer into them, you would be on a different path, the path of a Kafkan tale.[67]

The photographic metaphor is revealing here. Technologies of recording, which at first glance seem to work in service of the disenchantment of the world, making more and more of it available as archival information for sorting, classification, and scrutiny, also reveal the uncanny lurking in surprising places. The camera and the audio recorder show us the fugitives from the iron cage, caught in transit.

In his 1965 interview with Richard Schechner and Michael Kirby, a seminal text for the American avant-garde, John Cage, too, points to technology's capacity to discover the uncanny in the unnoticed ordinary, prophetically heralding rich new sources of artistic material. The new theater, he argued, could be made up of "things that don't connect with art as we conventionally understand it. Ordinary occurrences in a city, or ordinary occurrences in the country, or technological occurrences—things that are now practical simply because techniques have changed." He goes on, with poetic precision, to imagine a new kind of music made up "of sounds we can't hear because they're too small, but through new techniques we can enlarge them, sounds like ants walking in the grass."[68] Surprise, wonder, and reenchantment can attend the recording and playback of the world.

Looking Again, with Fresh Eyes

Just as the theater of the everyday forces us to rethink our reflexive habit of considering American experimenters in European terms, so too does it recalibrate our familiar narratives of American theatrical modernism (and what came after), making room for an alternative story that begins not with Eugene O'Neill's plumbing of reified depth psychology but with Thornton Wilder's assertion that every mind has its own reality, and with it, its own "realism." It asks us to rethink where we place the dividing lines of periods and movements, and the rupturing fissures of avant-garde and mainstream, conservative and progressive.

It also offers fresh perspectives on the work of many important figures in American theater. In some cases, my project here is also one of recovery and reappraisal, addressing what I perceive to be canonical omission, neglect, or misunderstanding. Considered as an attempt to refract the disparate perspectives of the many unique minds in the auditorium, the rigorous anti-spectacle of Thornton Wilder's empty stage presages later avant-garde experiments with attention and perception and belies his unjustly folksy reputation. Looked at in light of their common preoccupation with recording technologies, Method acting's studied mumblers and John Cage's musical experiments share a drive to redefine the relationship between unaesthetic noise and music, sound and sense—an affinity that shows a modernist formalism beneath the avowed essentialism of the Method's methods. Stuart Sherman's spectacles have been sidelined by examinations of the 1970s and 1980s theatrical avant-garde, even as his work has been embraced by art historians and scholars of performance emerging from visual art traditions. I aim to restore him to theater, his natural dwelling, and the secure home base that allowed him to range widely across disciplines. My last chapter and coda endeavor to bridge the interpretive gaps among seemingly outlying work, the "classical" American avant-garde, and artists like Wilder and Strasberg. Nature Theater of Oklahoma's deep immersion in the ideas of its forebears—Emerson, Dewey, Cage, Wilder, and the Judson Dancers, among others—reminds us that American progressive theater-making is now a tradition with its own canon, a line of artists as coherent and continuous as that claimed for the mainstream.

In my first chapter, I argue that Wilder's early one-act plays and *Our Town* cut an alternative path for American modernism. Turning to quotidian scenes, bracketing moments of seeing and hearing onstage, Wilder made the perceptual event ground zero for a new aesthetics of the everyday. Instead of naturalism's consensus view of reality and crowded visual field, he posited productive dissensus, filling the empty frame of a bare stage with his audiences' diverse perceptions, shifting rapidly between vantages and insisting that spectators do the same. I place Wilder between the aesthetic ideas of Emerson and Thoreau, the latter attempting to blur art and life in order to construct individual mental dwelling places, the former insisting on constant departure from all fixed systems (what Branka Arsic, in her recent roots-up reappraisal of the philosopher, terms Emerson's complex philosophy of "leaving").[69]

In chapter 2, I juxtapose John Cage's theory with Lee Strasberg's work in closed tape-recorded sessions at the Actors Studio and Elia Kazan's early films. I suggest that Cage's paradigmatic revaluing of noise and music, and his blurring of the boundary between aesthetic and unaesthetic sound, together with his emphasis on new forms of music produced with the aid of new recording technologies,[70] provides a useful framework by which to understand Method acting's reevaluation of the difference between sound and sense in theatrical and filmic performance—aided, of course, by film and tape recording's perfect visual and aural recall. Walter Benjamin observed that film makes "surgical" incursions into reality,[71] revealing the usually invisible aspects of everyday speech and behavior—stuttering half-movements, unmindful gestures, placeholder demi-words like "um" and "uh." But, although such inarticulate flourishes were the visible hallmarks of the Method's process of digging through the self for buried, true experiences, for the psychological unconscious, these bodily signifiers only really became visible, reproducible, through filmic recording. In this light, the Method becomes an early example of intermedial performance, produced as much by the ability of the camera and microphone to pick up stutters and mumbles as by any kind of dredging of the soul.

Chapter 3 considers Stuart Sherman's minutely scaled spectacles: motile collages made up of everyday objects arranged in unexpected combinations, creating startling compositions and unforeseen affinities. I discuss this gigantic series of tiny performances as an ongoing perceptual investigation, a decades-long search to find a stage idiom capable of illustrating the vertiginous push-pull of everyday consciousness: the ways in which experience takes us outside of ourselves and into the material world, while the objects that surround us invade our thoughts and sensations. For Sherman, language structures our relations with the material world, even as the material world shapes our use and understanding of language, in a constant, unresolvable dance of words and things. To him, consciousness is the record of the friction produced by the rubbing of the mind against the world.

Finally, my fourth chapter discusses the work of the contemporary New York experimental ensemble Nature Theater of Oklahoma as inheritors of Wilder, Cage, the Judson Dancers, and even the Method's mumbling, synthesizing American theater's long-standing preoccupation with transforming perception by staging the everyday, with its drive to enhance perception through technology. Nature Theater has turned John Dewey's notion of "consummation"—the redemptive transformation through enriched attention of experience into art—into a foundational formal principle for their theater, realizing it on a colossal scale.

In some ways, the aesthetics of the everyday conceived by these artists are historically contingent: Wilder's everyday plays respond to new experiential divisions in conceptions of time and space prompted by the standardization of clock time on the one hand, and Einstein's relativistic revelations on the other. The plays revel in the new perspectives afforded by racing automobiles and other fast-moving vehicles. Lee Strasberg's recording obsession and Marlon Brando's noisy acting were products of the new ubiquity of recording technology in postwar America. Stuart Sherman's interdisciplinary experiments were a result of the 1960s and 1970s avant-gardes' promiscuous artistic cross-pollination. Nature Theater of Oklahoma's mining of vast swathes of preserved conversation could only be possible in the era of nearly boundless digital memory.

But other concerns cut across time. Although this study proceeds roughly chronologically, from Thornton Wilder's early modernist experiments to Nature Theater of Oklahoma's twenty-first-century epics, I intend it to be read associatively as well as laterally. Arresting affinities can be glimpsed by jumping between the decades. For example, Wilder and Sherman share an artistic interest in blurring the interval where perception escapes the borders of the self, and in reversing the priority of theatrical (and experiential) foregrounds and backgrounds. Lee Strasberg and Nature Theater of Oklahoma share a faith in the revelatory capacity of recording to bestow a second look at perished experience, and a delight in speech's cast-off sounds: ums and uhs, half-turned thoughts, conversational false starts, the grain of talk. Reshuffling the chapters, Sherman's decades-long project of retuning perception so that visual static could become perceptual music is analogous to Method acting's reconsideration of the difference between signifying and nonsignifying matter in speech. Closing the loop, Nature Theater of Oklahoma and Thornton Wilder share the aspiration to review sweeping vistas of perished experience, creating artistic shapes that allow spectators to see again that which always escapes. These affinities suggest a constant concern with creating new theatrical strategies to reframe the everyday that remains vital across the decades. We can track a recurrent set of themes that remain continuous despite the shifting nature of the reality they address: a concern about both the value and danger of habit; a desire to hold on to experience that seems to be moving too fast; and a persistent imperative to look to the small, abject, and unnoticed aspects of daily life first.

I am not proposing a narrative of direct causation. But in many cases these artists do share influences and precedents, or were inspired by each other. Nor am I suggesting that the movement from fictional representations of everyday events and sights to the importing of found objects and found text harvested from daily life and put directly onstage is inevitable or inextricable. Nevertheless, a line can be drawn from Wilder's disavowal of what he called the "editorial" impulse, his preference for putting what he called "facts" on stage; to Strasberg's attention to the uncanny aspects of speech, inaudible except to the unbiased ears of the recording apparatus; to Sherman's attempts to short-circuit visual sense-making, and with it, language; to Nature Theater's vast epics constructed on the shifting foundation of consciousness's transcribed stops and starts. All these artists, in various ways, are suspicious of what Hans-Thies Lehmann has called the "fictive cosmos":[72] the illusionistic theater's concern with presenting internally coherent worlds, set off from that of the auditorium or that outside the theater's walls—a lingering hangover of idealism.

Looked at still another way, the chapters constellate around particular aspects of the everyday in performance, proffering case studies meditating on the theatrical possibilities of everyday objects (Sherman); speech (the Method, Nature Theater); quotidian streams of consciousness (Wilder, Nature Theater); visuality (Wilder, Sherman); and the everyday's paradoxes of scale (Wilder, Method, Sherman, Nature Theater). In this way, I hope that my selections sketch a genealogy and imply other entries on the tree, and that my consideration of these artists can illuminate the work of others.

Some readers might find the pioneering experiments of the 1960s theatrical and performance avant-gardes conspicuous by their absence here: Happenings, the Judsons, the performance collectives, and so on. I have two reasons for these strategic omissions. The first, pragmatic, one is that 1960s performance practitioners' recourse to quotidian materials and democratizing aesthetics is well known, and well documented. I couldn't hope to offer a better survey of that decade's artistic experiments than Sally Banes has in her various books, notably *Greenwich Village 1963*. Describing the various art forms that converged on quotidian aesthetics in the early 1960s, she notes that in the New York performance scene

> one no longer made plays or dances or films about people falling hopelessly in love or falling from power, or even people unable to fall in love. Instead, people in Happenings, Fluxus, new dances, Off-Off-Broadway theater, Pop Art, and underground films ironed clothing, combed or shampooed their hair, and shaved their legs. They smiled, slept, smoked cigarettes, went to the movies, sent their audiences to the movies, played cards, read newspapers, got haircuts, played hopscotch, played ball, and roller-skated. They made love and made lunch. In their very banality, these activities became charged with meaning. For in examining them—activities which everyone engages in, but does differently—the simultaneous variety and unity of human life seemed evident.[73]

These experiments have clear affinities with the theaters I discuss here, but also signal differences. Banes notes that a key characteristic of these attempts to transcend the border between art and life was a concomitant desire to flout the institutional limits that became metaphors for that border: to transgress the boundaries of the stage, or even the theater, to leave the canvas frame and museum behind. While the artists in this book undoubtedly share versions of the egalitarian politics of the 1960s, and the commitment of those artists to devising forms that are both innovative and inclusive, experimental and gregarious, for all the reasons I've elaborated above, they've been less inclined to abandon the structures and viewing habits of the theater. For them, theater's generic expectations are opportunities, not problems.

The second and related reason is that because these 1960s experiments with the everyday are so well known, and so well written about, they have a tendency to overshadow what came before and after. In order to really see the American theater of the everyday as a crucial genealogy, even a tradition, it's necessary to look past the 1960s in both directions. When we do, we see that the everyday was already a vital source of artistic inspiration long before Happenings or the Judson Dancers, and has remained a wellspring ever since.

It's worth pausing to point out, though, just how consonant the Judson Dancers' work in particular was with the tendencies I describe as characteristic of the theater of the everyday. We have only to remind ourselves of the relentless momentum of Yvonne Rainer's landmark *Trio A*, never allowing spectators to rest in the contemplation of any one gesture, and its deliberate disavowal of conventional high points in favor of pedestrian movements performable by almost any practiced body, to see the affinities, in both pace and ethos, with the equally relentless work I discuss here. (Carrie Lambert-Beatty's revelatory analysis of Rainer's work in the context of 1960s media culture in her study *Being Watched* has had a powerful influence on my thinking about the imbricated relationships between technology, perception, and artistic form throughout this book.)

Some of those figures nevertheless preside in the background here. John Cage's direct influence or illuminating comparison underwrites just about every postwar artistic experiment, and his ideas infuse my chapters about the Method (where he provides an alternative interpretative paradigm), Sherman (where he is an unseen foundation), and Nature Theater (where his example permeates their work, top to bottom). Other artists from that intrepid era will appear as touchstones: Rauschenberg, the Judson Dancers, Warhol. These citations are intended to be allusive, not exhaustive, suggesting connections rather than merely prescribing interpretive avenues.

There are two polemical points undergirding my approach in this book. I believe that our scholarly desire to separate theater and performance studies from literary studies has sometimes led us to neglect the important thinking about performance done by playwrights, or to elide the deliberately dramatic qualities of performance-based pieces. The everyday is a particularly vital arena in which to reappraise these priorities, since dramatic texts like Wilder's nevertheless deeply depend on the experiential moment of performance to acquire their full meaning—to a degree, I argue, that was nearly unprecedented in American playwriting. And performances as seemingly vanguard and nondramatic as those of Nature Theater of Oklahoma still employ the dramatic imperatives, old as Aristotle, of reversal and recognition to achieve their theatrical transformations, reminding us that such conventions form the deep structure of our day-to-day experience outside the theater. It's also a gesture to artistic plurality in a wider sense. I share Marc Robinson's enlarged view of the American canon, an American theater as diverse as the country it embodies and reflects upon. Outliers and mainstream artists often have more in common than we think.[74]

These theaters complicate questions of priority and authorship in the composition of dramatic text. Even Wilder's plays, the most conventionally dramatic of the examples I consider here, leave large gaps to be filled by the experience of his spectators. And as we move closer to the present, these theaters further confound ideas of authorship. Method acting's routes to authenticity involved the disruption of dramatic text by performance. Stuart Sherman relied on strings of carefully composed images to scrutinize the operations of language in the absence of words. Nature Theater of Oklahoma assembles its scripts retroactively, culling and editing text transcribed from the unpredictable utterances of interview subjects. In each case, these theaters frustrate the distinctions that are best expressed by Diana Taylor's notions of the archive and the repertoire: between the authority vested in textuality and textual culture on the one hand and intangible and often ephemeral experience, affect, and kinesthetic memory on the other.

This brings me to my second critical precept. In a field often preoccupied with theories of embodiment, I think spectatorship, the experience of the majority of people who will encounter a theatrical object, is an undervalued and undertheorized activity. Too often we equate sitting still with stilled thought, and attention with political passivity. Part of the goal of my research is to show how important reimagining spectatorship has been to the American theater. American artists were already engaged with emancipating spectators from habituated ways of seeing before Brecht, and long before Rancière, construing looking not as passive absorption but as active construction. The American theater-makers I examine do not consider aesthetics to be an autonomous realm separated from the drudgery of quotidian life. For them, artistic experience occurs on a continuum with everyday consciousness, not in rarefied intervals bracketed into seclusion. This preoccupation presages some current thinking in affect studies. As Ben Highmore put it in a recent essay, more attention must be paid to what he calls the "countertradition" of aesthetics that considers the "interlacing of sense perception and bodily dispensation."[75] Moreover, works of theater and performance provide vital clues to the spectatorial cultures of previous periods—their characteristic "structures of feeling," to employ Raymond Williams's illuminating concept.

This includes the nascent affective structures of our own time: our burgeoning digital culture is rife with opportunities to restage, reframe, and reimagine quotidian experience, unsettling the difference between experiential dross and aesthetic gold. Twitter transfixes passing thoughts; Instagram preserves short-lived sights, Vine (sadly, now defunct) looped telling gestures; Foursquare reminds us where we walked and where we ate dinner; Facebook makes the arc of human life visible in a ready-made timeline. This book demonstrates that developments in American theater anticipated the aspirations behind these efforts. *Our Town* is now a place in cyberspace, and each of us can take a second look at more and more of our perished experience—at the price, perhaps, of surrendering some of its aleatory strangeness to preframed narratives. My coda analyzes Richard Maxwell's recent actorless performance piece *Ads* (2010) as staging our culture's increasing hauntedness by all these archived revenants of everyday experience. The piece suggests future directions for the American theater of the everyday, as it continues to claim new artistic territory.

Finally, since the daily lives of authors are immanent in their words, and their ideas are germinal in their routines, I can only guess that some of the impetus behind this study emanated from my situation as an expatriate Canadian living in the United States for more than a decade. Finding the country at once profoundly familiar and lastingly strange, ever more my home and also never fully to be, I was comforted to find a group of theater artists, kindred spirits, who shared my continuing astonishment at its baffling, conflicted immensity. I felt at home in their estrangement. Now, finishing this book after recently returning to Canada, I remain, in my thoughts and affinities, lastingly American, and like the artists I consider here, an exile at home.

Chapter 1

✦

Brightness Is Seeing in a New Way

Thornton Wilder's Everyday Departures

Thornton Wilder wrote on the move. He liked to say that he measured his composition by the daily walks he took while thinking about it, so many miles to the page. The physical momentum helped him keep words and ideas in motion. As he once put it in his journals:

> Having always "got" my writing on long walks I have learned to prevent its solidifying, its "jelling" in my head; always when the moment of writing comes it is ready for that moment's novelty, excitement, and surprise.[1]

Though frequently identified with the deceptively homey setting of *Our Town*, his masterpiece, he was a vagabond for most of his life, fleeing the blandishments of literary fame to find the solitude he craved abroad, or in remote places. As with the lifestyle, so with the man: many acquaintances remarked upon the extreme motility of his disposition and moods (mercurial, but always genial) and the rapid-fire rhythms of his speech. He moved between literary genres and modes equally restlessly, alternating prose fiction and drama throughout his career. Skipping among professions, he would refresh his literary efforts with scholarly intermezzos, and enrich his theatrical theorizing with practical experiments. His quixotic years-long research project to fix the precise dates of Lope de Vega's hundreds of plays, an eccentric hobby, took place against the backdrop of a frenetic itinerary leading him across oceans and continents. As Penelope Niven, Wilder's niece and his most perceptive biographer, puts it, Wilder "had to get away from home in order to be himself."[2]

Of recent commentators, David Castronovo comes closest to capturing this aspect of Wilder's life and work when he calls him a "protean writer,"[3] fluidly moving between genres and styles. But this image of literary shapeshifting, with its implication of chameleon-like disappearance behind the mask of an adopted form, doesn't quite account for Wilder's interest in transition, particularly during the phase in his theatrical experimentation I wish to consider here. He was fascinated by the spaces between images, words, and scenes, preoccupied by intervals of entry and exit, when one thing ends and another is about to begin.

If there is one figure that characterizes Wilder's most innovative theatrical work, it is that of departure, of leaving. I am thinking here of three one-act plays written at the end of the 1920s—*Pullman Car Hiawatha*, *The Happy Journey to Trenton and Camden*, and *The Long Christmas Dinner*—and, of course, of *Our Town*.[4] I see the three shorter plays as a matched set, representing Wilder's most advanced early thinking about the theater, and there is evidence that he saw them this way too. In the beginning stages of his ardent friendship with Gertrude Stein, a relationship with profound intellectual ramifications for them both, it was those three plays—out of the half-dozen collected in *Six One Act Plays*—that he recommended she read.[5] I concentrate on this group of plays for several reasons. First, there are clear continuities among them as a single body of theatrical experiment. All three short plays rehearse the stripped-bare stage that is so much a part of *Our Town*'s effect. *Pullman Car Hiawatha* and *The Happy Journey* feature the mediating presence of a Stage Manager figure. While working on early versions of the play that became *Our Town*, Wilder considered having a "long Christmas dinner" comprise the play's second act.[6]

But perhaps more importantly, all four works unite the staging of everyday events with images of speed and restless movement. They are plays about perception, about irreplaceable experience, and about the continuities between aesthetic understanding outside and inside the walls of the theatrical auditorium. If Wilder believed, as does Ann Douglas, that modernism was, above all, a "momentum,"[7] it was because he believed that thought and experience were also racing velocities, and that received theatrical forms couldn't keep up with the true pace of human thought and feeling.

In these plays, Wilder's characters and situations are a blur of constant motion. Sometimes he dramatizes scenes of geographic travel, as in *Pullman Car Hiawatha*, or the family car trip staged in *The Happy Journey*. Sometimes these voyages are more allegorical, as in *The Long Christmas Dinner*, which, with the God's-eye view of a medieval station drama, turns time into space, observing the births and deaths of succeeding generations in a single family as entrances and exits across a cosmic stage. And of course, there's *Our Town*, which sets a whole historical moment, and the fragile human figures that populate it, into receding movement. Wilder once compared the action of the play to a telescope tracking a vanishing object.[8] The town of Grover's Corners, New Hampshire, is not just distant, it's actively disappearing, further removed with each attempt to resuscitate it. Speed is perhaps not the first attribute that comes to mind when considering Wilder's work. Decades of critical myopia have associated him more closely with the tar pit stickiness of nostalgia. But anxiety about daily life's relentless momentum, tempered by Wilder's simultaneous acknowledgment of the necessity of keeping pace with that momentum, is everywhere in these early plays.

Foregrounding this aspect of Wilder's work is the best antidote to accusations of nostalgia. Grover's Corners is not being brought closer by its theatrical revival; it's becoming more remote, and Emily Webb's example points out the impossibility of returning. It's vital to remember Emily's plangent realization from the play's final act: "It goes so fast," she says. "We don't have time to look at one another."[9] These lines apply as much to the theatrical situation's focused mode of looking as to everyday life's more vagrant glances. What would it mean to really see each other? Is it even possible? As the everyday plays indicate, Wilder thought that it was only possible to bring a changing self into momentary alignment with a changing world during moments of self-conscious transit between emotional or mental states. For his spectators, the possibility lay in the tantalizing interval fleetingly visible between one image mastered and abandoned by the gaze, and another taking shape to replace it.

Many critics, keen to redeem what they frequently perceive as Wilder's stalwart optimism from the darker depths visible in the plays, have clung to his metaphors of motion as evidence of an unshakeable belief in progress: in the Protestant-liberal-evolutionary view of history as constant material, social, and intellectual improvement, the movement of humanity closer to perfection, either in religious or secular-humanist terms. So, for example, Lincoln Konkle, in *Thornton Wilder and the Puritan Narrative Tradition*, links Wilder, through his New England roots and religious education, to the Puritan tradition of seeing America as the proving ground for the working-out of God's plan, interpreting his onstage journeys as latter-day Pilgrim's Progresses. Konkle views *The Happy Journey* as an affirmation of "national progress,"[10] and *Pullman Car* as expressing "the structure and theme of progress, providentially determined on all levels."[11] (In the book that seems to have inspired Konkle's book, Amos Wilder, the playwright's brother, and an incisive literary critic, points out the pitfalls of explaining Wilder's writing too much by reference to the family's stern New England antecedents.)[12] Although Paul Lifton, in the most recent full-length study of Wilder's plays, is more attentive to the plays' ambiguities, he still suggests that Wilder's journeys "frequently parallel inner voyages of spiritual discovery."[13]

When readers are less comforted by what they find, the interpretations favor the pessimistic obverse. In his recent book considering the parallel careers of the two Wilder brothers, Christopher Wheatley argues that the journeys enacted in the plays represent an untethered America, loosed from the old bonds that formerly knit it together, religion chief among them. He sees *The Happy Journey* as a celebration of "piety" and *Pullman Car Hiawatha*'s passengers as lost in solipsism, deaf to the divine mysteries unfolding around them.[14] Most dubiously, he concludes that the plays represent an unequivocal "affirmation of conventional values."[15] (Marc Robinson, the keenest of Wilder's contemporary critics, gives us a salutary reminder of the danger of making Wilder's plays appear either too dark or too light, suggesting instead that his characters meet crisis with "clear vision, direct language, common sense, and respect for fact—a vigorous, flexible simplicity, disarming to the degree that it is undeterred.")[16]

The best corrective to both the too-sanguine view of progress and the too-simple picture of cultural decline, like many such adjustments, comes from Wilder himself. Speaking about the difficulties of imaginative narration, he once argued that the problem of telling about past lives "lies in the effort to employ the past tense in such a way that it does not rob those events of their character of having occurred in freedom." Wilder calls "unacceptable" any style of writing about the past that freezes the "historical in a determinism."[17] Or, we could even say, freezes the theatrical instant in a too readily prescribed interpretation—Wilder has too much tact, too little presumption for that.

In what follows, I'll depart from these teleologies, while reaffirming the central place of figures of journeying in Wilder's theater. The providential readings of Wilder think too much about destinations on the horizon and not enough about movement—which is always Wilder's primary focus. My argument here is that Wilder believed mostly in motion itself: in relentless change as the only constant factor of human life and human perception; in the impossibility of standing still in any attitude, feeling, or sensation; in the necessity of being transformed with the world's transformations. For Wilder, constant change was the key to a new, quintessentially American, theatrical aesthetics—rejecting much of European modernism—and a new ethics of spectatorship pitched to the rigorous demands of being, feeling, and thinking like an American in the modern world. In the first part of this chapter, I'll discuss Wilder's affinities with theories of art and experience developed by transcendentalist and pragmatist philosophers. This prologue will set the stage for my readings of the four everyday plays.

Seeing movement even in apparent stasis, and asking spectators to see it too, was Wilder's artistic answer to his own inescapable awareness of everyday life as both stillness (repetitions of habit, thought, and surroundings that seem to deny the bare fact of constant change) and remorseless transit. For Wilder, the everyday was also a proving ground for his democratic ideas about art. If the smallest thing can be beautiful, beauty is more in the mind of its beholders than in the conception of artists, and we must reappraise our insistence on the grandiose conflicts of conventional drama. The ability to see the beautiful in the mundane was for Wilder a uniquely American capacity: born among the Puritans, ripened at Walden Pond, and continuing with his own theater of the everyday.

Despite Wilder's avowed Americanism—artistically productive, but never parochial—and his own searching appraisal of the American literary and philosophical tradition in books like *American Characteristics* and elsewhere, there has been a tendency to explain Wilder's aesthetic innovations in terms of European models. Wilder's innovations have been traced to Brecht, symbolism, Pirandello, and even the traditional Chinese theater. His family lived in China for a time during his boyhood, and Wilder himself made reference to his use of "Chinese dramatic techniques" in *Our Town*. But I'd like to consider Wilder's works in terms of his thoughtful engagement with American transcendentalist, pragmatic, and process philosophy, and in particular with these schools' ideas about aesthetics. He shares these thinkers' common concern with constant motion as the true ground of human consciousness, and everyday experience as the wellspring of aesthetic awareness. In his various published works, Wilder quotes liberally from Thoreau and William James. (I'd also argue that Emerson, never Wilder's favorite, is nevertheless present between the lines.) Moreover, Wilder was a contemporary of John Dewey, and, having taught at the University of Chicago, where the Philosophy Department was deeply saturated with Dewey's thinking, must have been aware of his work. Both men were pedagogues and progressives. But more importantly, Wilder's everyday plays, like Dewey's aesthetic ideas, represent experience as itself a kind of stage, the scene of incremental transformation effected through changes of perception.

In this way, Wilder is an inheritor of what Branka Arsic, in her radical recent reappraisal of the philosopher, terms Emerson's "complex philosophy of leaving."[18] Though a devotee of Thoreau, frequently citing his clarion call for "simplicity, simplicity," and finding in *Walden* a model for American consciousness,[19] Wilder is unfailingly scornful of Emerson in his letters and journals, accusing him of pomposity and superficiality. But perhaps Wilder protested too much. Isabel Wilder, his sister and faithful amanuensis, once wryly noted the unacknowledged intellectual affinity between the two by suggesting that "the shoe pinched."[20] When Emerson says that "the deepest pleasure comes, I think, from the occult belief that an unknown meaning and consequences lurk in common every day facts,"[21] he sounds very like Wilder's famous maxim saying that *Our Town* is an attempt to find "a value beyond all price for the smallest events of our daily life."[22]

Arsic frames her study with a suggestive passage from Emerson's essay "Compensation": "Every soul is by this intrinsic necessity quitting its whole system of things, its friends, and home, and laws, and faith, as the shell-fish crawls out of its beautiful but stony case, because it no longer admits of its growth, and slowly forms a new house."[23] Arsic argues that Emerson's philosophy of leaving was an answer to his enervating awareness of everyday life as repetition and routine, a succession of habit-dulled days—despite knowing that life was in constant flux all around him. These lines could serve as an epigraph to Wilder's everyday plays, concerned as they are with departures that free characters from accustomed habits of thought, painful but necessary quittings of familiar surrounds (sometimes on the edge of death). For spectators, too, they require quittings of habitual ways of seeing, thinking, and feeling—the creation of new houses to replace the old. As Arsic reminds us: "This deepest pleasure that comes from experiencing the familiar as inexperienced, hence alluring—because it entrusts us again with our world and makes us want to live in it—is a function of nothing less than the recovered possibility of the happiness of a common day."[24]

Houses of Thought

You could even say that Thoreau and Emerson represent opposing tensions in Wilder's work, neither ever fully mastering the other. If Thoreau is the philosopher of staying, of constructing new dwellings and, with them, new ways to live, amid the raw stuff of everyday experience, Emerson is the philosopher of leaving, the reminder that, for changeable creatures like ourselves, all such accommodations are temporary in a changing world. Wilder's everyday plays stage a tension between Thoreau-like moments of arrested attention—bracketed, framed, frozen; temporary resting points for the gaze and the brain—and Emersonian departures, the necessary abandonment of these resting places.

A key passage from Wilder's lecture on *American Characteristics*—published some twenty years after these plays, but so resonant with them that a careful reader can't help but assume that it codified ideas long ambient in his works—suggests that the temporary convocation of disparate minds assembled in a theatrical audience is the real community to which *Our Town*'s title alludes, and to which Wilder's theater of the everyday was addressed:

> Every American has a large disposition to believe that there is a truth for him, and that he is in the process of laying hold of it. He is building his own house of thought and he rejoices in seeing that someone else is also a-building. Such houses can never be alike—begun in infancy and constructed with the diversity which is the diversity of every human life.[25]

The Thoreau echo here is obvious. Each American is engaged with building his or her own mental Walden from the materials of everyday life, figuring out how to live and why. We might recall Stanley Cavell's brilliant reading of *Walden*. Cavell argues that, while composing his book, Thoreau's experience of daily life became thoroughly blended with his reading and his writing, that there was no separation between life and the writing of life, between the documented past of the book and the living present of the author. For Cavell, the quintessential parable of American independence is also a story about the productive blurring of art and everyday existence.[26] A section from Wilder's journals parallels this theme:

> America was founded by those who repudiated authority (king, father, custom); the sense of the aloneness of the individual unaided

> and unsuppressed by authority was enhanced by the vastness of the land and the multitude of beings; these mental attitudes increased in them the sense that experience is a process of making: place, time, and destiny are *to be made*; the objects about them are separate, self-developing, hence without any other emotional relation to ourselves than that which we may impose upon them by thought. Literature (and thought) is then the conferring of meaning on "process."[27]

If experience is a process of making, of conferring meaning on flux, it shares characteristics with art.

Whether the similarity is conscious or not, it's worth mentioning here that Wilder's everyday plays were written at roughly the same time as John Dewey was delivering the set of Harvard lectures that later became *Art as Experience*. The progressive functions of both experience and art that Wilder describes above are uncannily similar to Dewey's ideas. In *Art as Experience* Dewey argues, anticipating many of the most radical artistic experiments of the twentieth century, mostly still decades away, that aesthetic qualities potentially inhere in every experience, expertly practiced craft, or perfectly realized idea. The carpenter at her lathe, the mathematician at her blackboard, and the artist at her easel can all equally experience the creative moment, produce objects or ideas of great beauty, and convey that beauty to a beholder. A moment of startling, revelatory perception bracketed off from daily life can linger as memorably in the mind as any painting. Art in its more commonly recognized manifestations models this kind of enriched perception, but doesn't exist apart from it. The point is that the experience—of making or beholding—reach what Dewey calls "consummation," in which it arrives at a shapely structure, an organic form based on the realization of its own internal qualities.[28] As we saw in my introduction, Dewey's ideas neatly undo avant-gardist notions of the autonomy of art and bourgeois elite-cultural ideas of the rarefied sphere of art, necessarily separate from ordinary life, without resorting to his era's radical programs for political transformation. Dewey argued for a progressive conception of both art and politics: for ceaseless renovation of received forms with no teleological end point on the horizon. For Dewey, change—perceptual, political—simply leads to more change.

Wilder shares Dewey's intellectual restlessness, and his belief that the fruits of experience lie in the future. In Wilder's theorizing about American habits of thinking and feeling we see staged the same tension between movement and stasis, the urge to stay and the need to depart, that typifies his everyday plays. Even though the erecting of a unique house of thought is the life-project of every American—the crucial "conferring of meaning on 'process' "—Wilder continually returns to the idea that meaning and motion are inseparable. He suggests that there is only one way by which Americans can ever feel themselves in relation to other Americans—when they are "united with them in a project, caught up in an idea and propelled with them toward the future."[29]

As I have already suggested, Wilder's obsession with staging scenes of travel indicates that, to his mind, the theater is a place where, in transit between destinations, Americans might feel themselves in fragile relation to one another. Engaged with the project of making meaning and discarding it, of grasping a new image and leaving it behind, Wilder's spectators are most together when they're most apart—abandoning each fresh-built understanding, clearing the stage for a successor. When he notes, in "Some Thoughts on Playwriting," that theater is an art directed to the "group-mind,"[30] demanding the active cognitive collaboration of spectators, he doesn't simply mean that theater's illusions depend on the accumulated credulity of an audience. Rather, he refers to the constellation of a temporary community of irreducibly different minds, a town of individual houses of thought.[31]

This is a bracing corrective to the widely held idea that Wilder's *Our Town* represents a normative America. If each American inhabits a unique "house of thought," irreducibly individual in design and materials, then the gathering-together each night of Wilder's spectators at his play creates a "town" of perceiving minds looking out from their apperceptive dwelling places, with each spectator busily perceiving, and no two spectators perceiving exactly the same thing. This form of community of consciousness is explicitly alluded to in *Our Town* when the dead, dispassionate spectators to the travails of the living flip the play's perspective and locate the town of Grover's Corners among the audience members in the auditorium;[32] and in *Pullman Car Hiawatha* when the thinking passengers create a buzzing murmur matching that emanating from the auditorium.[33] It appears in *The Long Christmas Dinner* when Genevieve is tormented by afterimages of all the thinking and feeling expended in the family home over generations (and, by implication, in whatever theater the play is being performed in),[34] and when the passengers in *Happy Journey* have a sudden, world-expanding realization of how big America really is, how full, like the theater in which it is being performed, of other thinking, feeling beings.[35] All these instances in which the time and activity of the audience is joined to the time of the stage serve to remind Wilder's spectators that they are all witnesses to the same event, but are not necessarily seeing it the same way. For Wilder, the shared experience of common difference is a truer picture of America, in all its vastness. And creating frames for the individual perceptions of his disparate spectators became the basis of his theatrical experimentation in the everyday plays.

New Modalities of the True and the Beautiful

At this distance from the previous century's critical scuffles, perhaps it's time to recoup the "mid" from Dwight Macdonald's scabrous appraisal of Wilder as "Midcult."[36] One of the things Macdonald found most offensive about the purveyors of midcult was that they were neither high-mindedly modernist in the vanguard-of-the masses way, nor "authentically" folk-cultural, but sought to mediate between the two terms—basically, in his assessment, dumbing-down and diluting high art while pretentiously looking down on popular forms. While *Our Town* assuredly does not "do the feeling for spectators," the central charge in Macdonald's midcult indictment,[37] the idea of Wilder's theater as in-between registers and forms is apt and useful. As Amos Wilder reminds us, Thornton Wilder wanted to be modern without sacrificing the possibility that his theater might be available to all spectators: innovative but also democratic, progressive rather than revolutionary.[38] We might think again of Cavell's Walden: art intervenes to give shape to experience, even as experience provides the raw material for the making of art. Wilder's in-betweenness attempts to accomplish a similar function. As he once said: "Art (significance) doesn't begin when the curtain goes up or end when it goes down."[39]

Let's call his theater "medial" rather than midcult. Wilder was undoubtedly invested in creating his own artistically productive version of in-betweenness—mediating between stage and auditorium, between everyday life and art, between a vanished cultural past and an unknown future, between the tangible, observable world of daily life and an enormous universe. In his bold address "Culture in a Democracy," he would eventually militate against all cultural leadership by elites—not just the aristocrats of the classical tradition, but the cadres of modernists, too (he cites Eliot, the high priest of literary newness).[40] Wilder was opposed to all teleologies of taste, revanchist or radical. He proposed instead a liberality of imagination, an unguarded appreciation for what he called elsewhere "new modalities of the true and the beautiful,"[41] the new forms of art that democratic culture would eventually propagate. Anyone who finds Wilder stodgy should pause to consider his early and enthusiastic embrace of pop art, a later generation's attempt to transfigure the commonplace, expressed in terms uncannily akin to his own artistic aims with *Our Town*—"a joyous effort to accommodate all that is tiresome and joyless in national life . . . to digest it in creativity."[42] As Wilder once put it: "I do believe in perpetual modification of the basic received ideas of society, a constant reform."[43]

The aspiration to create progressive forms of art, with its echoes of Dewey's ideas, that are nevertheless, at least in theory, available to anyone, unites Wilder with the other artists I will consider later. By bringing everyday experience to the stage, he didn't seek, like so many European modernists, to abolish distinctions between art and life, or to destroy the institution of the theater. Rather, he sought to use the theater's very apartness, its distance from quotidian life, its status as an interruption of routine, as well as the conventional expectation that the stage is a place of high drama and not humdrum sights, in order to provide clarifying distance, the chance to see brightly, in a new way.

In all the everyday plays, the stage is deliberately figured as a space in-between, the site of perpetual modifications: between destinations as in *Pullman Car* and *Happy Journey*, between life and death in *The Long Christmas Dinner*, between both past and present and life and death in *Our Town*. Wilder is careful to mark this visually with a stage that continues into the wings (and perhaps beyond) on both sides in *Pullman Car* and the opposing portals of life and death in *Long Christmas Dinner*. Even Grover's Corners' name invokes a crossroads, an in-between place, only partially glimpsed—set between past and present, life and death, the beginning of a theatrical evening and the end. Wilder is always scrupulous about reminding readers that his plays present only a small piece of a larger whole: one confined section of a busy train, a single carload of passengers on a highway, one dinner table on successive Christmases, a couple of households in a bigger town (itself only a crossroads in a larger landscape).

This isn't the naturalist slice of life, where a precisely measured section is sheared off reality, its modest sample size and precise borders assuring the veracity of what's onstage. Rather, Wilder's small pieces point insistently to the immensities surrounding any commonplace scene or instant of perception, and to the impossibility of ever seeing the whole. The proper context of any moment of reality is unknowable; only in transit between perspectives, during shifts of scale and register, can glimmers of provisional truth be spotted. The plays are, as Marc Robinson eloquently points out, perpetually and uneasily poised between rehearsal and performance:

> The stage we look at—enclosing a repetition of the now-inaccessible first performance, and before that, first rehearsal, and still further back, first draft—recedes even as the play asserts, no less vigorously than in any other theater, the irreproducibility of the performance we're watching . . . [Wilder] tells us, with equal conviction, that his play is finished and unfinished, grown and growing, inanimate and animate, written and being written.[44]

Motion and stillness held in irresolvable tension is, of course, also the central paradox of playwriting, one that assumes special importance in light of Wilder's preoccupations in these works. The playwright transfixes future motion in the stillness of text, creating motive potentialities in arrested words. Writing mediates between the temporarily stilled velocity of the author's consciousness and the reigniting propulsions of theatrical performance and spectatorship.

Wilder's Stage Manager—a figure with omniscient author-like knowledge, who is, nevertheless, explicitly not the author—is this conundrum brought to life. He's caught between text and enactment, rehearsal and performance, inside and outside the frame, both narrating and embodied, a character and a non-character. He restores liveliness to the text before reabsorbing enacted scenes into narration. In both *Our Town* and *Happy Journey*, the Stage Manager first appears leaning on a proscenium pillar, between stage and audience, fiction and reality, then and now. He's both a spectator and an actor. He possesses an author's omniscient foreknowledge, but he is also a careful tender of the moment-by-moment experience of the play, parceling out imaginative fodder. He doesn't just narrate, although he does do that. Rather, he indicates, points to things, manages perspective, moves a scene along so it doesn't become too much subject to one way of feeling or seeing. As soon as spectators become accustomed to a particular framing of a scene, a mode of representation, a stable assignment of background and foreground, he tactfully shifts it. His refrains are: "Now that'll do"; "All right"; "That's enough of that."[45] (In the *Happy Journey*, though the Stage Manager doesn't explicitly narrate, he keeps the play in motion by stepping into, and out of, the minor roles that mark the borders of the scenes—tactfully cuing shifts in locale and mood, while also keeping the otherwise almost-naturalistic quality of the scenes from tipping over into a too-neat alignment of theatrical and fictional realities.)

Wilder keeps his theater suspended between poles because the human mind, too, is always in between coordinates—caught between experience and memory, self and sensation. It's not that, as Macdonald suggests, Wilder wants the best of both tenses, but rather that he fears human minds get the worst, that clutching at the past or reaching for the future prevents them from seeing the present. As he once put it to an interviewer: "What stands still turns to pillars of salt . . . the world is full of bright people and brightness is seeing things in a new way."[46]

Reality in Motion

Wilder's determination to keep reality in motion, to show it as always in the process of being made, lies behind his emptying of the cluttered realist stages of his time. At the end of the 1920s, Wilder found himself at a crisis point as both a playwright and a spectator. He began to "lose pleasure in going to the theater," certain that the theater of his time was "fulfilling only a small part of its potentialities." As he later put it in his preface to *Three Plays*, he resolved to begin writing "one act plays that tried to capture not verisimilitude but reality."[47]

All of Wilder's everyday plays take place on a deliberately bare stage, and this bareness constituted a deliberate refutation of realism's visuality. What was radical about Wilder's dramaturgy, then, was not simply his turn to the everyday, but his certainty that realism and naturalism were inadequate for representing reality. More than this, he thought that such empirically based genres of imagining the real were intrinsically un-American; in fact, that a truly American theater could not be naturalistic because American life was not "naturalistic" in that way. For Wilder, a true imaginative libertarian, America's diversity could never be reduced to a reified image of the real, and the irreducible plurality of an American audience could never assent to such an image.

A key to the artistic aims behind Wilder's empty stage lies in his opposition of the "density" of European experience with the nomadic, processional mode of American experience in his *American Characteristics*. He writes that everyday objects and habits in the old country "whisper that life has its repetitions, its recurring demonstrations that all is well—happy thought, that life with all its menace, its irruptions of antagonism and hatred, can be partially tamed."[48] Americans, however, he goes on to suggest, are "differently surrounded,"[49] in relation to everything and nothing, everyone and no one, every time and no time.

What, after all, is theatrical naturalism but a renewed claim about the "density" of everyday life, one in which each object, utterance, person can be indexed to the precisely calibrated socio-scientific coordinates of race, milieu, and moment? Many naturalist writers, of course, Zola and Strindberg among them, argued for a new conception of tragedy based on these nineteenth-century determinisms. But the other side of this causal relation is the comforting notion that everyday life's material and social components share the same meanings for everyone. To this density, the "bric-a-brac"[50] Wilder saw as his theatrical mission to clear away, Wilder opposed radical bareness, the mind's empty stage against the clutter of the old world's accumulated customs.

For Wilder, it was the everyday and not realism that represented the way forward. The distinction, as I make it here, might at first seem counterintuitive. Isn't realism the lingua franca of depicting quotidian events, characters, and scenes? But the difference is crucial to understanding both Wilder's theater and that of the artists I will consider in subsequent chapters (when even more stridently non-realist work can still usefully be considered as theater of the everyday). To start with, realism implies a consensus view of what constitutes the real, proposed by theater-makers, and ratified by spectators. It takes the constituent stuff of everyday experience and fixes it, stabilizes it, makes it the validating but forgettable backdrop to more important events. Peter Brooks eloquently argues in *Realist Vision* that realist art creates scale models of the real, manageable miniatures, that "give us a way to bind and organize the complex, and at times, overwhelming energies of the world outside us."[51] As Brooks goes on to lucidly suggest, realism, a form dedicated to registering through sight the presence of things in the world,

> tends to deal in "first impressions" of all sorts, and they are impressions on the retina first of all—the way things look. . . . It is on the basis of first impressions that the greatest realists will go on to far more encompassing and at times visionary visions, ones that

> attempt to give us not only the world viewed but as well the world comprehended.[52]

Brooks is primarily concerned with literary sight, the ways that realist fiction transposes its linguistic effects to the mind's eye. But his insights apply perhaps even more aptly to the theater, where seeing is believing (or not). Bert States has aptly described this latent animism of the realist stage—the notion that the stage itself encodes charged meanings, waiting to explode—as the expectation that "everything is in view, lying in wait."[53] Wilder's plays about the everyday expose and attempt to reorient the visual habits of realism in two intimately connected ways. His bare stage disturbed the relationship between foreground and background, reality effects and dramatic episodes; and his obsession with motion unsettled the difference between stillness and flux.

Unsatisfied with the illusive firmness of theatrical first impressions, Wilder undermined the possibility of such stability altogether by starving the eyes of spectators accustomed to visual surfeit. While his plays appeal constantly to the eye, they do so in unaccustomed ways. Wilder is most interested in second (and third) impressions: jolting reframings of quotidian scenes that compel renewed attention to sights normally taken for granted; enlarged surrounds that amplify the fragile importance of everyday events while dwarfing them with the enormities of cosmic time and space. It's precisely by denying the reality of first impressions that he reaches his own encompassing visions. (A *Life Magazine* photo feature from 1938, when *Our Town* was running on Broadway—notes that the scenery-less play was giving its audience a "new thrill.")[54]

Most of Wilder's everyday plays are built around looking—and then looking again, this time with new eyes. Emily's return in *Our Town*'s last act is an impossible second glance at perished sights for both the dead girl and Wilder's spectators. *Pullman Car Hiawatha* takes in a quotidian scene of travel and then resituates it against the limits of human imagination. *The Happy Journey*, unfussy but insistent, accelerates motion and perception to show the fragility of human minds' claim on experience. *The Long Christmas Dinner* moves so fast that it turns everyday life's seeming interminability into a brief variation on oblivion. For Wilder, realism and habituated dullness were synonymous, both inside and outside of theater. The idea was to prevent the real from solidifying into an "ism," rather than to reproduce staid forms to reify it. Wilder's theater of the everyday is a democratic mode, prying apart habitual arrangements of perception to allow the elemental particles of everyday life to be reassembled in idiosyncratic shapes. To him, everyday experience is irreducibly individual and so should aesthetic experience be.

In Wilder's plays about the everyday, spectators are constantly confronted with a singular visual paradox: compositions made up of stationary figures, often seated, that are nevertheless understood to be in constant motion. The train travelers in *Pullman Car Hiawatha*, the car passengers in *The Happy Journey to Trenton and Camden*, the rapidly aging generations in *The Long*

Christmas Dinner—all are in rapid transit through space and time, their conveyances roughed in with the few simple chairs that Wilder stipulated be the only furnishings onstage, even as they remain confined to the boundaries of the stage. Given how often these figures are tasked with observing some action outside the immediate vicinity of the stage—remarking on rapidly passing scenery in *Happy Journey* or *Pullman Car*, stopping to gaze at a New Hampshire moon in *Our Town*, rhapsodizing the same icebound branch in *Long Christmas Dinner*—they inevitably bring to mind the other crucial group of seated figures making simultaneous journeys through space and time, Wilder's audience. That this parallel is deliberate is evident in the number of times onstage characters locate some fleeting sight in the audience, identifying seemingly stationary spectators with transitory, changeable panoramas. Wilder continually prompts spectators to see movement behind stillness, and to pay attention to their own seeing. He reminds his viewers that they themselves are always in motion, whether they're aware of it or not.

Perhaps the most disturbing instance of this phenomenon comes in the third act of *Our Town*, when the deceased inhabitants of the hilltop cemetery outside Grover's Corners resemble nothing so much as the real-world theatrical audience facing them. Wilder stipulates that the dead are arranged in rows, and like good spectators, they stare fixedly ahead of them, disregarding the many similarly disposed figures all around. Meanwhile, in a stunning reversal of perspective, the town itself, the scene of human pushing, striving, and stumbling that the dead dispassionately observe—and that spectators have spent the two previous acts likewise observing—is transposed onto the auditorium. For a few eerie early moments at the beginning of the play's final act, we are the spectacle. The dead are watching us, the living, as we change and die before them. For Wilder, stillness and becalmed contemplation are the prerogative of the dead.[55]

Wilder's subtle deployment of autobiographical elements in the plays amplifies this uncanny sense that the plays are looking back at their spectators. They seem, in fact, to be looking directly at him. In *The Happy Journey*, Ma and Pa remark on the architecture of the Lawrenceville School, where Wilder lived and taught for several years. The passengers in *Pullman Car Hiawatha* see the University of Chicago, where Wilder also taught, as they approach the city. Amos Wilder speaks eloquently of Thornton's attachment to the New Hampshire locales of their boyhood, scenes that resurfaced in *Our Town*.[56] Emily, the namesake of Emily Dickinson, was also the name of the daughter of a beloved Lawrenceville colleague.[57]

Branka Arsic's interpretation of Emerson illuminates the optical effect of Wilder's bare stage. She suggests, explicating Emerson's theories of visuality, that human beings "inhabit their visual field in the same way that they inhabit language." A framed perspective solidifies the objects it contemplates in the same way that language grasps the objects it signifies. Perspective "names" what it frames:

> It signifies the ways, as Emerson puts it, in which the eye of the subject has integrated a "mass of objects" into a coherent subjective picture, just as a name collects a variety of properties into a fixed identity . . . Through its distortion of the visible, perspective isolates us within idealism, since it is idealism that teaches us the difference "between the observer and the spectacle."[58]

Arsic goes on to make a suggestive distinction between "gazing" and "glancing" in Emerson's thinking about perception. The "gaze," a clutching at experience, attempts to master, stabilize, and hold fast what it sees; the "glance," the roving method of aleatory sight, the mode of everyday looking suddenly caught by some fugitive sight, "sees the transition itself."[59] She opposes "the trained, sedate and focused eye" to "one capable of catching minute changes," able to see "through a thing in the moment of its transformation."[60]

There is a large ethical dimension to this distinction between ways of seeing. Gazers effectively ask for the world to remain stable as they contemplate it, and implicitly expect to remain the same while they watch. Glancers accept that what they are seeing is in flux, and that they themselves are, too. Gazers see an unbridgeable gulf between spectator and spectacle; glancers find themselves in what they see. As Arsic points out, Emerson pleads for alertness to "every thing"[61]—the opened space between the usually conjoined words pointing to the chasm between seeing an undifferentiated "everything" and contemplating the gaps between, the telling differences, in "every thing." Wilder's empty stage is nothing but gap, the space between objects almost infinite, since, as he once put it, "our claim, our hope, our despair are in the mind—not in things, not in scenery."[62]

Wilder's characters are glancers. Their wandering eyes constantly interrupt his dramaturgy. (Indeed, *The Happy Journey* is made up of practically nothing but glances.) Wilder's everyday plays are full of moments when he stages his characters' attention being momentarily caught by something: a blurred road sign, an icebound branch, a glimpse of the moon. For Wilder, these intervals become the record of a fragile, unique mind's claim upon the world outside, the purest instances of the unrepeatable fact of perception, tiny artworks in themselves. For spectators, too, they are the kind of passing moments that are just as likely to be forgotten as remembered. After all, they're not consequential to the plot. These figments only assume their full measure of importance later on, when, like Emily, audience members must confront how much experience they've already lost. Seen this way, Emily's return from the grave isn't a scene about the supernatural appearance of a ghost, or an argument about any metaphysical idea of an afterlife to return from. Rather, it's a theatrical thought experiment: an impossible instance of revived perception, twice-experienced experience. But revisiting the scene of already-experienced sights, smells, and sounds causes Emily to fall into pernicious theatricality. She doesn't just live it again; she watches herself live it again.

Peter Szondi's key insight that *The Long Christmas Dinner* is "a secular mystery play about time"[63] could apply to all of these plays. (*The Long Christmas Dinner*, of course, is actually very short.) Each, in its way, is concerned with the mysteries of sharing time and experience. As Stephen Kern points out in *The Culture of Time and Space*, the opening decades of the twentieth century were characterized by a crisis in the perception of time, a rupture between private and public modes of experiencing its passage.[64] Almost simultaneous with the completion of the long process of standardizing time zones that ensured mechanical time could at last be told in a uniform way, Einstein's insights about relativity shattered the idea that time could be universal or absolute. Time became subject to speed, vantage point, and location, dependent on perception, and the relation of observer to observed—a theatrical conception of time, in fact.

This distinction between time as a remorseless, universal, geological force and time as measured by the contingent experiences of disparate minds is central to Wilder's theater.[65] A theater filled with spectators is like a train car filled with passengers, an automobile filled with riders, or a communal dinner table. All three are situations of common time and shared experience that bring the private time of individuals and the public time of an assembled group together, creating occasions at once shared by proximity and refracted by disparate minds. These journeys, defined more by duration and experience than by generic conventions or theatrical expectations, became Wilder's way to flout received definitions of dramatic structure, and to split realism into its constituent parts.

At this point, it's helpful to return to Fredric Jameson's incisive reading of realism. He argues that realism, a deeply schizophrenic mode, always contains within itself the seeds of its own dissolution. To Jameson, these are the "antinomies" of realism: its hidden schism between fable (plot, story, narrative) and experience, or what he calls "affect," sensations too inchoate to fall into preexisting emotional categories.[66] Citing Barthes, he notes that the choices and actions faced by realist characters are frequently exceptional—he calls this "marked time," a fateful chronology elevated from quotidian cycles—even as the most humdrum details bind those actions in place with sensory detail that serves no direct plot-advancing function. (Barthes famously called these superfluities "reality effects.") Put another way, according to Jameson, realism is riven by an unacknowledged contradiction between narrative and sensory experience. The momentous events depicted by the narrative frequently pull the artwork away from the ordinary circumstances that its descriptive elements work so hard to evoke.

Throughout *Our Town*, dramatizing this split concern with public and private time, fable and affect, Wilder intersperses theatricalist moments when the time of the spectators is reconnected to that of the performance. At the end of the first act, the Stage Manager invites them to go smoke a cigarette;[67] at the close of the second, he carefully notes how long the intermission will be;[68] at the end of the play, he wishes them good rest.[69] At many points in the play, characters and audience members stop to savor the same sights and smells together—or the suggestion of them, anyway. The beautiful moon and the fragrant heliotropes in the concluding moments of the first act are the precursors of the precious details Emily wishes she'd noticed in the third.[70] For Wilder, as for John Dewey, shared experience is the greatest human good, precious in its contingency.

"On the stage it is always now," Wilder wrote; "the personages are standing on that razor-edge between the past and the future, which is the essential character of conscious being."[71] But Wilder's "always now"[72] is far more fine-grained than simply the realist theater's magic proposition that events are really happening, and happening for the first time. It's a "now" predicated on the idea that, in the words of Alfred North Whitehead, a philosopher—as his diaries and letters attest—who was often on Wilder's mind, "every occasion in the existence of a conscious being is unique . . . happens but once."[73] Every one of these singular occasions is both an arrival and a departure. The theatrical now is something constantly constituted and reconstituted by spectators—a succession of unrepeatable instants departed from almost as soon as they arrive. Just as every moment of experience pits a finite mind against a huge universe, every moment of a theatrical performance tests fragile presence against disappearance.

Wilder's theater deliberately pits the repetitions inherent in the theatrical process against the indivisible singularity of any audience member's perceptions. The performance has happened before, is happening again—and has never happened quite like this and will never happen like this again. Wilder's is a theater dedicated to tracking the advancing narrow knife-edge of the present, while stripping the stage of those visual markers that would tie it to a previously established solid-state reality—perpetually caught between recollection of the past and anticipation of the future. He advocated a mode of spectatorship attuned to catch the flickering instant of transition between states. "The pure event" he adds, borrowing a locution from Stein, is "more interesting than any comment that can be made upon it."[74] For Wilder, the "pure event" meant primarily the perceptual event, the ineffable cognitive alchemy that occurs when perceived object encounters perceiving subject, or when perceiving subjects subtly reorganize themselves around the perceived object.

Wilder was moving toward a conception of theater as "pure" experience—simply befalling spectators and leaving no traces behind. (His ideas of experiential purity may have been partly derived from William James, whose injunction against being impressed with the "abject truth"—the merely empirical truth, divorced from subjective understanding—Wilder cites in his preface to *Our Town*.)[75] For Wilder, this abject notion of truth was synonymous with realism's obsession with material verisimilitude; the more important reality to represent was the encounter of the human mind with the world outside.

Elsewhere, he writes that, throughout theatrical history, the various forms of moralizing drama were merely an alibi for the "exhibition of pure experience," even "experience for experience's sake."[76] But this version of purity was radically *im*-pure by most existing artistic standards. By arguing that art is mostly constituted by the minds that perceive it—and by writing plays structured to empty the stage of almost everything except the imagining of his audience—Wilder makes a virtue of the phenomenon that Michael Fried would eventually decry as "theatricality"[77] in minimalist art: the tenet that no aesthetic criteria or qualities inhere in the artistic object. Rather, that relationality, the meeting of observer with observed object, wholly constitutes the aesthetic event.

In a telling coincidence, Fried and Wilder both employ the same figure, a car trip through New Jersey, to articulate their respective views of the relationship between art and objecthood. Fried's essay quotes the artist Tony Smith's description of taking his students for a midnight drive along the partly finished New Jersey Turnpike. To Fried, celebrating the unruly perceptual chaos of looking out the windows of a car hurtling along the highway is the ultimate image of the minimalist nullification of artistic standards.[78] But Wilder's *The Happy Journey to Trenton and Camden* stages experience hurtling toward a car's passengers in order to dramatize the aleatory nature of everyday perception, and the beauties to be found in the happenstance of experience.

Looked at in light of the experiments with attention and perception that, several decades later, would characterize the project of the American avant-garde, the radical bareness of Wilder's stage appears as practically an empty frame in the sense that thinkers like John Cage would come to think about as the function of art: as a purposefully voided receptacle waiting to be filled with the aesthetic consciousness of spectators. You could perhaps even say that the tracks under Pullman Car Hiawatha lead to Cage's *4' 33"*.

Wilder's bare stage was the result of his thinking about experiential "purity." Put simply, the less he staged, the more his spectators had to picture themselves. His stage was not simply denuded of scenery. It was stringently empty, his plays packed with gestures of vacating, stripping down, wiping clean. Often, it is as if even leaving scenery behind after the conclusion of a performance would be too much of a gesture of permanence in the face of fleeting time. At the end of *Pullman Car Hiawatha*, the chalk marks on the stage denoting the passageways and apertures of the titular railway car are about to be washed away by a team of cleaning ladies—the stage scrubbed back to its bare boards, readied for the next performance, while redoubling the audience's sense of the ephemerality of the one that is concluding.[79] (The performance begins with the Stage Manager laying down the marks, already asserting that they will be a temporary intrusion on the boards' nakedness.) *Our Town* begins with the few naked furnishings that will indicate its places being brought on by the Stage Manager, emptiness populated, rather than a fictive scene discovered. And Wilder is careful to note that the already sparsely furnished stage should become starker as the piece goes on, forcing spectators, like poor Emily Webb, to conjure the material details of previous scenes—details always absent, but now twice absent—from memory. As he remarked in a letter to an admirer: "when Emily 'returns' there is not even the table and two chairs: all, all is in our minds."[80]

This points to an interesting paradox in Wilder's visuality. As Marc Robinson observes, "Wilder's characters are careful not to envision what they cannot see."[81] Ma Kirby, for instance, won't rest easy until she sees her daughter. But Wilder's blank stage demands that spectators constantly flicker between imagining things they cannot see—chickens being fed, beans being strung, gas being pumped, Christmas dinners being eaten, Midwestern landscapes flashing by—and paying close attention to the ways the tangible human beings before them invoke these presences. For Wilder, the objects are always secondary. Human attachment, use, and experience are all.

In his writing, too, Wilder was driving at bareness. Over and over in his essays, letters, and diaries, he returns to the notion of a theater that could be "mere" or "pure" description, free from the "editorial presence"[82] innate to the novel's stream of subjective narration or the realist theater's mania for tethering drama to precisely graphed social coordinates. Or even, perhaps, from the intervention of any authorial manipulation at all:

> *Our Town* evades every possible requirement of the legitimate stage. It is pure description, entirely devoid of anything even resembling conflict, expectation or action. The only other drama in all literature that I know of that is as static is the Trojan Women.[83]

The more "realist" passages in his plays show Wilder's easy fluency in establishing place and persons with accent, idiom, and reference across a broad spectrum of social classes and locales, but the particular is always deployed in service of a larger generality. As Wilder once wrote of Dickinson, the particular only points to the general. His spare, plain language, deceptively folksy in its mastery of idiom but utterly unsentimental in its deployment of common usages to present uncommonly stark facts, was meant to provide a minimum of interference between the listener and the immensities described. The refracting prism of style would not blunt the force of his precise, indicative sentences. In *Our Town* or *Pullman Car Hiawatha*, the Stage Manager's speeches are an exercise in making the maximum amount of raw reality present in the theater—the immensity of the cosmos (whether conceived in scientific or theological terms), the weather outside, population statistics, the geographical contours of the landscape surrounding the visible scene—with a minimum of representational presence. As Wilder wrote to Stein while writing the play that became *Our Town*:

> My play #1 is as far as the stage has gone toward "mere" description. A New Hampshire town; its daily life; its living; its dead; its weather; its geology; its sociology; its mores as seen by an archaeologist a thousand years from now, its birth and death statistics and how Mrs. Gibbs ironed Doctor Gibbs' shirts—all in one great curve: quod erat demonstrandum.[84]

It's vital to remember that, for Wilder, particularity was the best route to allegorical universality. By hewing close to a New Hampshire setting, he's not daubing it in rose-hued colors, or holding it up as a cultural paragon, but is simply proposing it as one, contingent, however beloved by him, shape a human settlement could take. Wilder's ambition to create a theater of pure description prefigures the impulses of later artists of the everyday to put found objects, found text, found sounds, or amateur bodies onstage. Freeing art of the editorial impulse was John Cage's project, and that of many later artists, too. Wilder's theater predicts Lee Strasberg's efforts to hear the unfiltered grain of everyday speech; Stuart Sherman's attempts to see past language and habit to alternate quotidian worlds; and Nature Theater of Oklahoma's herculean efforts to make visible the artistic genius of casual talk.

I turn now to more detailed readings of the three short plays that together constitute a poetics for Wilder's new theater of the everyday. *Pullman Car Hiawatha* puts thought into perpetual motion, making constant departure the basis for a new epistemology and theatrical poetics. *The Happy Journey to Trenton and Camden* traces the self's permeable borders, suggesting that spectators are constituted by what they see and how they see it, both inside and outside the theater. Wilder makes space in the theater for an enlarged sense of humanity's affective changeability, treating emotions as scenery, and emotional life as constant transit between feelings. *The Long Christmas Dinner* sets the perceptual event against the parade of generations, contrasting personal (and theatrical) time with geological and historical time. These readings will set the stage for my consideration of *Our Town,* which places the most fragile and evanescent of quotidian experiences against the vast backdrop of a cosmic surround.

Almost Never Seeing: *The Long Christmas Dinner*

Unlike the characters in its companion plays, those in *The Long Christmas Dinner* never leave home, but despite remaining at table, they travel faster and further than Wilder's other journeyers. In its deliberately brief span, the play surveys ninety years and multiple generations as the temporary traffic of a narrow stage (one early reviewer compared its techniques to stop-motion film's ability to reveal the slow working of nature by collapsing time).[85] When Peter Szondi describes *The Long Christmas Dinner* as a secular mystery play about time, he does so by noting all the syncopated ironies in the play: time heals (but we see that it also destroys); things don't change (but they do, so fast we can hardly believe it); time passes slowly (it flies by before our eyes). Throughout, Wilder stipulates that the pantomime dinner routine should go on uninterrupted as the generations ebb and flow, running from cradle to grave[86]—a figure for the habituated routines that underwrite everyday time's repetitions, what Siobhan Phillips calls "a central problem—or opportunity—of this life: quotidian repetition, that possibly enervating, possibly empowering, recurrence endemic to daily time."[87]

Many of the play's ironies have to do with fragile memory and perishable perception. The similarities among the dinners, of course, only make the differences more apparent. Each fresh variation points to the poignant differences, as members of the family depart, age, and die. (The repetitions multiply exponentially if we consider the play's repeat performances.) But despite the play's hurtling velocity, Wilder periodically slows time down to the same pace inhabited by its spectator, then allows it to accelerate again. In these brief intervals, the action, as it will be again in *The Happy Journey* and *Our Town*, is that of seeing together. In every generation, at each dinner, some member of the family notices the same icebound branch and remarks upon the singularity of the experience in virtually the same words: "Every least twig is wrapped around with ice. You almost never see that."[88] The statement is first ironic, and then poignant. (The repetition of lines insisting that characters "look" or "see" is the counterpoint to all this irony—pointing to the singularity of each sight.) But each character is also right. We've never seen *that* person register that sight before, and each instance is actually altogether unlike the one that went before. If they stop to think about it, the play's spectators themselves might realize they're not the same, either. They're minutes older than the last time they saw the diners see the branch, minutes closer to their own exit from life's stage. As they look, and we look at them looking, and so at ourselves looking, the fragility of the onstage stillness during these isolated moments of perception is the fragility of human consciousness itself.

As Marc Robinson notes, the plain beauty of the line about the frozen branch is exactly equal to the evanescent moment of aesthetic perception it encapsulates, holding it still for an instant—freezing it—against the current of time that will sweep it away.[89] The line itself, as well as Wilder's direction that the stage be bathed in "sparkling winter sunlight,"[90] comes almost directly from Thoreau's journals, where it cues a meditation on the necessity of finding beauty in everyday things close at hand:

> Every leaf and twig this morning was covered with a sparkling ice armor; even the grasses in exposed fields were hung with innumerable

> diamond pendants, which jingled merrily when brushed by the foot of the traveler . . . Such is beauty ever—neither here nor there, now nor then, neither in Rome nor in Athens, but wherever there is a soul to admire. If I seek her elsewhere because I do not find her at home, my search will prove a fruitless one.[91]

But despite its homely setting, the beauty to be found everywhere in the everyday is ultimately unstable, liquid. Thoreau notes that "the scene changed at every step" and with every change of perspective, "as the head was inclined to the right or the left."[92] That glittering ice can't last.

Wilder's play similarly reminds us to see flux in seeming stability. What we can never actually see in day-to-day existence, what Wilder's play is constructed to disclose, is life at a distance, the arrow of time latent in every moment of daily life's seeming repetitions. Wilder asks that there be no curtain for the play, staging a moment of gradated transition from life to theater:

> The audience arriving at the theatre sees the stage set and the table laid, though still in partial darkness. Gradually, the lights in the auditorium become dim and the stage brightens until sparkling winter sunlight streams through the dining room windows.[93]

The play presents human life as a series of entrances and exits almost too fast to be registered. Wilder's notes for the play dictate briskness and momentum above all. After each death, each departure, he asks that the "tempo pick up its time at once,"[94] that the play quit its previous scene and move relentlessly toward the next. Just as the "least twig" is "wrapped with ice," so too is the temporary traffic of the stage surrounded by oblivion. The characters enter from the pre-existential void and exit to death's imponderable unknown. In between are restless movements, unexpected departures, temporary comforts.

Wilder pits the brief moment of human perception—onstage and in the auditorium—against the ceaseless transit of generations. Meanwhile, the world outside the house is changing rapidly—streets are paved, automobiles appear, the town grows.[95] (And, contrary to some overoptimistic readings of the play, these changes are not just evidence of progress and improvement. War breaks out, the family is dispersed, and its members become unhappy or self-satisfied.)

For audience members, this syncopated movement, as time quickens and stalls, running alternately at the slowed speed of focused perception and the accelerated pace of history, means that they must constantly historicize their own spectatorship, confronting the temporary nature of both their claim on the perishing performance and their rapidly running lives. This is the full import of Genevieve's anguished exclamation that she "can't stand" being in the house anymore because of the accumulated "thoughts" that come through the "very walls of the house" like soot: "the feeling about this house of the years grinding away."[96] Like the house, the theater itself is full of the maddening echoes of the spent murmuring of human consciousness.

A Recovered Language of Transformation: *Pullman Car Hiawatha*

In *Pullman Car Hiawatha*, Wilder stages an image of the theater as group-mind at work, clearing space to attend to the murmuring of consciousness itself. The scene is an overnight train ride from New York to Chicago on the night of December 21, a date with twinned significances. It's close to Christmas, and so suggests the prospect of epiphanic revelations. But it's also the date that the Pilgrims, apocryphally at least, disembarked at Plymouth Rock, inaugurating the long, complex, and frequently thwarted voyage of American democracy.[97]

Contemplating the train's passengers, who are disposed about the stage in attitudes of travelers' repose, and seated in "compartments" sketched on the floor with chalk markings, the Stage Manager invites the audience to listen to their thoughts. What issues forth from the stage then is an audible but purposefully illegible "murmuring-swishing noise."[98] Out of this fugue of choral sound emerge and subside solo voices speaking streams of ordinary cares and ruminations. One passenger ticks off a list of gifts bought for relatives; another obsesses amorously; a doctor reads from a medical journal; an insomniac tosses and turns; a businessman regrets impulsive investments.[99] Each thinking voice picks up from the previous one. The line of figures onstage is continuous in the work of thinking, even if they are all entirely separate in thought. Each asserts a fragile claim to unique expression, only to disappear again into the hum below. (These disappearances foreshadow the eventual death of one of the train's passengers, a reminder that every mind's hold on the world is only temporary.)

This enigmatic murmuring echoes the silent but similar buzzing going on throughout the auditorium as the assembled spectators do the work of absorbing the play, while also, no doubt, finding their own minds, like those of Wilder's passengers, dragged away from the stage every so often by the gravity of everyday concerns, the subconscious labor of the mind worrying away at previous hours. Spectators must weigh their own insistent internal soundtracks against the knowledge that all around them, similar cognitive work is being done by minds like theirs but utterly different, all soloists in the murmuring symphony of the thinking audience, the group-mind. (As we'll see in my final chapter, the idea of an immense thinking murmur of quotidian consciousness running nonstop across the country, making and discarding artistic shapes, is an image shared by Wilder's latter-day inheritors, Nature Theater of Oklahoma.)

In this cognitive circuit established between stage and auditorium—a temporary community founded on nothing but the recognition that many people are sitting together having diverse experiences in shared company—spectators are simultaneously brought closer together (they're all thinking and seeing together) and reminded of their irrevocable apartness (no two of them are seeing the same thing, and others' minds are fundamentally unknowable). This, in turn, suggests the millions of other American minds, and billions of other global minds, at work outside the theater's walls, all busily making sense of experience. Wilder creates an interval of the thinking sublime. The world we know is a shifting point orbited by uncountable minds, all with an equal claim on reality. ("Hundreds," thousands," "millions" are the important words in *Our Town*, Wilder once said.)[100]

The action of the play begins and ends with passages evocative of an everyday train ride. (Visiting a scene, then revisiting it—enlarging its surround, then forcing comparison with previous perceptions—is a dramaturgical device Wilder will return to in *Our Town.*) Starting with the murmur, and continuing with further orchestral elaborations on its theme, Wilder dramatizes experience as a process of making: the creation of contingent shapes for consciousness's constant hum. The thinking murmur is the ground note for the rest of the play, and, indeed, for the entire theatrical situation: the sound of earth amid the music of the spheres;[101] the counterpoint of mobile thought held against the stilled version embodied in scraps of quoted literature, philosophy, and homily;[102] a reminder of evaporating theatrical time as measured by spectators' and performers' experience of the proceedings; a celebration of the interpretive power that underwrites the play's representational leaps. Events rise up out of, and return to, the murmur, just as the audience's sense of the play emerges and takes shape amid the stream of sensory information and unbidden thoughts coursing along their own mental tracks.

The constant flux of thought is contrasted with the many forms of fixity suggested, and subverted, by the play, mottos and quotations as stable slices of congealed ideation, language and theatrical representation as modes of giving shape to thought's unnamed figments. Consciousness itself, the play reminds us, is a speeding train we can't get off of without becoming mad, or ceasing to be. One character, Harriet, disembarks early, suddenly dead. Another, the Insane Woman, was never really on board. Like the assembled dead in *Our Town*, her mind is with us, in the auditorium. She is the only character who looks out, the way we look on.[103]

The audible murmur of thought is juxtaposed with the inaudible secrets heard by Harriet as she is led away by angels to death, and with the private knowledge acquired by the madwoman, secrets too terrible for we ordinary thinkers and strivers, still riding the train of life ourselves. (Wilder clearly notes that the Insane Woman "is unconsoled" by what she hears.)[104] Or perhaps, rather, the secret of existence is leaving itself. Like Emily in *Our Town*, Harriet wants to stay most at the moment when she is most compelled to depart. Harriet's list of goodbyes—her childhood home with its "steps and doors and wallpapers," her teachers, her church—is at once entirely particular to a Midwestern childhood, and wrenchingly likely to have correlates among spectators' own private lists, personal tallies they may not realize they possess until they see her making hers.[105] In *American Characteristics*, Wilder talks about the serial form of the list as a democratic poetic device aptly suited to suggesting American magnitude, spilling details readers can cognitively rearrange themselves. Each item, precise, concrete, tangible, is a cue to imagination: in one sense "merely" descriptive, but overwhelming in the aggregate. Each entry indexes a vast affective, cognitive, behavioral surround, an entire house of thought. The list captures in language stray instances of congealed perception, mnemonic fragments like those Wilder stages in *The Happy Journey* with his characters' vagrant looks out the car windows.

As the speeding train races on through the Midwestern night, as the performance cuts irrevocably through theatrical space and time, Wilder keeps finding new vantage points to put before his spectators. The play stages intellectual inheritance not as continuity and growth but as restlessness and rupture, the constant supplanting of previous authorities by new ones, themselves to be soon left behind, culminating with the appearance of a new university, the University of Chicago, on the horizon, "the best of them all" (perhaps because its curriculum was still in flux when Wilder wrote the play). The University of Chicago here seems to stand in for a new paradigm for education, the culmination of the epistemic journey made by *Pullman Car Hiawatha*. But the train never really arrives. The passengers disembark, but as they do, the train is wiped away.[106]

The paradoxical project of the play, as articulated by the Stage Manager, is to graph the "position" of the speeding train—to, impossibly, fix points in disappearing time and space, in empirical reality, with weather readings, cartographic pronouncements, local landmarks, but also philosophically and theologically, culturally and historically. Extracts from the entire Western philosophical tradition mingle with commonsense homilies from folk culture, biblical proverbs, bits of beloved poems, and other intellectual flotsam.[107] (These coordinates, written by speech on the air, are no more stable or durable than the chalk marks with which the Stage Manager plots the outline of the train.) The play marks its movement by shifting among theatrical styles too, allowing a recognizable representational mode to coalesce before disrupting it and moving on. Attempting to transfix the progress of a racing train, Wilder suggests, is like trying to plot any instant of a theatrical performance or to arrest the quicksilver movement of the brain. The effort to locate is more important than the always-superseded result. (The play's title hints at another departure that occurred long before the play begins, the exit of the hero Hiawatha from the American scene, and from American history, and, with him, a whole vanished culture and way of being.)

As the train continues along, Wilder playfully exhausts all the inherited idioms, high and low, of the American theater. Modernism forms one track: naturalism, in the precisely observed swatches of train life presented at the beginning and end; expressionism, making the inner tumult of his madwoman figure visible; and classically inflected symbolism with allegorical figures and mythic scale (he even stipulates that the pretty girls dressed up as the Hours should look like a famous painting by the American symbolist Elihu Vedder).[108] But these high-art inflections are juxtaposed with the cheerful amateurism of the Sunday school pageant, and some hints of Follies-style spectacle. Christian and temperance drama show up, too, when angels appear to summon Harriet to the afterlife, and when a grim-faced Midwestern matriarch pleads for sobriety with a teetotaler song. Wilder hints at melodrama with Harriet's death's-door departure, and the madwoman's heightened pleadings. (And perhaps even with the play's railcar setting, tying his characters to the ceaseless movement of the train rather than the tracks.) Wilder's theater is free of the gentrifying hierarchies that typified thinking about the future of the American theater—or, indeed, American intellectual culture—at this time. He refuses to separate high from low, art from folk forms, literary from popular, canonical from commonsense.

Similarly, in the train's speeding course through the registers of human wisdom, Wilder refuses to segregate the titans of philosophy from the often forgotten but incalculably influential purveyors of homily. The train traverses the conventional history of Western philosophy as one line of stations in the night: Plato, Epictetus, Augustine. Yet Wilder records the presence of these ideas not so much as definite points on the rising chart of human knowledge, but rather as another kind of blurred scenery speeding past: not linear progress, but a series of way stations inhabited and abandoned. Tellingly, the texts in the classical series all have to do with life as a brief shadow of some higher reality, with the aleatory nature of existence that imbues life with one form rather than another, or with the constant striving of the living world.[109] And Wilder balances this high road with a contrapuntal line staging a series of common American cultural touchstones: Stevenson, Lowell, Service, temperance sayings, and others.[110]

With these juxtapositions, Wilder takes a pragmatic view of philosophy and its place in human thought. Every brain is a sea of bobbing fragments shaped by what's useful, what's remembered, what people like his characters tote around in daily life. These jumbled bits of text create an intellectual collage of high and low wisdom—masscult, midcult, and highcult—as the pieces of found text literally jostle one another for the spectator's attention in a theater of the mind. They're ironized by being misquoted, or forgotten, performed insufficiently loudly or at the wrong speed. Wilder subtly points out the ways that we use or misuse such texts in our daily lives, unsettling the fixity of print with forgetfulness, tempering sturdy book learning with the vagaries of human recall.[111]

The play's conception of identity is equally unstable. The Stage Manager, laconically stepping in and out of roles, script in hand, reminds us that the other performers, too, are only temporarily embodying their roles, filling berths on the imaginary train, and will shortly step out of them to resume their everyday lives. As the players stand in for natural features (a field), built additions to the landscape (a couple of small towns), philosophical mottos, folk-wise homilies, abstract theological principles, living characters and undead revenants, theatrical representation itself is stretched, compacted, pulled tight, allowed to go slack. The patent absurdity of an actor claiming to represent a field is set against the no less absurd, but far more commonplace, theatrical proposition that one human being can truly embody another.

Pullman Car Hiawatha thus models a radically democratic representation. Tramps and porters, doctors and lunatics, fields and towns, philosophy and theology, Sunday school pageants and symbolist art, the living and the dead, the animate and the inanimate, all have a "right to be in this play," as the Tramp puts it.[112] Realism alone, Wilder clearly suggests, isn't ecumenical enough to depict American realities. (Wilder's inclusion of a railroad watchman, present only to say that he's doing his job and everything is fine, a humdrum appearance antithetical to most conventional definitions of dramatic importance, is both another reminder of the other usually unsung set of observers that keep the theatrical experience chugging along, the spectators, and the incredible multiplicity of human labor which, when it struggles along competently, finds no reflection in theater's crisis-happy stages.)[113] What is the proper context for an object seen in everyday life? A bridge, sighted outside in passing, might be a forgettable detail of an ephemeral landscape. But what about the man who died building it? What realist depiction can include him? Every mundane object or scene in Wilder's universe is an index to the human world that surrounded it. This is the perceptual archaeology to which Wilder will return when writing about *Our Town*.[114]

It's significant that one of Wilder's very few black characters appears in *Pullman Car Hiawatha* at precisely the moment at which the play's democratic concerns become manifest. The Stage Manager invites the car's Porter to take his turn to speak, but he blushes, stammers, and demurs, saying that his thoughts wouldn't be very interesting to the audience: he's only thinking about his life insurance policy and his home in Chicago. The gesture is ambivalent. We could see this moment as a token liberal-humanist gesture of inclusion, but Wilder's failure to put more words in his character's mouth is telling. Unlike many contemporary writers, Eugene O'Neill prominent among them, Wilder hesitates to impinge on a reality he cannot fully understand. Wilder deliberately does not presume to speak for his character. He asserts the Porter's right to address the audience, but he also defends his right to privacy. In the presence of a presumptively white audience—he's writing in the early 1930s, for a theater that was still deeply segregated—he simply declares the Porter's right to be as everyday, as preoccupied with workaday concerns, as any American, and insists that the everyday reality of America, and the unfulfilled project of its democracy, necessarily include black experience.

Pullman Car's treatment of time is as vertiginous as its representational experiments, sequentially dilating or contracting the theatrical now. If, as its allegorical characters suggest, minutes are gossips, hours are philosophers, and years are theologians, then Wilder's play asks its spectators to perform each of these roles—alternately getting in close or taking the long view, dwelling in the perishable present or thinking about ultimate things.[115] As the play transits rapidly between styles and interpretive frames, spectators are asked to consider the illusory stabilities of abstract thought. Requiring the liquid movement of consciousness to freeze itself into stable concepts (homily or philosophy, piercing epigram or ponderous cliché) is like asking a breathing, changing human being to temporarily live as a fixed character provided by a script. Theater, Wilder suggests, is akin to thought itself in that its representations are capable of sudden changes in scope, scale, degree, or mode. The play, activated by performance, turns common nouns (the field, the bridge), and proper names (the towns of Grover's Corners and Parkersburg, Ohio) into active agents, into verbs, setting stillness into motion. (Arsic, reading in Emerson's wake, talks about the impossible ideal of a "recovered language of transformation" consisting of "pure verbs . . . ascribed to no one" that might liquefy "identities and beings into processes and becomings.")[116]

Even as the play personifies its objects and settings, it abstracts its personages. Few characters are named, and the Stage Manager's stepping in and out of subsidiary roles reminds us that all identities on this stage are provisional. The only people who have names are those singled out by suffering—the Insane Woman, who sees the audience watching her; Harriet, who dies suddenly in the night; and Phillip, her husband, likely changed by this incident forever. Harriet perhaps becomes a "character" because she's no longer alive and changing and so can be fixed in place.

The play concludes with a vision of the University of Chicago's towers on the horizon and an elided quotation from a hymn by Cardinal Newman, author of "The Idea of a University." Harriet's version omits that the singer "loved the garish day," but that's what the entire play reminds its spectators to do: situating the prosaic moments of a train ride within the immensities of life and death, this world and the next, the philosophical tradition and the American democratic project. For Wilder, theater becomes the model of a more expansive university, and a more democratic conception of aesthetics, where high and low culture, philosophy and homily, people and objects, modes of representation exalted or amateur, can mingle.

Human Scenery: *The Happy Journey to Trenton and Camden*

The Happy Journey to Trenton and Camden begins with departure from the routines of everyday life. The Kirby family leaves their cozy New Jersey home and takes a road trip, journeying to nearby Camden to visit Beulah, the oldest

Kirby child. Put outside their habitual surroundings, put into suspension, they notice more. (As in *Our Town*, a pantomime sequence at the beginning establishes the unnoticed routine of the street, an unremarked-upon hubbub that contrasts sharply with the family's determination to see *everything* once they're driving.) The family matriarch and patriarch are apprehensive about leaving the familiar behind. He "anxiously" checks and rechecks his preparations for the journey. She "anxiously" checks her hat.[117] We shouldn't allow the seeming coziness of the scene to distract us from its sharp modernism. *The Happy Journey* was written only about two decades after the futurist manifesto, and Wilder is dramatizing a very similar scenario—modern life, grasped in fragments, out the window of a moving automobile that "travels seventy miles in twenty minutes," as Wilder once put it.[118]

Most of *The Happy Journey* is devoted simply to pointing things out, catching fleeting sights in motion as the family car speeds on. As in *Pullman Car Hiawatha,* the characters are fixing temporary, unstable coordinates for the action. The central action of the play, in fact, in both form and content, is seeing. The purpose of the "happy journey" is to see Beulah. Most of its events have to do with registering and interpreting sights along the way. Throughout, we might think of Emily's plangent realization at the end of *Our Town* that we never really see each other because we go too fast. *The Happy Journey* shows us a group of minds taking the time to notice and being changed by what they observe. Because, as Wilder prescribes in his stage directions, the "car"—four plain kitchen chairs arranged by the Stage Manager—faces the audience, the play's spectators are, in a sense, always the destination. (As in *Our Town*, the Stage Manager serves as narrator and authorial surrogate here, moving the furniture and filling in minor characters' lines, mediating between the reality of the performance situation and the onstage fiction.) Arrayed, like playgoers, in rows—the chairs in the backseat are raked for maximum visibility—the family's seated postures and constant spectatorial alertness are the uncanny mirror image of the onlookers in the auditorium.

Because audience members can't see the scenery outside the car—because, in fact, at many points they *are* the scenery (the "car," after all, is heading straight for them)—they must watch the family watching, and so also watch themselves watch. These moments of shared perception, registering a sight, discussing it, finding shared meanings, matching minds, are precious for being transitory, fragile, and contingent, as the play's conclusion, in which we learn that Beulah has recently lost a child, and narrowly escaped death herself, makes clear. The sights the family points out are the kind that, in everyday life, might immediately fade from memory: roadside signs, restaurants, a roaming dog, a blossoming weed, a yellow house, a lovely sunset. Onstage, they're twice-perishable for being evanescent restagings of already evanescent perceptual events. As in *The Long Christmas Dinner* and *Pullman Car Hiawatha*, Wilder suggests that life and death are present in every moment of a unique mind's contact with the world—even more forcefully in the theater, where disappearance underwrites every performance. (There's "only one Loolie in the world"[119] and only one of each of us, too.) The end-of-play revelation that Beulah has recently lost a child, and almost died herself ("Are you glad I'm still alive, pa?" she asks)[120] is prefigured by the perishability of all the things the passengers (and spectators) notice, and then lose, together.

With these moments devoted to dramatizing instances of shared perception, Wilder invites a complex contrast between purposeful looking, as in theatrical spectatorship, the absorbed gaze that seeks to master the onstage scene, and non-purposeful, glancing attention, the roving mode of everyday life, such as that practiced by the Kirby family as their eyes flit from roadside sign to roadside sign, passing sight to passing sight. The play asks us to consider how we're watching, and if perhaps we might be better served by a more motile approach. (Our own watching is thus intimately linked to our own mortality, the fixity of the gaze a synecdoche, perhaps, for the final fixity of death.) The members of the Kirby family notice more because they're in motion, but the play reminds us that we're always in motion, even if we don't realize it.

When the family stops to get gas and stretch their legs, Ma Kirby falls into conversation with the gas station attendant. They make small talk, matching class backgrounds, religious affiliations, moral outlooks.[121] It's the only sequence in which the Stage Manager steps wholly into character, the play's only moment of prolonged human contact outside the family unit that is allowed the fullness of theatrical embodiment. The present-tense enacting of the scene quietly underscores that it's an encounter that becomes most meaningful in its apparent meaninglessness, two human beings falling into temporary sympathy with each other based on painstakingly aligned worldviews. Wilder invites us to share the drama of two minds attempting to construct a common world. That it's more than likely these are two people who will never see each other again, that each for the other is human scenery speeded past and soon to vanish, only makes the ephemeral relation more poignant.

The scene becomes a metonym for the theatrical encounter. Theater, too, is also about sizing up, finding commonalities, constructing affinities (or marking differences) with the strangers we find before us, beings always destined to remain strange despite the apparent intimacy of the shared time we spend with them. The theatrical relation is built on forging empathic and intellectual connections to these others, vivid connections we too will soon discard when we leave the theater, remaining in memory only as shards of their former brightness (if we can preserve them at all). And then, too, there is our strange intimacy with the other spectators all around us, the other passengers in our shared vehicle, momentarily connected to us by experiences held in common, but destined to remain otherwise unknown.

Throughout *The Happy Journey* Wilder's characters, and with them the play's spectators, find beauty in the most banal facets of ordinary American life, caught on the fly. Ma Kirby models a kind of attention that finds beauty in the seemingly abject, and un-noteworthy. She likes a weed by the side of the road, a pretty dog that runs by, a roadside sign. The act of perception, of noticing, creates the aesthetic experience. When the characters remark on the clumsy estrangement of language performed by an attention-mongering billboard, the exchange encapsulates the play's aesthetic project in miniature. The Kirby scion asks why "right" is misspelled "rite" on the sign (which advertises trousers). The reply: "So that you'll stop and ask about it."[122] Late in the play, Wilder stages another theatrical metonym. The family is most delighted by seeing Beulah's written directions fulfilled by the unfamiliar scenery racing past outside the car. Writing is being fulfilled by performance, immediate experience paradoxically confirmed by writing.[123]

Wilder subtly dramatizes the porousness of the barrier between inside and outside the mind. The family thinks and feels as much in response to what they see together, and to being in motion, as to any internal promptings. Ma Kirby's thoughts leap from the "pretty dog" she espies and follows with her eyes, to "the pretty advertisement for chesterfield cigarettes."[124] The sight of a funeral procession cues meditations on mortality. As Wilder depicts thoughts and feelings simply befalling his characters, following a logic set by the happenstance of perception, he prompts spectators to consider how the play is interacting with their own minds, how it is directing their musings or spurring free-roaming tangential associations.

For Wilder, consciousness is a theater whose entrances and exits are never predictable. The wafting of quotidian cognition holds more strange surprises than any melodrama. After a little of this drifting, the Kirby son is led to the dizzying realization that 126,000,000 American minds are in that very moment likewise surveying the world, seeing their own sights. Overwhelmed, he remarks: "What a lotta people there are in the world, ma."[125] We shouldn't forget that he's facing the audience while he says this. Like the cognitive circuit in *Pullman Car Hiawatha*, or the echo-haunted house in *The Long Christmas Dinner*, this is a statement incorporating the play's spectators, inviting them to trace the permeable membrane between their own observing and their own thoughts, and to contemplate the community of brains in the auditorium similarly following the doings onstage.

Emotions, too, are more like the scenery the family passes by in transit than climactic theatrical events: there, sadness; there, joy; there, ruefulness. Wilder's point isn't just that our emotional lives are far more mutable, and even strange, than the conventional theater allows them to be, but also that they can have as much to do with the everyday world outside us as they do with the internal logics of our affective being. Like glimpses of a roadside flower or a pretty little dog, feelings, too, suddenly befall us, having as much to do with the imbibing of a shared atmosphere as the eruption of significant interior turmoil. The play skips rapidly from meditations on mortality to ecstasies of well-being to family strife to shocked silence to abject repentance to joyous liveliness to dreamy silence to family closeness in the course of only a few pages, as spectators mark the borders of the shared feelings, and appraise how they themselves might be keeping up. (The family's mobile feelings contrast with the fixity of Beulah's mourning at the end—a grief Ma Kirby acknowledges, but takes care not to dwell on, gently directing her daughter back toward the practical task of feeding the family. The play ends with the imperative of continued motion: "We just go on, honey, doin our business.")[126]

As Branka Arsic points out, explicating Emerson's theories of affective life, both laughter and sorrow, the handmaiden emotions of comedy and tragedy, are "practices of 'figuring,' 'fixing,' and stabilizing; they set and protect boundaries, mediate ruptures, minimize changes . . . in isolating us they alienate us from life, which is always mobile."[127] The images of laughing and grieving man "suggest human beings consistently neglect what is happening to them. We either flee from danger and grief, laughing them away, or flee from pleasure, mourning its absence, and we do that because we fear the discontinuity that may result."[128]

In *The Happy Journey* Wilder embraces emotional discontinuity, finding a place for all the orphaned feelings that usually get skipped over to create delineated states in the theater. As Ben Highmore points out, most art, and most thinking about the function of art, radically simplifies the emotional lability of moment-to-moment experience: "What happens to fear, anger, disappointment, contentment, smell, touch, boredom, frustration, weariness, hope, itchiness, backache, trepidation, and the mass of hardly articulated feelings and moods that saturate our social, political, and private lives? Aren't these the elements (rather than beauty and the sublime) that fill most of our lives most of the time?"[129]

Theatrical spectators, Wilder suggests, are like passengers taking a journey in the same car. Empathy is as much the unthinking response to shared affective atmospheres and to common sights as it is the answering of ethical imperatives. As Wilder's characters pass through these stations of feeling, so too are his spectators compelled to scrutinize their own attachment to the proceedings. Are they simply falling into sympathy with the performers onstage, seduced like them into moods governed by a particular emotional climate? Are they tumbling into reveries based on imaginative restagings of the sights flitting by the car window? The play urges spectators to contemplate the drift of their own affective progress as it moves in and out of sync with the action onstage, to be attuned to transitional feelings, tangential stirrings, the emotional scenery we usually speed past on the way to theater's more memorable destinations. In *Pullman Car Hiawatha*, Wilder's democratic theater had room for objects and people, geography and cosmology, philosophy and homily, folk art and high art. In *The Happy Journey*, mundane sights, fleeting emotions, and little epiphanies are all big enough to suggest the frail, precious singularity of the perceiving minds that register them.

The Least Important Day Will Be Important Enough: *Our Town*

Wilder's shorter everyday plays arm us to see *Our Town* more clearly, a play so familiar in both its controversies and its felicities that we can take it for granted, the way Emily Webb does the precious daily doings of her household. Like her, we should learn to look again at the things we don't usually notice. And it's especially important to stop to notice what it means for Wilder's characters to stop to notice things in the play. Like *Pullman Car Hiawatha*, *Our Town* is full of moments designed to fill the stage with the murmur of thought emanating from the auditorium. And like *The Happy Journey* or *The Long Christmas Dinner*, at many intervals in the play, a scene slows or stops as characters quite literally halt to smell the flowers, or to gaze at the moon.

These pauses are crucial because *Our Town* moves so fast. It's vital to keep this restlessness in mind because we have a tendency to think of Wilder, through the darkened glass of decades of critical misreading, as a homebody, a dramatic Norman Rockwell. Generations of high school productions of *Our Town* have blazoned that image on our collective psyche. But the more we look for the idealized, cozy version of Grover's Corners, New Hampshire, that we've been accustomed to expect, the less likely we are to find it. If we look carefully, what we do find, in fact, is not a secure conception of home at all, but constant motion—not cozy happiness but ambivalence, anxiety, and loss. For Wilder, home is somewhere you leave, whether you want to or not.

In *Our Town*, neither Wilder's characters nor his setting can stay still. Each entrance is haunted by an exit; each moment of joy is shadowed by pain. No sooner does Wilder announce a new character like Dr. Gibbs, or Joe Crowell, the paperboy, than he vaults ahead to their eventual deaths, letting us know not to get too close, reminding us that everything we're seeing is an artifact of an ever-more distant past.[130] Emily and George's courtship might appear to be the image of bygone bobby-sox romance—books carried, phosphates at the drugstore—but the halting confession of their flowering affection is accompanied by tears, fear, and profound uncertainty, a premonition of more final departures. And almost as soon as they find each other, they part again.

These departures are only the most literal signs of the play's preoccupation with movement. The Stage Manager takes care to remind us that he's seen it all before, that the urgent human striving we see before us—love, loss, anguish, anxiety, birth, marriage, death—is simply part of the passing show, impossibly tiny when set against the backdrop of eternity. Emily and George's wedding goes by in the blink of an eye, and we're distracted from fully registering it by the "chatter" of one of the wedding guests, a poignant early illustration of Emily's sad realization that we go too fast to truly see each other. Wilder notes in his stage directions that Mrs. Soames's rhapsodizing about the loveliness of the occasion should first "drown out" and then "cover" the wedding vows—a sign that our eyes should be repeatedly pulled away from the action, too.[131]

The little town of Grover's Corners moves as fast, faster even, than the trains and cars of Wilder's earlier everyday plays. Only *The Long Christmas Dinner* comes close to matching its velocity. (We might think again of Wilder's description of *Our Town* as a telescope tracking a vanishing object.) The play's three acts cycle through one day—a morning, an afternoon, a chilly evening—dispersed across years, and spanning the hallmarks of entire lives: departures, homecomings, marriages, and especially deaths. Three years pass between acts 1 and 2. The play multiplies speed between the second and third acts, when nine years elapse. Despite the Stage Manager's ironic assertion that "things don't change much around here," we watch the whole onstage society transform.

The more time we spend with the characters onstage, in other words, the further they move away from us. Everything that seems so permanent about *Our Town*—the stolid New England values, the precious local traditions, the sense of being rooted so durably in a precise landscape and culture—is entirely temporary, a blip on the geological radar. Wilder isn't evoking the timelessness of small-town life. He's reminding us that everything solid melts away into time, as the theatrical performance before us is already doing. This is what he means when he compares watching *Our Town* to archaeology, as he does in his essays about the play. Even as he asks spectators to restore sensory vividness to bygone experience, he's also reminding us to think of everything we see on stage as already part of the past and to imagine how future generations will see our own moment from an equally distanced remove.

Because the play is always accelerating, hurtling from departure to departure, it's especially important to note the intervals where Wilder slows down and allows his characters to, quite literally, smell the flowers, to savor the aroma of a garden, to gaze at a glowing moon. In these moments, short respites from the play's remorseless momentum, we're united with the people onstage, seeing as they see, noticing their world as they do, conjuring up our own memories of similar sights and smells.

These passages of onstage perception, akin to what Joseph Roach has called "liturgical silences,"[132] are complex. In one sense they unite spectators with the actors, as both groups strain to imagine the sensory details demanded by the situation, recalling sights or smells from their memory banks. The act of attempting to retrieve such sensory figments prepares the way for the devastating scene of Emily's impossible return to her past in the third act. Such quotidian data are both precisely what Emily misses most and the hardest things to preserve in memory. It's remarkable how often she says that she's "forgotten" or "didn't know" things in this section, which is supposedly devoted to a happy return to the familiar.[133] For a play often seen as nostalgic, Rockwellian, it's surprising how unstable her vision of home is, how full of departures and traumas. As in *The Long Christmas Dinner*, death huddles closely around the quotidian scenes onstage, because Emily visits from and returns to the world of the assembled dead in the third act, but also because of all the loss she notices when she returns, all the characters who've aged or died or gone away, all the sights, sounds, and smells she can't recall. (Wilder links experiential vividness with inevitable loss in the play's opening lines when the Stage Manager notes that the "morning star always gets wonderful bright the minute before it has to go.")[134]

In these final scenes, the absence of tangible scenery and objects to ground the shared imagining of everyday life onstage means that spectators are confronted with a double absence, attempting to re-summon details they were forced to conjure from memory in the first place. Throughout *Our Town*, Wilder makes the consoling routines that underwrite everyday life literally invisible. The audience must cognitively fill in the blanks in order to see breakfast being prepared, milk being delivered, beans strung for canning, chickens fed.[135] Here again is the thinking murmur from *Pullman Car Hiawatha*, the community of minds at work in the auditorium. These are perhaps the most present-tense passages in a work that plays havoc with time. And seeing these routines in motion, pushed into relief against an absent backdrop, tells us something about everyday life and about history that factual records never could. We all carry out daily procedures that are like these in their routineness (even if we don't can beans ourselves), and these habits are at once the quantum structure of history, generations of lived human experience, and the texture we lose to memory's vagaries. To return to Jameson's terms, affect inevitably surrenders to fable, sensation to narrative. But affect—urgent, unnamed experience—is what we yearn for.

This is the primal paradox about everyday perception that Wilder's play is artfully constructed to confront. Those tiny details that most clearly root us in place and time, in an idea of home, are the first to be tuned out, the constant ground of our thoughts, but made invisible by habit, even when those details are ultimately the ones we will someday miss most. Everyday consciousness isn't a naturalist stage, Wilder reminds us, crowded with precise material details ratifying specific facts about our lives, but one made bare for thought by the process of instantly forgetting everything we preconsciously decide to ignore. The pantomime forces spectators to pay attention to the performance of humdrum activities that might otherwise be filed away into the background so as to focus on the usually more pressing theatrical imperatives of plot and character. This is Wilder's point about everyday life outside the auditorium, too. We're so focused on the "plot" that we lose track of the background.

Spectators are compelled to simultaneously imagine the details of the New Hampshire world being sketched before them, to speculate by analogy about corresponding routines from their own lives, and to become aware of all the other minds at work in the auditorium imagining those details. In a realist play, these activities would fall into the category of what Barthes called "reality effects," details extraneous to the narrative that ratify the fidelity of the fictional world to the world outside.[136] But here, their invisibility makes them paradoxically more present, shifting focus onto these vital but often forgettable tasks. (We might recall the enlarged conception of "art" hinted at in the play: as Mr. Webb wryly suggests, in reply to the Lady in the Box—like the Stage Manager, a medial figure, poised between the play and its spectators—the inhabitants of Grover's Corners don't have much use for literature, fine art, or classical music, but they sink into aesthetic rapture before a sunset.)[137]

Eventually the audience, returning to the play's early scenes along with Emily, is put in the strange cognitive position of missing things that were never really there, precisely the situation of memory attempting to recall sensory information from a vanished field of everyday data that was never given a full measure of attention in the first place. This is the hidden import of Wilder's well-known assertion that *Our Town* was intended to find a value beyond all price for the smallest details of our everyday life.[138] The value of such bygone particles of experience is beyond price precisely because its value was never really properly assessed—*could* never be assessed—in the first place. They vanished before they could be properly appraised. Arthur Miller once accused Wilder of forgoing true "loss," thus falling "short of a form that will press into reality to the limits of reality,"[139] and failing to achieve the moral profundity of a true tragic vision. But loss is part of the molecular structure of Wilder's theater, endemic to the thinking, perceiving—and so always losing—nature of human consciousness. *The Death of a Salesman* is Willy Loman's tragedy. *Our Town* is everybody's tragedy.

And as spectators try to summon memories to lay alongside Emily's, they're confronted with the inescapable fact that events from earlier in the evening have also slipped away. Like Nature Theater of Oklahoma's *The Life and Times*, discussed in my final chapter, *Our Town* blurs life and art by making the vanishing experience of the latter stand in for the equally fleeting experience of the former. Call it the perceptual sublime: these works invite us to contemplate the vast worlds of experience we've lost over our living years, and all the beautiful sights we will lose in the future.

This is an important complication of Wilder's statement that *Our Town* is a historical document depicting "the way we were" in "our growing-up, in our marrying, in our doctoring, in our living, and our dying."[140] In provocatively claiming that his play is a faithful record of daily life in turn-of-the-century New Hampshire, Wilder is, in fact, gesturing to an idea of history-as-absence not unlike that proposed by Diana Taylor in *The Archive and the Repertoire*. A true history of Grover's Corners would have to include those feelings, perceptions, and experiences that are impossible to record: what it was like to string beans, eat breakfast, smell the heliotrope. Many of the things that make Grover's Corners what it was can be present only as absences—or double-absences as performances of an absence. The embodied history of the play, into which future feeling, thinking beings can step, is, in this sense, a more accurate testament than the dry statistics provided by the newspaper buried alongside the script in the town's cornerstone.[141] Wilder's audience must act as perceptual archaeologists, resurrecting the sensory world of his vanished New Hampshire community. For him, the tantalizing history to recover is the cosmic murmur itself. (This juxtaposition also brings back to mind the family genealogical table hidden away somewhere upstairs in *The Long Christmas Dinner*, an ultimately less satisfying picture of the passage of generations than seeing bodies parade across the stage, thinking, being, seeing, feeling. That table is, in turn, juxtaposed with another kind of history: the maddening echoes of all the thinking and feeling expended in the house, and the theater.)

Wilder contrasts the pace of perception, the fragile grasp of consciousness on the world, with the heedless transit of geological time. As he does, he invites us to think about the smallness and the bigness of our own minds: no one will ever see the play again in quite the same way that we do, but thousands have seen it before, and thousands will see it again. *Our Town* is only ours because it's already gone.

Wilder's everyday plays unite spectators in the continuous effort of creating, and the bravery of abandoning, new-built houses of thought, as they struggle to keep pace with all the play's departures. These mental exits anticipate their own, when they gather their possessions about them and return to the workaday world, departing the imaginative houses they've built around themselves that evening, retaining whatever fragments they can preserve of the vanishing life of the performance—departures that, in turn, presage even more final leavings. And if, as Wilder once wrote of Goethe, in the process of being confronted by the smallness of their minds and lives in the face of the immensities of space, time, and historical moment, they feel as if they have "shrunk, shrunk, shrunk,"[142] they have shrunk to their proper scale as individual voices in the ceaseless choir of the world's murmuring.

While he didn't make use of technologies of reproduction onstage, Wilder educates spectators in a mode of attention that subsequent artists concerned with the everyday would amplify with audio and visual recording, giving close scrutiny to the most perishable, transitory, and usually ignored aspects of everyday experience and emotional life. He taught audiences to look in the margins and really see, to rethink the difference between background and foreground, consequence and inconsequence, importance and unimportance, art and nonart. For his inheritors, too, the least important things would be important enough—perhaps even the most important, since the smallest thing is the biggest test of what *we* can make important.

Chapter 2

✦

Mediating the Method

I BELIEVE "THAT THE USE OF NOISE . . . TO MAKE MUSIC . . . WILL CONTINUE AND INCREASE UNTIL WE REACH A MUSIC PRODUCED THROUGH THE AID OF ELECTRICAL INSTRUMENTS."[1] Thus runs the cross-page mantra intercut into the opening passages of John Cage's prescient essay "The Future of Music: Credo." Cage's ideas were, of course, germinal for the American theatrical avant-garde. Chance operations, perceptual experiments, and found materials continue to be important concepts for latter-day progressive theater-makers. But my argument here is that Cage's early writings also anticipated another, earlier, theatrical and filmic movement: Method acting.

This is not a chapter primarily about Cage. It's about the Method, but not about the factional squabbles and terminological disputes that have predetermined much scholarship about the American inheritors—many might say usurpers—of Stanislavski's legacy. For my purposes, it doesn't matter whether Stella Adler or Lee Strasberg was the more scrupulous apostle of Stanislavski's early or late thinking, or whether Stanislavski finally abandoned or embraced the concept of affective memory. My subject here is the relationship between the Method and media: the central importance of technologies of recording to both the philosophy and aesthetic evolution of the Method. The conventional narrative of twentieth-century acting suggests that the Method and cinema were simpatico because film allowed for a greater degree of naturalistic detail—permitting performances to become smaller and more lifelike. This story is promulgated by scholars like Richard Blum, who argues, in his *American Film Acting: The Stanislavski Heritage*, that "with actors trained in variations of the Stanislavski system, branching out from the Actors Studio and other experimental forums, screen acting became a natural extension of Stanislavski's search for realism."[2]

The arch-formalist Cage and the arch-essentialist emotional archaeologists of the Method might seem to have little in common. But I think his ideas explain certain features of the American Method better than Stanislavski's do. My suggestion is that Cage's paradigmatic revaluing of "noise" and "music," his blurring of the boundary between aesthetic and unaesthetic sound, together with his emphasis on new forms of music produced with the aid of new recording technologies, actually prefigure Method acting's reevaluation of the difference between sound and sense in theatrical and filmic performance, aided, of course, by film's perfect visual and aural recall.

I begin from the premises that, sectarian conflict aside, by the late 1950s a picture of Method acting had become widespread in the American imagination—and that such a picture, despite the protestations of Method pedagogues, was a largely accurate portrayal of the new style of acting advanced by the performers who studied at the Actors Studio, the institution most closely identified with the Method. Contemporary critics differ widely in their assessment of the condition, but all agree about the symptoms. America's actors were in the throes of an epidemic of impaired speech: mumbling, slurring, broken thoughts, inarticulate feelings.

This chapter is about how acting became noisier: about how the formerly nonsignifying matter of speech became an essential part of postwar performance, and how the rustle of the recording apparatus was intrinsic to that process. Cage will be my stalking horse. Cage is an alienation device. If Cage's experiments with analog recording made him more sensitive to the universe of ambient sounds that attend every moment of supposed silence, the Method's embrace of recording achieved a similar effect, bringing orphan sounds into theatrical speech.

Feelings without Words

The scene is New York City, 1958. That year, in two disparate arenas, American culture was attempting to come to grips with the difference between noise and art. A 25-year retrospective concert of John Cage's work at New York's Town Hall helped create an intellectually coherent canon out of Cage's experiments, which critics had often treated as puerile provocations or exercises in whimsy to be regarded with bemused toleration. For some forward thinkers, noise was becoming intellectually exciting material for experimental music, whereas the audible audience outrage preserved by the recording of the Town Hall concert testifies to the continuing rearguard pique of more conservative sensibilities.[3] Cage himself couldn't have imagined a more apt illustration of his theories than this aleatory auditory event, preserved for posterity by the recording apparatus.

Meanwhile, in newspapers and weekly magazines, a furious and analogous debate was warming up about the merits of Method acting, a new performance style pioneered by the constellation of actors working under the tutelage of Lee Strasberg, Elia Kazan, and Robert Lewis at the Actors Studio in New York, the obsessive secrecy of which only heightened curiosity about it. To its opponents, Method acting seemed to augur a wholesale demolition of linguistic fluency in what Robert Brustein, one of the Method's most eloquent denouncers, called the "spoken arts": radio, television, film, and theater.

In a magisterial essay titled "America's New Culture Hero: Feelings without Words,"[4] Brustein warned that Method acting's new proletarian archetypes threatened to surrender political thought along with language. Unlike the prolix heroes of the 1930s generation, they couldn't find the rousing words to summarize their predicaments. He also worried that these actors were, by implication, willing to abandon the entirety of the classical canon, since their halting delivery was eminently unsuitable to the rhythmic strictures of Shakespeare or the ornate cadenzas of Shaw. Already the terms of this debate might sound eerily familiar to followers of Cage's critical fortunes. A whole tradition is perceived to be at stake in the reweighing of the difference between music (art) and noise (not-art).

Here is Brustein's ruthless description of Method acting's antihero:

> Of medium height and usually of lower-class birth, his most familiar physical characteristic is his surly and discontented expression. His eyes peer out at the world from under beetling brows; his uncombed hair falls carelessly over his forehead; his right hand rests casually on his right hip. He is extremely muscular and walks with a slouching, shuffling gait. He scratches himself often, slumps in chairs, and almost never smiles. He is also identified by the sounds which issue from his mouth. He squeezes, he grunts, he passes his hand over his eyes and forehead, he stares steadily, he turns away, he scratches, then again faces his adversary, and finally speaks. What he says is rarely important but he has mesmerized his auditor by the effort he takes to say it. He has communicated not information but feeling; he has revealed an inner life of unspecified anguish and torment.[5]

Brustein blames Marlon Brando more than any other performer for bringing the barbarians to the gates of verbal virtuosity. More precisely, he indicts Brando's rendition of Stanley Kowalski in Tennessee Williams's *A Streetcar Named Desire*, both onstage and (especially) on-screen, in Elia Kazan's 1951 film version of the Broadway production. From Brando's Stanley, according to Brustein, sprang James Dean, John Garfield, Paul Newman, Eli Wallach, and a host of other mumblers, grimacers, flinchers, and fumers—actors whose difficulty forming a sentence threatened to overshadow the dramatic predicaments of their characters and whose illegible speech pointed to a more discomfiting illegibility in their interior lives.

I deliberately juxtapose these two events—the Brustein debate and the Cage concert—in order to rethink Method acting from the perspectives of mediated perception and mediated artmaking. Most scholarship about the Method considers it largely from within its own precepts. How authentic was its vaunted emotional authenticity and how authentic could it ever actually be? How adequate was the experience of its practitioners to prepare them to portray the marginalized social types they often played? How slippery was the process of emotionally identifying with characters outside the mainstream of American culture, simultaneously celebrating them as antiheroes and co-opting them for mass culture? What assumptions about gender, race, and sexuality did the Method's purported universality elide or repress? These are the essential questions that the Method's critics have asked in recent years.[6] All of these lines of inquiry relate to the Method's purported exploration of the depth psychology of an authentic self and the understandable squeamishness induced in modern readers by the near-obsessive recourse to vaporous terms such as "truth," "reality," and "honesty" in the public statements of the Method's practitioners and teachers.

The Method, in Strasberg's conception, brought the vast trove of affective experience registered in the unconscious mind into rehearsal rooms and auditoriums. But in what follows, I'll consider the Method as an investigation of a different unconscious, what Walter Benjamin called the "optical unconscious," those uncanny aspects of everyday life revealed by the surgical incursions of the camera and microphone into reality.[7] The Method's most salient legacy may have more to do with media than with emotional recall, with the ways recording had already changed performance and spectatorship. The debates about Method acting were symptomatic of a new postwar landscape of theatrical performance and a new conception of everyday life in which theater was only one of many possible modes of encountering spoken art, most of them mediated to a greater or lesser degree by technologies of recording. These technologies of reproduction and transmission were becoming ubiquitous: squalling radios, TVs rattling in the background, Muzak in elevators. Life was getting noisier. Moreover, in this new economy, actors were more likely than ever to move between media—TV, radio, film, stage—and face the competing demands each form made on performance.

For listeners such as Brustein who were accustomed to fluency and smoothness in the spoken arts and to media products that attempted to minimize the traces of their own recording or broadcast, Brando's performances mixed music and noise, sense and strangeness. But what Brustein called inarticulateness is actually a more complicated proposition about the relationship between noise and music, sound and sense, aesthetic and unaesthetic elements in acting and, indeed, in art—and about the ways that recording technology was intervening to transform our understanding of these relationships. The German media theorist Friedrich Kittler has described the disruptive effect of the advent of audio recording on human perception, beginning with the phonograph: "The phonograph does not hear as do ears that have been trained immediately to filter voices, words, and sounds out of noise; it registers acoustic events as such. Articulateness becomes a second-order exception in a spectrum of noise. . . . The undermining of articulation becomes the order of the day."[8] If we take Kittler's proposition seriously, then the preference of Method actors for mumbling, for blurring speech into sound and meaning into noise, might be the product of the ways the cameras and microphones that constantly surveilled them were altering what it meant to watch and listen to acting. Mumbling brings the wider spectrum of noise into the realm of performed speech.

Method acting marked a crisis point in acting's translation to the big screen. (We shouldn't forget that dialogue had been a part of the cinematic experience for only about twenty-five years by the time Brando started doing his best to make his lines inaudible.) To use Cage's terms, Method acting was noise becoming music onstage and on camera, a form of music produced with the aid of electrical instruments.[9] In this way, I think we can see the Method, and its wildfire effect on the American imagination, as a watershed event in the process that the cultural theorist Juan A. Suárez, taking his cues from Kittler, calls the "reinvention of the everyday," the process by which noise, in the cybernetic sense of nonsignifying matter, became "another name for the otherness that modernism . . . discovered in the heart of the quotidian."[10] As he describes it:

> Modernism and the everyday life of modernity were actually full of noise: not only the clang of machinery and the din of traffic . . . but also occurrences and recesses that simply refused to yield sense. The material cause of this ever-present opaque component was the analog media—sound recording machines, film, and photography—that were the hardware of modernity and of modernism. . . . Through their nondiscriminatory receptivity, technologies of electronic reproduction register the automatism of the world. They capture sense and nonsense and mix signifying matter with opaque traces and textures—an involuntary gesture, the distracting fold of a fabric, the grain of the voice.[11]

Mediated representation, he goes on to argue, "thus reveals an uncanny double of the quotidian—a shadow realm of meaninglessness and contingency alongside the intelligible. Relayed by the camera or microphone, 'reality' becomes pregnant with secrets, and the known constantly slips into the unknown."[12]

My suggestion here is that Method acting, abetted by recording technology, quickly became an art of trace and texture, involuntary gesture and vocal grain, and that this was not simply the result of one medium (film) being more suited to representing the real than another (theater). Instead, I'll argue that Method acting was always poised between media. Recording undergirded the exercises and thought of Lee Strasberg, the Method's Svengali. And upon closer scrutiny, Brando's infamous mumbling reveals itself to be a canny medial experiment.

Alone Together: Lee Strasberg's Public Privacy and Private Publics

In an unpublished fragment written around 1930 and eventually collected in the volume *Culture and Value,* Ludwig Wittgenstein speculates about an impossible theater of the everyday:

> Nothing could be more remarkable than seeing a man who thinks he is unobserved performing some quite simple everyday activity. Let us imagine a theatre; the curtain goes up and we see a man alone in a room, walking up and down, lighting a cigarette, sitting down, etc. so that suddenly we are observing a human being from outside in a way that ordinarily we can never observe ourselves; it would be like watching a chapter of biography with our own eyes—surely this would be uncanny and wonderful at the same time. We should be observing something more wonderful than anything a playwright could arrange to be acted or spoken on the stage: life itself.—But then we do see this every day without its making the slightest impression on us! True enough, but we do not see it from *that* point of view.[13]

The passage's paradoxes crowd around the slanting "that" of its last line—*that* point of view would provide a second look at what we never see for the first time: the everyday. It would combine the perceptual singularity of primary experience with the clarifying benefit of aesthetic distance. In Wittgenstein's thought experiment, the subject is observed without being disturbed into performance; everyday life has been transposed into the theater without any alteration to its essential everydayness. What technologies of seeing or staging could possibly allow for this glimpse at the secret progress of an ordinary life?

Some two decades later, a version of this scene—and its aspiration to an uncanny glimpse of quotidian life caught unaware—became a cornerstone of the work of the Actors Studio, as led by Lee Strasberg. The "private moment" exercise was a foundational element in his acting pedagogy, both in private sessions and at the studio. To perform the exercise, an actor would attempt simply to behave as if he or she were alone, unobserved and engaged in some prosaic behavior or task. But there was nothing simple about it.

Strasberg's conception of the private moment is almost mystical. It is at once "precise and concrete"[14]—nearly thinglike in its undivided being—and deeply, immanently subjective. It is the product of intense self-scrutiny but is also the vehicle by which an actor can hope to transcend the confining falseness of theatrical self-consciousness. Strasberg suggests that the actor begin by watching him- or herself, taking careful note of moments when he or she notices that "'I'm thinking not just about myself, but of this particular thing about myself. When that happens, I usually do this and this—which I would never admit to anybody except in some indirect way'" (118). As I will elaborate shortly, Strasberg's vagueness is at once a gnostic wariness of defining subjective sensation, a way of preserving the quintessential privacy of the exercise, even in speech, and a by-product of the recording technologies that created the preconditions for Strasberg's conception of privacy.

The pupil would then go on to imaginatively reconstruct the scene of this elusive privacy at the studio, beginning with sensate realities and working outward to more complex dynamics. To this end, Strasberg encouraged actors to bring objects from their private environments to the studio to help create the fine-grained texture of solitary experience: "books, records, and other small physical objects" (118). These objects were intended to "strengthen [the actor's] sense of being alone. He tries to create the room until he can say to himself, 'That's the couch and that's the table,' until he can see and touch and smell the objects in that room, until the room has the kind of reality that any reality on the stage should have" (118).

As Strasberg's commentary elucidates, the studio's staging of privacy did not mean voyeuristic peeping at colleagues' hidden peccadilloes or the exuberant confession of taboo topics, although some iterations of the exercise at the studio undoubtedly tended in that direction. It was something weirder and altogether more paradoxical, an attempt to renegotiate the theater's contract with publicity and, even stranger, with having audiences at all:

> We do private things when we are alone, and we know they are really private when we cannot continue them if somebody comes into the room. Whereas if somebody interrupts when we are doing a personal thing, we become shy or a little embarrassed, but we go ahead and do it anyhow. . . . A made-up privacy would not have the same results, because there would be nothing to encourage the actor unconsciously. (118–19)

In an intriguing aside, Strasberg once suggested that "the private-moment exercise is particularly useful in training because it obviates questions of interpretation" (119). Why does privacy obviate interpretation? Perhaps because in the true private moment—as in Wittgenstein's parable—life is simply being itself, without referent. It's not theatrical because the spectator, although there, is not *really* there, and the actor, although there, is not there to be *seen*. The actor is not trying to represent anything; the spectator is not trying to read anything beneath the surface of the action, is not aware of herself or himself as a spectator. The paradox presented by this exercise—that the actor should deliberately labor to behave as if he or she were alone in one semipublic forum, the acting school, which was intended to prepare him or her for another public forum, the theater or the film studio—is the paradox of Method acting itself.

Privacy was a paramount concern for the Method's pedagogues and acolytes and a structuring principle for the studio's work and Strasberg's teaching. No one but members of the studio or rare invited guests could observe a working session. (This reticence is maintained to this day.) And these sessions were kept almost vanishingly brief: an hour or so in most cases. The dramatic material with which actors worked was apportioned into small units with small casts, monologues or two-handed scenes, and was often discarded partway through a session in favor of impromptu exercises. Most of Strasberg's trademark pedagogical tools—emotion memory, the private moment, the song-and-dance exercise—could be practiced (or were best employed) only by a solitary student.[15]

And the Method's notorious discomfort with language, a quintessentially public instrument—quickly abandoned during exercises, mangled by emotive deliveries—is perhaps also another aspect of this concern for privacy. (Although the short excerpts and small companies were undoubtedly partly a concession to the exigencies of getting a group of working actors together to rehearse, the studio's obsession with solitude also suggests that solos and duets were preferable in order to make the work onstage as private as possible without violating theatrical necessities.)

How could this ideal privacy be created? How can you have an audience that is not an audience? How can actors, and acting teachers, be alone but still attentively observed? My argument here is that analog recording was the implicit presence in the Actors Studio's paradoxical dance of public and private. Suspicious of language's mediations of inner realities, the Method substituted the mediation of technology: the tape recorder, the movie camera. The Method's immediacy was deeply mediated, its mediations intended to provide access to unmediated reality. Tape provided the preconditions for Strasberg's theory and practice at the studio. The recording apparatus, the perpetually attentive audience that is not an audience, mediated between the privacy of the Actors Studio's closed sessions and a wider public eager to penetrate the secretive laboratory's mystique. The camera (and audio recorder), which were both prying eye and neutrally observant machine, performed a similar function for reticent performers such as Marlon Brando, whose obsessive worrying of the border between private and public in his acting, with his own body as both medium and message, mirrored Strasberg's preoccupations.

The Actors Studio's very self-conception was as a medial site situated between the demands of the commercial theater and those of everyday life, of commerce and art, of life and theater. And in its exercises, dramatic roles mediated between the actors as they were and the actors as they could be. Work on acting was also work on the self. Strasberg's pedagogy was intended to have a transformative effect on the actors' everyday lives and their professional lives. In many places, Strasberg's commentary circles around the idea that the studio's goals centered as much on revising the daily lives of its actors as on improving their craft: "Neither life nor talent stands still. Standing still leads inevitably to retrogression. . . . The work here is not [just] for artistic purposes, for something that satisfies your soul and nothing else" (32).

The techniques of Method acting were intended to mediate between inner life and outer expression, between real, spontaneous feeling and thought and their onstage correlates, between the resources of the actor and the demands of the director. Because so much of the Method's mandate fell in such liminal zones, in precisely the places where the lines between life and art became fuzzy, it's no surprise to discover that so much of the Method's energy went into perfecting techniques and concepts intended to resolve the distance between incommensurable philosophical oppositions: surface or reality, sign or symptom, truth or artifice. The Method's medial status was an unending source of anxiety for its practitioners (am I doing this right?) and a major source of perplexity for its critics.

In her brilliant analysis of the Method's vexed status in postwar thought, Marianne Conroy points out that the studio's self-conception as a place between cultural registers was part of what irked commentators:

> The arguments brought to bear against Method acting thus delineate an historically specific kind of cultural controversy: in that struggle, high and low culture worked in concert to shore up residual modernist values against an emergent middlebrow cultural style. Method acting elicited such reactions because its practices confounded the central assumption that enabled modernism to map the cultural universe into simple hierarchies: the high/low distinction between aesthetic autonomy and commercial necessity. In effect, in the approach to performance associated with the Actors Studio, an aesthetic disposition toward technique was adapted to the demands of commerce, so that technique became visible not only in its aesthetic effects, but also as part of the publicity content of performance. In thus mixing the aesthetic and the commercial, the Studio destabilized the founding oppositions—between high and low culture, prestige and popularity—through which the actor's role in bearing cultural values had been constructed.[16]

To this ledger of destabilizations, I would add the Method's troubling status as a style caught between media—between theater and film, liveness and recording. In his statements at the studio, Strasberg always couched his descriptions of the studio's goals in the language of high modernism, as a sacred precinct, a refuge held apart from commerce, mass entertainment, and the media landscape of postwar America, and one that was dedicated to the search for artistic truth as a self-rewarding quest. But he was also very aware that a large part of the studio's mystique was due to its relationship to Hollywood. On the first page of chapter 1 of *Strasberg at the Actors Studio: Tape-Recorded Sessions*, he weeps—this emoting is carefully noted by the transcript—while remembering poor departed "Jimmy Dean" (27). Practicing his preaching, Strasberg neatly combines an adroit use of affective memory with a reminder of the social capital the studio accrued through its association with star actors such as Marlon Brando and his eager disciple, the doomed actor-martyr Dean.

This in-betweenness is reflected in the studio's literature. The major works of acting theory by key members of the Actors Studio (*Strasberg at the Actors Studio* or Robert Lewis's *Method—or Madness?*) evidence several commonalities. First, they weren't actually written per se, but are rather transcripts of classes or lectures given to closed audiences ("informal," as Harold Clurman's preface to Lewis's book of transcribed lectures calls them).[17] Second, they're long. *Strasberg at the Actors Studio* runs to more than 300 pages, and *Method—or Madness?*, though less unwieldy, is still perhaps more compendious than its substance should permit. Third, they're rather vague, throwing around airy, unqualified terms such as "truth" and "reality." Fourth, they devote almost as much time to dispelling illusions about what the real work of the studio is as they do to documenting that work. The ways the outside world grievously misunderstood the Actors Studio was apparently a hot topic of discussion at the studio. *Strasberg at the Actors Studio* is especially self-referential, devoting many pages to the debunking of myths it reifies with its very vagueness. It is a huge book that still preserves the privacy of its subjects, providing chapters and chapters of public pronouncements by a guru who, we are repeatedly reminded, cannot be truly understood by anyone who hasn't seen him at work in the studio. Finally, recordings, the hidden medium behind the transcripts and thus behind the books, are frequently called in as evidence to support the truth-claims of Method teachers. And usually—and this fact is especially significant—they are cited without actually being played.

When Lewis argued in his famous public lecture series on the Method (later transcribed and published as *Method—or Madness?*) that the Method was not responsible for the notorious mumbling of its most lauded acolytes, he brandished as evidence a recording of the celebrated Italian actor Tommaso Salvini, the performer Stanislavski reportedly trumpeted as the "greatest speaker he had ever heard."[18] He brandished the record—the transcripts indicate the gesture—but he didn't let the audience hear it, saying that although he (Lewis) didn't have the equipment handy to play the album, spectators could take his word that the recording was "definite proof" that Salvini wasn't a mumbler.[19] Although by 1958 the already-ancient disc must have been full of hisses and pops, static and skips, markers of the recording's material life, Lewis was sure he could hear past the noise and get to the music. (A little later on in the same lecture he referred to recordings of the actor Alexander Moissi's voice, again for evidentiary value.)[20] The Method paradoxes recur. Lewis was performing an exclusive lecture in private for invited guests that was being transcribed for publication. He was being recorded, but he couldn't play a recording.

An even more evocative example appears early on in *Strasberg at the Actors Studio*, the compendious volume that was for decades Strasberg's sole public statement of his theory and practice. Waxing elegiac about his acting heroes, Strasberg arrived at a surprising place, a description of what might be called the primal scene of Method acting. I will quote it at length because it is so revealing about the importance of recording to the Method's methods. Strasberg introduced the anecdote by rapturously expounding upon a definition of "great acting"—a "true relation between impulse and expression"—while lamenting that "very few of us are sufficiently free so that body, mind, spirit, thought, and verbalization are able to combine in full and true expression" (66). He went on to say that he was fortunate to have witnessed this ineffable commingling just a few times, in only a very few performers: Eleonora Duse, Feodor Chaliapin, Giovanni Grasso, Jacob Ben-Ami, Laurette Taylor, Pauline Lord, and the Moscow Art Theatre and the Group Theatre at their best.

With these illustrious stage luminaries as prologue—the leading lights of previous theatrical generations—the reader might be taken aback by what succeeds them as the apotheosis of this much-lauded "full and true" expression:

> I am reminded of an experiment we did here quite a few years ago when Clifford Odets brought in a tape on which, in preparation for writing something, he had recorded his aunt and uncle talking. We copied off the words and had one of the actors read them, which he did—very nicely, very simply, very well—and seemingly logically and sincerely. And then we put on the recording. It was a howl in a strange, exciting way, because the sound of human life was so totally different. We heard how real people said those words with fullness of excitement, vividness of response, and sudden poetic leaps of expression. The way in which his uncle could switch from some ordinary remark (*shouting passionately*) "TEN YEARS OF MY LIFE!" and back to (*chattily*), "Well, I mean, she's an idiot," was fantastic. This was dialogue spoken by an ordinary man with an accent and a choked voice, but that ordinary voice became so vivid and expressive through the coming together of emotion and sound and meaning that it was thrilling. It would be flabbergasting to hear that tone on the stage. (66–67; Hethmon's emphasis and stage directions)

So many startling ideas crowd to the fore in this passage that they might as well simply be overtly enumerated. First, for Strasberg, recorded everyday speech surpasses conventional theatrical performance in both authenticity and expressive dynamism. What seemed simple, logical, and sincere pales beside the richness of transfixed spontaneous expression on tape, despite the unavoidable fact that the recording alienates the sound of authenticity from the scene of delivery, separating speech from its original gestural and corporeal accompaniment. (This alienation is, of course, what allows it to be savored as the *sound* of authenticity. The recording skews apart seeing and hearing.) And Strasberg defines the recorded voice—the "tone"—that serves as his paragon of vividness, expressiveness, and the confluence of emotion and meaning by its limitations: the accent, the choked quality. And it perhaps even becomes such a paragon of expressivity *because* of these obstacles rather than in spite of them. Strasberg's description deliberately elides the spatiotemporal chasm between recording and listening. In the moment of hearing the tape, Strasberg believes that he has access to the original, embodied moment of utterance.

This elided interval between inscription and transmission serves as Strasberg's positive example of another surmounted hiatus: the "true"—true because seemingly unmediated—relation "between impulse and expression" (66) in acting, the overcoming of interference in the actor's body so that impulses can flow easily from initiation to expression, privacy to publicity, without being compromised. (Once again, as with Lewis's record, the noise of the medium—static, the whirring of tape reels, the hiss of speakers, any distracting background sounds—is entirely repressed.) Recording points the way to the truth, the reel to the real. One communication medium, tape recording, allows Strasberg to think medially about another, the actor's body.

Finally, the tape is so precious and illuminating precisely because, presumably, the aunt and uncle were unaware of its presence—or at least they don't seem to be in Strasberg's description—and so were not "performing." They were simply being themselves, in a state of uncontaminated privacy. Strasberg's rhapsodies about fullness, excitement, and vividness suggest that the recording reveals whole swathes of experience imperceptible in any other way. In this anecdote and, I suggest, in much of Strasberg's work and thought, the quintessentially medial problem of acting—what intervenes between impulse and expression, enabling or inhibiting—is resolved by the unforced fullness of "reality" as uncovered by the medium of tape recording. If only acting could approach the truthful reproduction of actuality rendered by tape, a transcript not just of words—like impoverished dramatic text—but of the very grain of reality, preserving accents, habits of speech, sudden emotive flights, the self's relation to objects.

Though the Method is most commonly associated with dredging up traumas registered in the deep folds of the unconscious mind, this anecdote links it more forcefully with Benjamin's optical unconscious, the strange swathes of everyday experience that the recording's democratic gaze reveals. Strasberg makes fetishes of the aleatory aspects of the tape. It's the unforeseeable flights the speakers make, the counterintuitive, "surprising," quality of the expressive dynamics—the rubbing of a choked voice and immigrant accent against the words—that constitute its claim to authenticity. There's an explicit political point here, immanent throughout Strasberg's statement. The hardscrabble speech of the immigrant rebukes the more polished diction of the mainstream and, we can assume, more assimilated actor. And this margins-over-mainstream narrative has a corollary in the anecdote's reappraisal of aesthetic values, favoring the choked and limited over the eloquent and fluent. However, in typically paradoxical Method fashion, the critique is ambivalent. In order to be savored as the sound of authenticity, the recording must be stripped of its (Jewish, working-class) origins. The particularities of accent and diction, together with the milieu that informs them, must be evacuated so that their sounds can become more flexible signifiers of a generalized authenticity.

What seems to attract Strasberg to the recording is the sound of difference as the true sound of everyday life, the unpredictable terrain revealed by the tape recorder's unbiased hearing. And, crucially, that difference is a question of formal qualities—dynamics, timbre—not identity or character. The ordinary is inextricably linked with the uncanny and the uncanny with the recorded. For Strasberg, recording allowed a second look at the everyday. It made that superabundance of meaning visible, and permitted him to see from "that" point of view that Wittgenstein imagined.

Once we are attuned to the significance of recording for Strasberg, technological metaphors seem to be everywhere in his writing, particularly in his descriptions of the private moment and emotional memory exercises, the two linchpins of his practice. Strasberg's working vocabulary contains many words with connotations redolent of recording and transmission, media words that jar in the context of the studio's supposedly hermetic freedom from the bustling, noisy, commerce-minded world outside, a world that, as Strasberg is careful to note, most certainly includes the mass media of the culture industry.

In several places in *Strasberg at the Actors Studio*, he describes affective recall in terms that suggest tape or vinyl as much as they do the more ineffable reaches of the nether brain. He affirms that the unconscious mind is adept at storing precise transcriptions of sensory or affective experience that only await the right stimulus to surge again to the surface, achieving a kind of cerebral-affective playback: "I mean employing the unconscious or subconscious knowledge that we have stored away but which we cannot easily or quickly put our hand on by means of the conscious mind" (83). Moreover, because this emotional-perceptual archive contains only the already-experienced—the recorded—its contents are safe to peruse again. The now-inert but still vivid secondhand impressions can be "played" again and again by the savvy Method practitioner, without fear of being taken over by the recycled feelings.

Similarly, in his descriptions of the actor's body and the actor's onstage affective life, Strasberg often sounds as if he's talking about crossed wires or kinked cables that are producing static in the line. He is forever trying to unblock blocks, clear obstacles, relax knotted tension to allow for the unhindered communication of impulses from interior to exterior. At one point, deploying a particularly apt analogy, Strasberg compares actors to machines not unlike the tape recorder of his Odets anecdote:

> The actor is an instrument that pays attention. Something happens to him as a result of paying attention which is pure expression. It is happening even when he thinks nothing is being expressed. . . . Inspiration is within the actor; something starts it off. If you push a button and no electricity is attached, nothing happens. Electricity only comes from where electricity is, not from where the button is. In the actor, both electricity and button are usually unconscious. Often the button seems to be external to the actor, but it is not. (85)

Strasberg's description of the proper means by which an actor can achieve imaginative texture onstage is a case study in the penetration of his thinking by technological metaphors. Averring that concentration cannot be abstract, he proposes exercises in the intense scrutiny of everyday objects that amount to perceptual recording, storing thickened experience for later recall and use. He proclaims that this type of concentration, "true concentration . . . always works" (95). Engaging with a hypothetical table by way of demonstration, Strasberg slowly pores over it as if panning a camera across its shape, tracking its presence across both space and time. How wide is it? How tall? How big are its parts in relation to each other? He doubles back and checks his perceptions again, sliding his attention along the table's dimensions, gathering data (97).

In these and other similar examples, the actor's job is conceived as registering sensate information for eventual playback. This process is transcriptive, not mimetic; notational, not expressive. The performer should, by implication, aspire to the neutrality of the recording apparatus, simply seeing, hearing, touching, tasting what is *there*. (Elsewhere, Strasberg remarks, perhaps ruefully, that because the human being's imaginative powers do not "function with machine-like precision," the actor's inscriptive capacities must be built up slowly, with much practice [109].)

Lest a skeptic think I am imbuing Strasberg's parable about the recording of Odets's relatives with too much significance, I'll point out that Strasberg, fulfilling the anecdote's claims for the revelatory capacities of recording, was in the habit of recording almost everything that happened in closed sessions at the studio, creating an aural archive that spooled out over days, months, years, and decades. Both champions and critics of the studio remark on the privileged place accorded the tape recorder in its daily routines. Setting the stage for *Strasberg at the Actors Studio*, writing in the key of hagiography, Hethmon's introduction describes a scene of anticipation akin to a Hollywood soundstage eagerly awaiting the arrival of a star. The students, comely and serious (they "look like an exceptionally attractive and intelligent group of graduate students") await the great man's arrival with a buzz of eager expectation: "the air is charged." Technical precision creates the aura of professional rigor: "A technician comes in, adjusts the tape recorder, and places a glass of water and a large alarm clock on the low stand in front of a movie director's folding canvas chair" (2).

Hethmon's description of the scene as like a film studio—prepped for recording—is hardly incidental. (Note the director's chair.) Performances at the studio are only preparation for the important work of critique, carried out under the attentive gaze of posterity, as represented by the tape recorder:

> Finally, whatever the scene, it will be over. . . . *The stage manager starts the tape recorder*, and one of the performers begins to talk about what he had tried to accomplish in the scene. Strasberg listens, sometimes asks a question, and finally calls on the other actors in the scene, one by one, to explain the problems they were working on. Occasionally the actors will be asked to repeat the scene, so that Strasberg can comment as it progresses. . . . Finally, Strasberg himself begins to speak. He may speak for ten or sixty minutes, but usually his remarks continue for only fifteen or twenty, because a second scene must be accommodated before the session ends about one o'clock.
>
> This is all. . . . The casual observer may be somewhat bewildered. "Is this the world-famous Actors Studio? Is this the birthplace and home of stars? Can these rather simple procedures be the famous 'Method?' " (2–3; emphasis mine)

As in the filming of a movie, where the brilliance of each take may be visible only upon repeated viewing, after seeming sloppiness or casual " 'mooching' " (3) has been alchemized into acting gold, so too, the editor suggests, does Strasberg's scintillating pedagogy emerge only in hindsight, upon review: "Only after one has seen in hundreds of examples his ability to bring the full range of his knowledge, experience, personality, and eloquence to bear on the particular problems of individual actors can one appreciate the authority he brings to the training of each one" (17).

Or, by implication, only when one has listened again to the tapes of those hundreds of examples. This expansive conception of duration is conditioned by recording. A similar sense of the scale of the studio's work frequently recurs in Strasberg's critiques, bearing witness to the high seriousness and vital importance of its project to redeem the American theater for Art with a capital A. He refers to "running" engagements with particular actors over months and years (34). Various actors repeatedly refer to watching their colleagues over long periods. It took two years for one actor to "train [him]self to look and listen and try to understand" (48). An actress points out that "some of us have watched one another four or five years, some of us ten years" (49).

Just as the capacity of tape for audio transcription is endless—subject only to time, opportunity, and the availability of raw material, looping endlessly back on itself, playing again from the beginning as soon as it ends, recorded over in an instant palimpsest—so too is Strasberg's sense of the size of the studio's project shaped by the boundlessness of his favorite archival tool. Even the carefully edited Strasberg of *Strasberg at the Actors Studio* frequently divagates, loops back, revisits the same anecdotes in a way that suggests the medium lying behind his messages. The critic Gordon Rogoff makes the point eloquently:

> Miles upon miles of recorded tape, even when someday they might be edited, may give—as they do in the Studio—a sense of presence and imminent discovery. But like exercises that do not necessarily lead to art, they cannot be expected to drift automatically into philosophy.[21]

Recording was the way Strasberg transformed his impromptu pronouncements into theory—and it was the necessary ground for that theory. Rogoff, the Actors Studio's administrative director from 1958 to 1960 and one of its most perceptive observers in print afterward, recounts the unvarnished version of Strasberg's classroom discourse:

> Where he is most at home—directly coping with an actor's immediate problems demonstrated moments before in a scene or exercise—he is still unable to match his passion to a clear expression of it. His sentences wind their way in jerky, fumbling patterns through cluttered underbrush, most of them masterpieces of how not to use the language. Studded with qualifiers, parenthetical clauses, and jumbled syntax as his message is, the only miracle is not that it is widely misunderstood, as he so often complains, but that it is understood at all.
>
> A written transcription of Strasberg's extemporaneous spoken words can be only partially evocative of the sound he makes; indeed, to transcribe him on paper is to transform what is essentially an astounding run-on sentence into a series of reasonably intelligible single sentences with commas, semi-colons, and full stops.[22]

Rogoff goes on to proffer just such a transcription, and the paragraph's seething stops and starts, abrupt divagations, and churning vagaries chafe the eye, while also reminding us how much careful grooming went into producing the more manicured prose of *Strasberg at the Actors Studio*.

But even in that regularized text, the editor is careful to preserve some flashes of the demotic, hectoring Strasberg, some tics of everyday speech to indicate not only that the transcripts preserve the heat of spontaneous problem-solving, but also that Strasberg is a hands-on, rough-and-ready man of practice, not an abstracter of the actor's task: "Huh?"; "I don't know"; "I forget" (259); "Nope!" (229); "okay" (151, 212, 275, etc.); "Gee!"; "Boy!"; "You see?" (89, 235, 370, etc.). These artifacts of the original scenes of utterance, fetishized survivors of extemporized speech, testify to the book's beginnings in impromptu talk, in immediate verbal objects. They attest to the status of Strasberg's remarks as unpremeditated responses to present performances, not commentary for a disinterested reader. We are always reminded that it is not just the words that carry the force of Strasberg's ideas, but the situation in which he delivered them and the power of the animating principles that gave them velocity. The many moments of inarticulacy vouchsafe that his doctrine is rooted in practice, not abstract speculation. The disavowal of fluency testifies to his authenticity. It is the "noise" of his speech, the surface vibration, that provides signs of this seismic stratum of subterranean meaning.

And it is these signifiers of Strasberg's natural speech patterns, intended to serve as evidence of his immediate presence, that are most the products of recording, of mediation. His Method theorizing requires Method reading. His readers must always scan for subtext, and ascribe experiential fullness to sketchily visible thoughts. The available texts of his classes evince the same flummoxing of fluency, the same preference for feelings over words that the Method's harsher critics indicted in the acting of Method-associated performers such as Brando. The speech crimes of Method acting seem also to have been the speech crimes of its major pedagogue. He too preferred feelings to words. Hethmon himself admits that Strasberg is sometimes difficult to understand: "Sometimes *what* he says, taken literally, does not make sense" (17). For Hethmon, though, this is further proof of Strasberg's teaching brilliance. The mostly unconscious problems of acting must be addressed by techniques that speak directly to the unconscious, as if by telepathy: "[Strasberg] is extremely articulate when he wants to be, but he is also aware that a great deal of the actor's functioning is unconscious, that ideas and rules and principles may or may not have any effect on his work" (17).

Strasberg's (tactical?) vagueness and prolixity on paper only reinforce the sense that the reader would have to have *been there*, at the studio in the heat of the session, to understand him completely. His gnomic pronouncements remain lastingly private even as he rambles on for pages in public. Like the transcript of reality in his anecdote about listening to the Odets clan, his dictated declamations can only gesture to a fuller truth. And reading through the sessions is itself a form of playback. The reader is invited to restage the discussions imaginatively, returning to the scenes of breakthrough or blockage, scenes we know really happened because of the book's origins in transcripts of recorded classwork, to pore over their import as acting parables. As though to further underline the transcripts' dimensionality, their origins in pedagogical performance, not isolated meditation, the book preserves Strasberg's gestures too, rendered as italicized stage directions. Strasberg snaps his fingers (229), stamps his feet (225). His words can't be entirely separated from his expressive body, even in print.

The real drama of the Actors Studio wasn't to be found onstage in snippets of Inge, Odets, or Chekhov. It began with the click of the tape recorder and hit its high points when the irresistible force of Strasberg's pedagogical will collided with the immovable object of a stubborn actor. The centerpiece of *Strasberg at the Actors Studio* is a confrontation between Strasberg and a recalcitrant actress, identified only as RR. Over more than fifteen pages, what began as a critique of scene work heats up into a one-act play, depicting a battle of opposing personalities as volatile as the best dustup from mid-twentieth-century realist drama. Clearly intending to make it a parable-play—call it *The Breakthrough!*—the editor presents the scene as dialogue, complete with stage directions depicting the main players' movements and emotional states. (Usually in *Strasberg at the Actors Studio*, the actors' transcribed questions or commentary provide cues for Strasberg's ruminations, but the speakers don't remain a part of the text that follows. They disappear obediently into the background of his monologue.)

The point of the episode isn't the intellectual content—the words themselves are mostly quite banal—but the record of a titanic struggle and the powerful feelings involved. Haranguing, hectoring, bullying, overbearing, Strasberg shouts, interrupts, urges, interrogates. Successively mumbling, weeping, half laughing, half and fully sobbing, the young actress screams incoherently, kicks furniture, curses, rages, protests, and eventually relents (227–41). She is blocked, full of dammed-up expression and emotion that needs to be "let out" (239). This catharsis, and not, crucially, a better performance of the soliloquy from *Romeo and Juliet* that she's ostensibly workshopping, is the true goal of the scene. And the measure of its success is not crisply enunciated pentameters but that the actress is left tear-stained, exhausted, and submissive, having made a mess of the room. One can only imagine how very tenuous the relationship of this psychodrama to Shakespeare must have seemed. (Strasberg notes that she almost broke the tape recorder.) The process is manifestly physical, and disturbingly paternalistic. Strasberg asserts his control—he demands several times that she "obey" (235)—over the actress's body, piece by piece, leading her in a series of fantastical movements: "Arms wide. Hold on to the chair. That's right. You have good hands. That's right. (*She sobs.*)" (238). As he does so, he repeatedly addresses her as "darling," "sweetie," or as a "girl." He employs such epithets more than seventeen times throughout the scene, a veritable litany of diminution, and one that is all the more striking because it survived Hethmon's editorial ministrations to make it into print. Clearly, the scenario is representative (228–41).

This sequence gives us insight into the gendered dynamics of Strasberg's soundscapes. In the scene above, Strasberg asserts his authority by attacking language. He performs his pedagogical power by forcing the actress to abandon the play she is working on to fulfill the idiosyncratic diktats of his classroom exercises. The Shakespearean example is surely not accidental. As a parable, the scene depicts the demolition of theatrical artifice—at one point, he notes that the actress, a former dancer, "has a flair for picking wonderful theatrical attitudes" (235)—in order to reveal a raw core of authenticity, the "full" expression that Strasberg knew was there, and that only he could extract and adjudicate. The drama of uncovering this buried reality depends on positioning the female student as an avatar of artifice and her performance as a false surface to be penetrated. The act of breaking down this facade is a precondition for confirming Strasberg's guru status, and tears are the signs of success. As Rosemary Malague has incisively argued, for Strasberg, the "Big Daddy" of the Method, breakdowns and breakthroughs were virtually synonymous.[23]

If the characteristic unit of noisemaking for the male Method actor was the mumble, we could even say that for the female members of the studio, the corresponding quantum of authenticity was the sob. Over and over again in *Strasberg at the Actors Studio*, Strasberg's classroom encounters with women end in tears. A similar scene, with HH, another student, who is described as "a very mixed-up girl . . . but obviously undisciplined and with strong personal problems" occurs some fifty pages later. It also culminates with weeping and thrown objects (344). And this triumphalist display of authentic tears wrung from difficult actors occurs elsewhere in Strasberg's archive, too. Shonni Enelow vividly describes revisiting the taped classroom session from 1966 that furnishes Strasberg with one of his examples of a "successful" emotional memory exercise in his memoir-treatise, *A Dream of Passion*. On the tape, Enelow hears "a series of pregnant pauses punctuated by screams, sobs, and short bursts of language."[24]

But, as Enelow reminds us, we shouldn't deny these actresses their creative agency, especially in the face of Strasberg's bullying.[25] Becoming adept at displaying the right sort of breakdown, adroitly dissolving a theatrical surface with truth-testifying tears, may have been one of the most important survival skills, one with both social and artistic applications, cultivated by women in Method classrooms and rehearsal halls. If breakdowns were breakthroughs, actors did well to master their characteristic rhythms, the music of redolent pauses, solvent sobs, and eruptive screams.

As we'll see a little later, these scenes uncannily double the narrative of *A Streetcar Named Desire* and, especially, of the representational politics of Kazan's casting of his iconic film. As a character, Blanche DuBois, too, has a propensity for "wonderful theatrical attitudes" and she is suspiciously voluble. Her decadent language is somehow of a piece with the perceived decadence of her past. She's an anti-Method figure, hiding the truth behind poetry. And the revelation of that truth is accompanied by a breakdown. Stanley acts as Big Daddy, wrenching the truth from beneath her evasive fictions.

Episodes like the ones described above confirm Brustein's worst suspicions about the Method's assault on the articulate acting demanded by complicated classical texts. But even more important, they also show clearly that for Strasberg, fluent language was too public an instrument, for either pedagogical discourse or theatrical performance, to be the vehicle for theatrical insight. To really do Method, you had to leave words behind, or find your way into the gaps between them.

In one intriguing passage in *Method—or Madness?* Robert Lewis describes the photographer Alfred Stieglitz waiting patiently in front of an office building for the right moment of exposure to capture an eloquent moment of urban loneliness. He makes an analogy with the Method's training techniques.[26] Strasberg, too, was fond of "waiting" during exercises, dilating the moment of performance, allowing actors to wander far off book and off scene, stretching out the performance until the fictive situation of the scene began to collapse into the reality of the studio exercise, until the right quality of veracity, of natural expression, began to appear in the acting. Just as Strasberg's faithful acolytes kept the tape recorder running to catch pedagogical genius in the moment of its efflorescence, Strasberg frequently kept the exercises going, creating intervals of open-ended receptivity—a mode of attention that matched the perfect audition of the ever-present tape recorder. The studio's near-obsessive habit of recording Strasberg's comments after each session suggests an aspiration to continuity in the archive: an ongoing metadiscourse conducted for the ears of posterity, apart from the demands of engaging with each day's scenes, dramatizing a lonely crusader's search for theatrical truth. His comments were conceived as both private and public at the outset.

In the published version of the sessions, because the individual actors Strasberg addresses are anonymous, identified only by letters, and because the reader has no access to the performances Strasberg expounds on beyond the barest descriptions of the material performed, the "drama" of the encounters is transposed from scenes to critique of scenes, from Strasberg addressing specific acting difficulties to Strasberg taking on the problems of the American theater at large and addressing acting problems in the abstract, a titanic monodrama of the lonely prophet crying out in the wilderness against mendacity, artifice, commercialism, and glitz and pleading for reality, honesty, and art.

Confronted with Strasberg's perpetual demands for more of these elusive quantities—more reality, more texture, more imagination, more art—what he calls the "sense of 'more-ness' that life has" (72)—we should think again of his anecdotal distinction between the performance of reality's transcript by a careful actor and reality itself as audible on tape. The latter, in his recounting, is fuller, richer, more dynamic, more unpredictable, more "more."

But Robert Brustein's jeremiad against the Method's cluttered speech raises the specter of another "more." For him, and spectators like him, the "more" revealed by Method acting's creative dialogue with recording was not an experience of fullness or vividness. It was actually frighteningly empty or obstructive: more obstacles, more strange blank spots, more meaningless noise and less music. Both Strasberg and Lewis, prompted no doubt by Brustein or the ire of critics who felt similarly (there were many, including Harold Clurman, Strasberg's old colleague from the Group Theatre days),[27] take great pains in their published statements to distance themselves from the Method's infamous mumblers. *Strasberg at the Actors Studio* and *Method—or Madness?* both contain lengthy disquisitions disavowing poor speech and affirming the applicability of Method techniques to all genres of theater, not just the proletarian antiheroes of American urban realism.

But perhaps they protested too much. The mumblers were the most faithful exponents of the Method's mediated aesthetic, the most faithful to the aspects of speech that only recording could reveal. Strasberg's (and Lewis's) consternation is entirely understandable. Techniques that were supposedly about unblocking the actor, freeing them to communicate, making their performances more full of the ineffable vividness of real, unperformative, everyday life had become synonymous in the minds of the public with stymied speech, inarticulate feelings, mumble-smeared delivery. But as both Strasberg's transcripts and Brando's iconic performances illustrate, these are aspects of the same thing. Taking recording as the arbiter of the real also means taking the noise of everyday life as the substance of everyday life. It also means absorbing the noise of the medium into that substance. In a 1956 lecture on the Method, Michael Redgrave articulated this reevaluation of noise and music, sound and sense, background and foreground, margin and center in particularly vivid terms: "The danger [of the Method] is that what is seized on and preserved, in this passionate quest for originality, is not the essential but the decorative, or even the waste product."[28] Just as the Method valorized characters from marginal social groups, it made abject perceptual data central to its aesthetic.

Reviewing the Actors Studio Theatre's inaugural 1963 production of Chekhov's *Three Sisters* for the *New York Times*, Howard Taubman noted that while Strasberg's approach was "unhurried, sensitive and full of relish for the details of Russian life," the plentitude of such details sometimes disturbed the relation between atmosphere and event. In particular, he pointed out that in the first act, "the chatter and laughter at the table in the background are so insistent and loud that it becomes difficult to follow what is happening in the foreground."[29] Even more remarkable, this conversational noisiness was matched by a corresponding busyness throughout the aural spectrum of the production. Taubman described a "constant concern for the literalism of the precise sounds in the distance, like the tolling of the bells, the calls of the birds flying south and the music of the band playing for the departing soldiers."[30] The same preference for "more," for texture over detail and sound over sense, that pervades Strasberg's thought and studio work seems to have infiltrated his few publicly staged productions from the era.

The Noise of Authenticity: Marlon Brando's Methods of Mediation

Back to Brustein, Brando, and *A Streetcar Named Desire*. I'm going to take Brustein at his word and look at Brando's early career performances as exemplars of Method acting. Despite Marianne Conroy's salutary reminder that the Brando fixation of the Method's midcentury critics was essentially revisionist—"to identify Brando as the singular exemplar of the Method style," she points out "is to overlook the intense rifts within that segment of the American acting community influenced by Stanislavski"[31]—I'm going to be just as monomaniacal. My idea here is that the Brando obsession was rooted not just in a confusion over methodology—whether his acting could be attributed to Adler or Strasberg or was properly Stanislavskian at all—but in a recognition that Brando's acting fulfilled a dynamic that was present in Strasberg's thought and work anyway.

Just like Strasberg, in fact, Brando's performances in the iconic early Kazan films, *Streetcar* most prominently but *On the Waterfront* too, use recording to mediate between public and private. For Strasberg, a way of making private sessions public also became a way of translating private speech into public thought, while retaining the aura of authenticity imbued by the original scene of utterance. For Brando, recording became a way of making the public art of acting more private. His performances, whether deliberately or not, obsessively worry the border between those two terms. Incorporating more noise into his delivery, he marks the precise interval where private impulse becomes public expression, simultaneously pointing to the presence of the camera and microphone by making sounds only they can register. Upon closer examination, his mumbling wasn't simple mumbling at all but a deliberate attempt to tamper with his instrument to produce new sounds.

Mumbling is itself a medial problem. Mumbling, stammering, and misspeaking are events in which the human apparatus of communication—the brain that searches out the words, the tongue and mouth that shape them—becomes interference instead of vehicle, and interposes itself between words and listeners. The nonsignifying noise that attends speech—the ums, the uhs, the clearing of throats, licking of lips, all the vocal stuff we edit out while parsing out the words—surges to the fore. This collapse is particularly acute in the theater, where the playwright's words preexist and surround the actors who will embody them as a kind of transcendental halo of meaning. In the theater, mumbling is static on the line.

If you return to the film of *A Streetcar Named Desire*, ground zero of the Method's campaign against good speech, with Brustein's complaints in mind, however, you discover that the problem is not simply one of articulation. It's not just that Brando mumbles, although he certainly does that, waging a one-man war on consonants throughout his scenes. It's also that he usually actually has something *in* his mouth, an object or morsel around which his character's words must flow. In practically every one of his scenes, Brando is chewing on something or other. He snacks, he sips, he bites, he chews, he drags on a cigar. And while he does so, he's also masticating Tennessee Williams's words, grinding them against the food or smoking paraphernalia in his mouth and, thanks to the attentive microphones and cameras, pushing the action of his mouth against the frame of the picture. (When he screams "Stella! Stella!" in that now-mythic sequence, you can hear his voice rasping against the limits of the recording apparatus, the invisible line where distortion begins.)

In the original Broadway production of the play, as Kazan's exhaustive director's notes for the production elaborate, Brando's oral fixations were intended to symbolize Stanley's brute sensuality. He loves to taste, to ingest, to display mastery over his environment by literally incorporating its objects into his body.[32] He's the ruler of his domain ("Every man's a king!" he roars at Stella), and the apartment is stocked with his favorite things—snacks, cigarettes, liquor. In most scenes, his first action after his entrance is to put one of these in his mouth, making his body part of his kingdom and his kingdom part of his body.

But once transferred to film, this metaphorical munching became a more complex proposition. Freed from the imperative of making himself heard in a Broadway-sized theater, Brando was also more free to mumble, slur, drawl, and elide. Think of Brando's occluded mouth as a kind of prepared piano. Like Cage, he was adapting his instrument to make noises most spectators hadn't heard before. Recall Clifford Odets's uncle on the Group Theatre's famous tape. Once again, but deliberately this time, we have a voice that becomes more "authentic" because of its (self-imposed) limitations. Brando's full mouth always threatens to choke his speech, and the struggle of words against morsels introduces an aleatory element into his acting, enhanced by the microphone's ability to catch happenstance sounds.

Put simply, when Brando was chewing, he couldn't fully anticipate the sound of his own voice. He introduced a chance procedure into his performance, created the conditions by which the uncanniness of the mediated everyday could slip into view. Like Strasberg, he wanted his audience to be taken by surprise, to experience the everyday as unexpected difference. His chance-operative chewing maintained the spontaneity of his acting while also undermining that slippery quantity that perpetually threatened the private truth of his performance, the inherent publicity of language. And perhaps, as for Strasberg, these by-products, the unforeseeable sounds created by Brando's experiments with obstruction, had a sturdiness that rivaled the material objects anchoring everyday life. Revealed by the camera, they were true because they were strange, immediate because mediated. Brando's acting purposefully haunts both ends of the audible (and recordable) spectrum. Just as he murmurs his lines, forcing spectators to lean in in order to discern his words, he also suddenly yowls or exclaims, jolting Blanche, and us, with the sudden dynamic shifts.

In *A Streetcar Named Desire*, Blanche famously yearns for magic, not reality. Her world of beauty, illusion, and artifice is deliberately set against Stanley's grasping world of material achievement, sensate pleasures, and hard facts. Brando's performance in Kazan's film quite literally put the terms of this debate at the tip of his tongue. Audience members (such as Brustein) accustomed to the more fluent performances of a previous generation of actors wanted the language of playwrights to trip nimbly from actors' lips, exquisitely modulated and articulated even in times of storm and stress. These performers were eloquent even in suffering. Marianne Conroy astutely points out that Brando's costars in the stage and screen *Streetcar*s, Jessica Tandy and Vivien Leigh, tutored in the English repertory system and old Hollywood, were models of diction under duress. She suggests that "through its casting and performance, *Streetcar* staged a struggle between acting styles that enabled Method acting to become visible as a distinctive style."[33] And these contending acting styles were coded along gender lines. Leigh's precise elocution and classical panache were deliberately pitted against Brando's growling, eliding delivery. Fluency in language, eloquence of expression, becomes a hallmark of effeminacy, even decadence.

Meanwhile, film was expected to translate the actor's body to pictures without leaving a stubborn residue behind to remind viewers of the materiality of those bodies. Brando's acting in the film version of *Streetcar* deliberately skews the bodily production of language away from the apprehension of meaning. In doing so, he encourages us to pay attention to aspects of everyday speech that we usually tune out, the nonsignifying "noise" of human communication. Brando's teething continually marks the border between inside and outside, the precise interval at which speech becomes public, the moment when utterance as a somatic product, the work of the breath, the lips, the teeth and tongue, the resonance of the body's echo chambers, erupts into the air to be harvested by listeners as semantic signals. Auditors of the film must work harder than usual to sort noise from sense, to separate semiotics from mechanics. His hand gestures, too, often trace this division. He holds his fingers to his lips as if measuring the vibrations of his speech, briefly rests a fluttering hand on his chest. The play of his performance is medial, tracing the line between inside and outside. Like the Strasbergian gestures preserved in the *Strasberg at the Actors Studio* transcripts, Brando's movements seem to refer to their own evanescence. These were spontaneous expressions, he wants to tell us, forged in the fleeting heat of feeling. A different take might have prompted different choreographies.

The film theorist Laura Marks has coined the term "haptic visuality" to describe film or video images that create an appearance of tactility by pulling the gaze insistently to their flickering surfaces, drawing the eye across textures or along contours. Such synesthetic pictures, she argues, foster a feeling of proximity that seems almost to bridge the chasm between viewer and screen, between seeing and touching. In her memorable formulation, these images "approach the viewer not through the eyes alone, but along the skin."[34] I expand upon Marks's idea somewhat here to include recorded sound effects that, combined with film images, work to suggest physical nearness. This notion helps to explain what viewers may have found either enticing or alien about Brando's acting. His material being remains perpetually present in his speech, creating perceptual noise by implying touch along with sound. He confuses the aural and the tactile, suggests corporeal dimensions behind cinematic flatness, subverts surface with depth.

But even as Brando's performance brings us closer to his body, it also pushes us further away. His acting makes a virtue of interference. By putting objects between viewers and his words, he reminds us of the presence of that other great hiatus between his speech and our listening, the camera and the editing room. He makes us aware of the gap between performance and spectation. For critics of the Method such as Brustein, in fact, Brando's entire rendition of the character was an obstacle between the playwright and his audience. As the prime exponent of an acting style celebrated for its purported immediacy, for bringing characters closer to us with real existing emotion, it's startling how Brando's performance holds us at a distance, interposes barriers. He simultaneously invites the camera and his audience nearer and rebuffs these urges to proximity. He often turns his back to the camera, twisting away from our gaze, even as Leigh, as Blanche, stays plainly visible, in full or three-quarter-view attitudes more redolent of stage-bound theatricality. (Leigh's Blanche, like the Method student in the classroom scene we saw earlier, has a dangerous propensity for "wonderful theatrical attitudes.") Staging intimate closeness and impenetrable privacy at the same moment, Brando's performance, at once mediate and immediate, reproduces the dance of public and private that recurs throughout Strasberg's work and thought.

As with Strasberg, this distancing reflects an important fact. It is precisely those aspects of Brando's performance that became the hallmarks of Method acting's immediacy and authenticity—the chewed-over words, the mumbled delivery—that were most mediated, most the product of technology and technologically enhanced perception. His performance is more "cinematic" because it relies so heavily on fidgeting, mumbling, and obstructed speech that only the democratic eyes and ears of the camera and microphone could pick up. The noisiness of his performance is indivisible from the noisiness of the medium.

Kazan's journal entries about *A Streetcar Named Desire* reveal that one of the key changes he planned to make while transposing his production to film was to accentuate the sonic environment of New Orleans, as a way to bring the panoply of the modern city to bustling life but also as a way to presage Blanche's psychic collapse.[35] Noting that the high-strung Blanche is sensitive to sounds, Kazan heightened the aural effect of a raucous urban milieu in the film—clamoring vendors, pealing church bells, traffic noise, and the chugging mechanical din of the factory. In one interpolated scene in which Stanley tells Mitch about Blanche's lurid past (a dramatization of a moment which happens offstage in the play), the dialogue is entirely drowned out by the thrumming of heavy machinery. The violence of the argument and subsequent grappling is juxtaposed with the relentless brute force of the assembly line.

Why is this important? I think there is a crucial connection between Kazan's resolve to make his film noisier in order to reflect the everyday life of postwar cities and the fact that Brando's enormously influential performance made acting noisier, abetted by modern technology, in this case, the recording apparatus of film. Brando's noisy acting is the corollary of Kazan's noisy city. (As if acknowledging the connection between recording and noisiness, at one point Brando as Stanley chucks a radio, the totem of the postwar media ecology, out the window after complaining about the cacophonous pop music Stella and Blanche are listening to.)

And race was a crucial ingredient in this soundscape. African American characters and voices fill the margins of Kazan's frame, another way to heighten the sense of his cacophonous urban scene, and African American music provides its emotive soundscape. Paige McGinley has eloquently pointed out the central role played by black music and black performers in Kazan's stage production, and in its soundscape in particular.

> With his strong directorial hand Kazan amplified the black presence in both plays and used both black actors and black music to navigate the realistic and expressionistic registers of each play's performance. Alternately acting as realistic sociological frame, nostalgic evocation of a nearly lost past, an expression of forbidden desire, and as a social and political conscience, blackness served as the bond that held these "unstable compounds" together onstage.[36]

Each of these things is even more true of the film, which deploys black faces in its swirling crowd scenes, black music in its soundtrack, black voices in its urban streetscapes, and black characters on its margins to heighten the cosmopolitan effect of its depiction of New Orleans, and to depict the urban reality of postwar America, at once intensely segregated and more diverse than ever before.

But I would argue that race factors into the film's soundscapes in still another way. Many critics, George Crandell prominent among them, have read *A Streetcar Named Desire* as a coded story about the fearful but alluring prospect of miscegenation, suggesting that Stanley is portrayed in ways reminiscent of historical stereotypes of African American men, who were somehow more animalistic, less civilized, less articulate, more full of unpredictable desire, and less governed by the intellect and moral judgment.[37]

This line of argument illuminates another aspect of Brustein's jeremiad. Towards the end of his essay, he suggests that the Method's depredations of spoken language paved the way for other pop-culture despoilments:

> It is significant that not only Marlon Brando and James Dean have become spokesmen for the adolescent generation, but Elvis Presley as well; for Presley is the musical counterpart of the inarticulate hero.

> For the first time in recent memory, popular music has discarded intelligibility, even on the most basic level. Beginning by ignoring language, rock and roll is now dispensing with melodic content and offering only animal sounds and repetitive rhythms.[38]

The unspoken part of this indictment, of course, is that the musical forms Presley emulated were African American. The "animal sounds" and "repetitive rhythms" were borrowed from the blues and R&B, indirect descendants of Williams's scene-setting "Blue piano played by brown fingers." Presley scandalized listeners by not sounding white enough. And it's perhaps not too much to say that Brando and his cohort didn't sound white enough, either. The uproar about the inarticulateness of the Method is also haunted by the specter of miscegenation, by the infiltration of African American sounds, rhythms, and slang into the daily speech of American cities.

Kazan's film ends by almost rendering Blanche incoherent. As revelations about her past overwhelm the present, she begins, for the first time, to stammer, to mutter, and to slur. In her final, decisive confrontation with Brando's Stanley in the film's penultimate scene, he asserts physical control over her body, tossing her this way and that, wrenching her limbs askew. We might think again of the classroom scene in which Strasberg indicts the supposed theatrical falsity of his female student's performance while asserting his authority over her body, limb by limb. Blanche ends up sobbing like so many actresses did in Strasberg's classrooms. And her collapse is aurally illustrated with echoing fragments of voice-over, pure recording. Dialogue becomes noise, and speech becomes atmosphere, as shards of Brando's previous lines are interspersed with pieces from her own. In the medial play of the film's soundscapes, recording trumps theater. The breakdown forcefully separates the diegetic realities of performance and dialogue. Her voice is pulled decisively from her body, in an operation only film can accomplish. In this reading, her final, shaky return to her customarily fluent diction in the film's final scene, with the famous observation that she has always depended on the kindness of strangers, becomes even more poignant. It asserts the fragile reinstatement of her voice in her body, the importance of fluency in the face of noise, and theatrical magic in the face of blunt filmic realism.

So the story of Method acting's romance with the camera and microphone is not, as it is often portrayed, just a narrow story of the triumph of more verisimilar filmic acting over the stagy artifice of theatrical acting or of cinema's defeat of theater as a mass-cultural medium. Rather, it's a story of how acting became noisier as everyday life did. (In this fable, Robert Brustein becomes a Blanche DuBois figure, undone by the cacophony of a grasping, mediated world unfriendly to his canonical sympathies.) As Suárez points out, "After the machine was there to register it, and after cultural production was done exclusively with or alongside machines, it was harder to keep out the racket."[39]

If we needed proof that Brando's habit of speaking with his mouth full was as much the expression of Method acting's creative dialogue with analog recording as it was a particular oral quirk of Stanley Kowalski's, his portrayal of Terry Molloy in *On the Waterfront* delivers the goods. In the second of his indelible early performances, his mouth is once again almost always occupied, and his habit of withholding persists. Here, chewing gum and sometimes pretzels are the objects of choice. (He even offers gum as a panacea to his vocally outraged sweetheart.) But more important, the film is even more adamant in aligning noise with authenticity than *A Streetcar Named Desire*.

The plot turns on the possession, and eventual confession, of secret knowledge by Brando's character, Terry Molloy. An unwitting accomplice and witness to a murder, he is nonetheless bound by the taciturn code of the longshoreman and refuses to turn stool pigeon. His problem is thus the Method actor's problem: how to align private imperatives with the necessity of public speech, how to disclose the truth without compromising it or himself, how to make interior knowledge exterior fact without cheapening it, how to identify the fit medium for that authentic expression. And the stuff in Brando's mouth makes this dilemma tangible. His speech is especially precious because every utterance must surmount obstacles. Each audible word is hard won. Throughout the film, we are conditioned to accept Terry as more "authentic" because he is less verbal (the film is full of prolix liars in positions of power) and because he must fight harder than anyone else to say anything at all. He used to be a boxer, but now his sparring partner is language.

Given all this, it's especially significant that when Terry finally confesses what he knows, to the sister of the murder victim, who also happens to be his love interest, his voice is drowned out by the blaring of ship's horns and the rattle of machinery, the workaday clamor of the docks. As with Kazan's additions to *Streetcar,* the making public of a secret is accompanied by the smothering of speech, and noise keeps private the terms of that revelation. We can just barely detect Brando's tones under the racket, but what we hear is texture, not detail, sound, not sense. Freed from the burden of conveying specific meanings, Brando's performance is "pure" confession, private feeling unsullied by the publicity of language—feelings without words, to return to Brustein's elegant phrase.

In this sequence, the noise of modern life completely drowns language but does not submerge feeling, which, we are meant to understand, is perhaps communicated more powerfully without being limited by words. And once again, noisy acting is the corollary of a noisy city. Technology both enables this mode of expression and conceals it, makes Brando's feeling public and keeps it private all at once. For both Kazan and Brando, the grain of authenticity is more valuable than its particular verbal phrasings.

This is perhaps the apotheosis of Method acting's embrace of recording as a hallmark of veracity. Truth is only possible when words are smothered by noise. The noise of the medium and the noise of everyday life become indivisible. The camera and tape recorder were the perfect solutions to the Method's queasiness about airing private emotions in public places, a way to pretend those public places were not public at all by providing an audience that wasn't an audience. In the final analysis, for the Method, truth is what the camera sees or tape recorder hears, a kind of impossibly, inhumanly, expansive perception but also a mode of paying attention that makes no hierarchical distinctions between sounds. To the microphone, the noise of machinery on the dock is indistinguishable from the noise of Brando's emotive confession. To perceive everything is also to perceive nothing. More can be less.

In a short essay called simply "Film," John Cage once predicted that film would come into its own when it learned to exploit zones of invisibility in the same way that musical experiments like his own had reimagined silence as fulsome sound.[40] Brando's early performances, mixing inscrutable noise with dramatic sense, static with communication, hinted at the quotidian's uncanny double, the shadow realm of meaninglessness and contingency lurking underneath the intelligible world.

Chapter 3

As in Heavenly Raiment: Stuart Sherman's Ecstatic Quotidian

> So often I experience moments in which my consciousness adjusts itself like a lens, moving into close-up on a particular object—the object itself is irrelevant, what is relevant is the result obtained: a near-total escape from the human world—the world of human consciousness experienced singly or in relation to others—into the non-human, the purely (dumbly) physical world, represented in one object, all the better to sharpen the point (the end-point) of one's focusing instrument.
>
> —Stuart Sherman, journal entry

> During the performance, especially, but also, to some degree, afterward, I keep asking myself why do I bother doing anything but these performances, this type of performance, which includes this type of creation—creation which brings me into contact with the very heart of existence, face to face with reality itself, then simply in reality and reality in me. I become real . . . not free, not enlightened, not—, not—. Simply real, and it is enough and it is everything.
>
> —Stuart Sherman, journal entry

Stuart Sherman's "spectacles"—the monumental sequence of miniature performances he worked at for more than 25 years between 1975 and his death in 2001—are a study in illuminating paradoxes.[1] Viewed as a series, the pieces constitute a remarkable body of continuous work, or even a single, ever-expanding performance piece, in more than eighteen parts, a decades-long durational project made up of tiny fleeting molecules of performance, as transitively beguiling as they are difficult to retain in memory.

Sherman devoted his artistic career to reimagining the everyday. His name for his work, an umbrella term encompassing not only his performance pieces but also his sculptures, drawings, and poems, was the "Quotidian Foundation."[2] He even published several issues of a magazine devoted to his projects called the *Quotidian Review*. His spectacles, serial dramas of abject objects made suddenly animate and eloquent, are the most tangible manifestation of this idea. But this expansive idea of a wider quotidian theater also reflects Sherman's understanding of everyday experience and the everyday world as theaters in themselves. For Sherman, thought and language are stages across which objects strut and fret, transmuted from inert matter to parts of speech or elements of cognition. Objects index endless dramas, latent potentialities of meaning and association, awaiting the right productive estrangement of vision to become manifest. In Sherman's world, there is no such thing as an inanimate object. Things are alive with meaning, voluble with language.

Moving briskly, at the edge of a conjurer's mesmerizing pace, he would rapidly retrieve series of small everyday objects from jumbled piles, often contained within an open suitcase. His props of choice were usually small, often mass-produced items, innocuous at first glance, but lambently strange upon closer appraisal. Maneuvering them into precisely arranged configurations on the surface of a TV-tray table, a smaller stage recalibrating the scale of the larger ones on which he stood, he would assemble dynamic collages, or stage startling transformations, holding his animated things in place just long enough for interpretive possibilities to bloom in spectators' minds, before unsentimentally discarding his object-actors, tossing them aside into the oblivion of an unsorted heap.

Each spectacle—excluding those featuring multiple performers, of which there were at least two—is remarkably similar in form, but absolutely singular in content. The basic setup, once established, remained virtually constant through Sherman's career, right down to the "costume" he wore while performing: sneakers, black jeans, a black T-shirt with a vivid carmine (or sometimes blue) workshirt draped open over it. The constant shape of the spectacles embodies an image of quotidian consciousness as a tension between habit and exception, routine and singularity, dualities Sherman's pieces constantly confront in their estrangement of everyday things and words. He created routines to disrupt routine, habits to puncture habits.

"The Portrait of Stuart Sherman," a routine from the *Eighth Spectacle* (c. 1979), embodies his restless view of artmaking and its symbiotic relationship to everyday experience. It begins with Sherman holding up a transparent piece of plastic in front of his face, transforming his living body into a kind of still life, both presence and image, portrait and performer. Turning on a tape recorder, he plays what sounds like the caterwauling of a jungle creature. Curling his fingers into claws, he rakes the air above the recorder. Putting a party noisemaker in his mouth through a little hole in the plastic that he still holds before him, he mimes sketching the contours of his face on the transparent surface—layering a drawing over his countenance, a portrait on a portrait—before blowing on the party favor to emit a celebratory peal, the punctuation to his image-making. He repeats the sequence, clawing at his face this time, tracing savage abstract marks over his face instead of the more subdued lines of the previous iteration.

This interplay between unnamed wildness and artistic creation takes on a clearer significance as Sherman jauntily dons a pith helmet, takes up a prop pistol, and points it at himself, clicking the trigger merrily. Making art, he is both predator and prey, colonizer and colonized. Each finished work, both a celebration (the noisemaker) and an act of violence (the gun), freezes some living part of himself and his thought into relics, taming the uncharted parts of his psyche while also irreparably altering them. As the routine goes on, he emphasizes the chronological recession of this process by recording the belches of the noisemaker and playing them back, each festive exclamation of accomplished form only the marker of the cycle beginning again. (He shoots the pith helmet, too, pointing out that the hunter is a temporary persona as well.)

The routine concludes in stillness, as Sherman, his constant motion momentarily arrested, stares at the motley pile of junk from which he has elaborated this complex portrait of the artist as pursuer and pursued, as though contemplating what he has wrought, and what he still must create.

First performed for an audience of one, the philosopher and theater critic Stefan Brecht, who also appeared in the *Second Spectacle* (1976), the spectacles were staged in theaters, galleries, lofts, and even occasionally on street corners, busker-style. Sherman's portable stage, the counterpart to his diary, was a blank page on which he would set things down, writing with objects. Each spectacle usually consisted of a dozen or so object manipulations—Sherman also called them "routines" and sometimes "tricks"—each at most a few minutes long; the *Fifteenth* (1991), one of Sherman's longer pieces at about fifty minutes, includes seventeen such routines.

Though the brevity and precise construction of Sherman's theater would seem to offer the promise of mastery, he packs ungovernable scope, more than any spectator can see or remember, into his exquisite pieces. His microcosms suddenly dilate into macrocosms. Some of the manipulations have titles, introduced by Sherman with arch emphasis. Others proceed unannounced. His placements are as careful as the combinations of manipulations can appear arbitrary. The routines build complex models, dilate on droll puns, anatomize linguistic vagaries, or graph the wavering structure of a thought from abstract conception to concrete realization. Some of the spectacles are baldly representational, "dramatizing" a preexisting thought, memory, or idea. At other times, they've clearly been constructed according to formal affinities in the objects themselves. Sometimes, in other words, Sherman is scripting the objects, but at other times they are directing him.

Although Sherman's pieces are intimately concerned with the ways that language undergirds thought, and with it, reality, they're virtually wordless, except for the odd phrase or sentence, which usually eventually decomposes into sounds, standing out all the more rudely for its obtrusion into Sherman's mostly visual theater. His theater of images always circles back to language, even as he continually strives to liberate objects from language's clutches. It's a theater of the eye that continually affirms the power of words to structure our relations with the world. His is an aesthetic of disparity, employing understatement, bathos, synecdoche, and metonymy. But it's also an aesthetic of magnification, expansion, dilation, and transformation.

The studied neutrality of his performing persona, and the relentless pace of his performances, aspects of his work that might initially appear forbidding, are, in actuality, invitations to his audiences to participate in making meaning. His deeply personal associations with his objects can become public by being blended with the audience's. He refuses to overwhelm their thoughts with his. In his theater, subjective feelings and ideas become objective, so that they might become subjective again, housed by new sensibilities. (You can see his accelerated tempos as simply an effort to match the speed and impersonality of everyday experience outside the theater, which befalls us first and is only made sense of later—or is forgotten, almost as soon as it's registered.)

As Sherman once put it in an interview with Trudy Scott, one of his most astute contemporary critics:

> What I present to the audience is what is presented to me. If I presented all kinds of emotional shadings, my interpretation would take precedence over the structure of the creation . . . I want to show how things relate, and that would be obliterated.

Scott's analysis of this principle cuts to the heart of Sherman's methods:

> Each action, then, is given the amount of time it would take to think of it. If Sherman thinks, "drinks from a glass," the idea takes no time at all. This gesture would appear, as it does in "The Erotic" [*The Eleventh Spectacle*], as lifting the glass to the lips, a brief, small tilt, and putting it down.
>
> As thought, the idea has no size, little duration; it can't be seen, a pinpoint in the brain. Although, to physicalize the reality of that thought requires concession to temporal expansion, Sherman still wants his work to be as faithful as possible to the experience of thinking, just as it happens. He wants the actions to be moments that are mere dots of time. He concedes, however, the necessity at times to suggest ramifications in his actions. He will pause, stand back and repeat a gesture occasionally to let register the density of the sequence. But these moments should not take "too long" either. Adhering to the time/weight of temporal existence bores him.[3]

Keeping up with the speed of thought—his, but also our own—is part of what makes Sherman's pieces tiring to watch. There's no slack time, no interval that isn't dense with nested meanings. He tosses objects away with the same pitiless drive with which the mind discards sieved perceptual data from consciousness. His goal is to match the pace of prelinguistic perception, preventing primary experience from coalescing into language:

> If I did it any slower, so that you had time to say "he is drinking from a glass," it wouldn't be the experience anymore. The idea of "drinking from a glass" should register retinally . . . anything else would be a lie . . . it would be an interpretation of the experience.[4]

Putting his spectators in a state of suspension, preventing them from weaving objects into the usual webs of associations, keeping the wider world in abeyance, too—these are the forms of ecstatic experience Sherman aimed to induce. By forestalling thought from hardening into words, or by dissolving such crystallizations, Sherman keeps spectators outside themselves, or at least outside their usual modes of making sense of experience. If spectators are outside themselves, however temporarily, perhaps they're inside the world again.

At once proffering and withholding, his pieces hint at a reunion with primordial perception, a return to a prelinguistic, pre-abstracted state when there was no difference between perceiver and perceived, objects and experience. (He once said that his pieces were intended to stage "a reconciliation between the physical world and the world of ideas, a reconciliation between mind and matter.")[5] But they're also a reminder of permanent rupture. We can't help transmuting experience into language, can't help letting our impressions be kidnapped and carried away by the words we're forced to clothe them in.

A routine from the *Twelfth Spectacle: Language* (1980) makes this point masterfully. Holding an inflated white balloon momentarily aloft, so that it obscures his face, Sherman allows the oval to be dragged down again by the weight of a heavy chain affixed to it. He then pops it, while intoning the word "balloon," rolling the round vowels around his tongue, savoring their aural absurdity, as though substituting their fulsome sound for the now-depleted object. He then puts the slack vestiges in his mouth, and mimes writing, presumably the word "balloon" again, with the pen that we now see is attached to the end of the chain. Holding the pen aloft, he says "balloon" once more, before dropping it to the table. He concludes the sequence by inflating an entirely imaginary balloon in front of his face, marking its fictive swelling with his hand.

This series of declensions-turned-equivalencies illustrates a simple but profound truth about language. Is a balloon still a balloon once it's permanently deflated? How odd that the same word refers to both the filled article, replete with both air and meaning, and the empty and irreparably damaged one. The same word can refer equally to a filled, actual balloon; a popped carcass of a ruined balloon; the word itself, as a piece of writing (which, of course, can't float, isn't pleasingly round, and has no dimensionality); and even a wholly conceptual balloon that isn't actually there at all, a space filled only with our own inferences, a verb with no agent, ballooning emptiness. And what does it mean that we can make these second-order, and even third-order, substitutions so effortlessly?

In the process, Sherman also reminds us that language does not always account for time or entropy, that timeless nouns don't consider the material life of the things they supposedly signify. With his lagging chain, ever more heavy, he illustrates the way language drags on experience, pulling perception down to its leveling level, even puncturing sensate singularities with its blunt categories (recall that the balloon is popped at the same moment it becomes a "balloon"). Sherman conducts a mischievous workshop in semiotic theory. By the time the object-balloon has become the written-balloon, it has already been a signifier, a signified and a sign; a perceptual impulse; a thought shaped into language; a series of characters on the page. The one balloon has been translated into many balloons, none of which is the original, buoyant white object.[6]

While performing, Sherman defers to the objects, maintaining a matter-of-fact impassivity, as though he doesn't wish to disturb them or us by presuming too much familiarity. No series of object articulations is obviously sentimental or imbued with especial importance. None is given more weight than any other, though he does occasionally repeat manipulations in a spectacle. But in those cases, the repetition is the only marker of significance, and spectators are left to wonder if this doubling back indicates structural importance, or a questioning of the very idea of structural importance.

Sherman also avoids dividing the spectacles into sections that might obviously correspond to the temporal progression, and attendant affective expectations, of more conventional theatrical performances. He eschews acts, climaxes and denouements, refuses to speed up or slow down for emphasis. His beginnings and endings are decisively stated, but also provisional. As Brooks McNamara points out, once Sherman's pieces were set, he preferred not to alter them in any way. A spectacle was "made up of the routines that comprise it at the first performance, and even though the order of the routines could be changed and material added or deleted, he considers it wrong to change anything. The performance, he feels, is as fixed and unchangeable as a painting."[7] As Sherman himself once put it: "Art is evidence, residue, relic, momentary concretization of beginningless thought and endless seeing."[8] And if art is indeed such a remnant, then it can only gesture to the workings of the speeding sensibility that has already left it behind.

In Sherman's thought, aesthetic ideas are also experimental postulations about the nature of consciousness. Where does experience end and thought begin? What's the difference between perception and ideation? If thought is indeed beginningless, it's also endless. Does thought begin in the mind and incorporate objects outside, or does it begin out there and travel back? How can we begin to mark the borders between one such cognitive state and another? These unanswerable questions of priority haunt Sherman's theater in its coeval embrace of rigorous structure and unruly diversity.

In his notes for performances, the drafts for the cue cards he kept in his shirt pocket as an aide-mémoire while manipulating objects, his routines appear as individual clauses in a single run-on sentence with no full stop, divided only by em-dashes. Picking up, by implication, where the last spectacle finished, and ending with an ellipsis to be closed by the next, the pieces suggest no real endings or beginnings beyond the occasion of performance itself. His handwriting, a nearly illegible scrawl racing across scraps of notepaper, rarely respecting the lines if any happened to be present, seems almost to reach for the graphic potential of a drawing. But Sherman was also in the habit of corraling his musings into typewritten good copies, presumably with an eye on posterity, but also as a meditative discipline, returning to his offhand thoughts, taking a second glance at firsthand accounts. (His habit of filming the spectacles, with a degree of frequency unusual in artists of his generation, perhaps accomplished a similar function in his performance practice. Recordings of about half of his spectacles are available for viewing in several archives.)

This view of artistic media as at once provisional, conjectural, points on the graph of consciousness, and also as necessarily fixed, perhaps explains Sherman's interest in serial structures. A career-long polymath, Sherman veered between art forms throughout his life. In addition to the spectacles, which were a constant presence in his artistic practice after 1975, he made short films, drawings, collages, and sculptures that arrested his theatrical object manipulations into static installations. He kept a rigorously edited diary for long stretches of his life and also wrote poems, aphorisms, book reviews, essays, and manifestoes. (His own classification system for artistic genre is typically border-confusing: "To think is to see, so to think in images—images that move (performance, film, video), images that stand still (sculpture/objects, painting, photography, collage, installation).")[9]

But even as he pursued artistic structures that flout the limits of event or objecthood, Sherman continually circled around the idea of containment, in both his diaristic writing and artistic production, finding fixed points in the flux. He was obsessed with the panoply of ways that objects can contain words or ideas, prompting nebulae of associations to bloom around practically anything we care to concentrate on. But he was also fascinated by the ways language itself contains and disposes objects, and the slippery manner in which the human mind contains both. We use language to arrange objects and we use objects to recall words. What we see, even when we're not aware we're seeing it, shapes what we think and what we say. An enigmatic line from Sherman's journals sums up this preoccupation, chasing a line of propositions that runs throughout his work: "He fitted his body into clothes, his thoughts into words, his feelings into gesture, his soul into his body."[10] To this list might be added the overmastering task of fitting all these fittings into art, an activity which, at its most profound level, consists of devising new, if temporary, containers for experience (or revising old ones).

A particularly eloquent 1971 drawing, "Ils sont dans le vrai . . . ils sont dans le vrai," presciently maps these paradoxes of containment, the tensions between fixed artistic form and relentlessly mobile experience, seeming almost to predict the structure of the spectacles. At once precisely schematic and almost childlike in its simplicity, the picture, rendered in colored ink on a sheet of plain typing paper, presents a diagram of the everyday world as both enclosure and ground for Sherman's human figures.

At the top and bottom of the page, identically sized long narrow rectangles outlined in reddish-brown and blue seem to represent earth and sky. In the middle of the blue figure, a yellow circle stands in for the sun. In the wider middle band of the composition, a larger quadrangle, in black, contains four identical stick figures with round heads, fit exactingly to its dimensions—a house. It's flanked by two upright green boxes—trees, perhaps. Each of the boxes is presented in outline only, borders restraining a measurement of space.[11] As John Matturi points out in his helpful essay on Sherman's works on paper, this is

> a drawing of four people in a house surrounded by earth, natural foliage, and sunlit sky . . . as the title suggests, it is the happy bourgeois family whose conventional life, according to Flaubert's niece's memoirs, received his unexpectedly un-ironic praise: "They live in truth, they live in the right manner."[12]

But Sherman's underlining of that second "dans" suggests further nuances of meaning. The family lives in the truth, in the sense that they inhabit reality ("vrai," of course, can mean both truth and reality), but they also live *in* the truth, in the sense that it preexists, surrounds, and contains them. Another dimension is added to this reading when we consider how emphatically the drawing addresses itself to the eyes of its viewer, how it cries out for completion by its audience. It's small enough and hieratic enough to be absorbed with a single glance, to be contained by the gaze. The drawing's theatricality sets up a circuit of paradoxes. The picture tightly contains an image of daily life seen as tightly containing its human figures, which is, in turn, tightly contained by the eyes and minds of viewers, who are themselves, of course, contained equally tightly by their own versions of the *vrai*, everyday life outside the art gallery or library. But that *vrai*, though the very image of continuity and unbroken sameness, is, in reality, in a state of constant change, as is the mind that contains the picture. Which, in turn, means that the picture, though its glyphs could not be simpler, is itself in a situation of unremarked flux, never to be seen the same way twice.

Sherman once told Trudy Scott that he turned to performance once he felt he'd exhausted the possibilities of abstract drawings, but he never left that medium entirely behind.[13] The vectors of his performances recall the stark, angular line of his visual art. If the trajectories of one of his spectacles could be plotted in time, the result would look like one of his planar, punctilious drawings. And the paradoxical structure of the picture that appeals to the eye's facility for containment, while gesturing to the spectator's own enclosure within ramifying networks of language, use, and habit, repeats itself in the spectacles.

If the drawings compress the messy experiential surplus of everyday sights into clean, geometric figures, which only remind us how much reality was left out in order to create such neat outlines, his performances accomplish a similar feat (with similar ambiguities). Certainly, they distill the moment of performance to radical simplicity, what John Matturi calls "orderly miniature worlds": a tiny stage poised on a bigger one, which, in turn, suggests the wider world outside—a single performer, a few humble objects moving in closely rehearsed sequence, a tightly constrained bracketing in time and space.[14] But each meticulously plotted turn in one of Sherman's spectacles hints at the infinite possibilities that weren't realized. And this enormity haunts his reductions. The precision and containment of the manipulations implies disorder beyond, the barely contained chaos of the crowded suitcase from which the trick objects emerged, the even-more multifarious tumult outside the theater where sights will simply befall us without the careful organization of a benign performer-conjurer.

These implied forms of disorder also anticipate the unpredictable blendings that would occur when his manipulations mixed with the reactive medium of a spectator's consciousness. "Unintended meanings are welcome," he once said.[15] On a very basic level, the work of "containing" the world is the work of sentience itself, both moment-by-moment and the labor of a lifetime, but it is ultimately doomed to failure. There is only one real beginning, only one real end. In his diaries, Sherman often mulls over the act of committing suicide, not as an actual possibility, but as a motive force to spur further artistic work "that will save me, redeem me, re-integrate me back into vital, breathed and breathing existence, a lived, life." He goes on:

> But this is only possible if I use the thought of self-annihilation and oblivion to perform acts possible only in the extremest separation from life or involved in life at a profoundly invisible level—so as, ultimately, to re-emerge into the everyday world, clothed in everyday skin, as in heavenly raiment.[16]

The *Seventh Spectacle* (1976), one of Sherman's few group works, deliberately strains against the limits of spectators' capacity for containing visual experience, matching an extended series of succinct and mischievously idiosyncratic manipulations to a dizzying array of performers, old and young, male and female, fat and thin, long- and short-haired. It challenges us to make sense of the unmanageable multiplicity presented by the series, even though the *Seventh*'s careful composition, its bracketing off from daily life, reminds us it could not be more precisely structured. As dozens of actors step onstage from some unseen holding area to briefly arrange an equally vertiginous array of props, each manipulation painstakingly choreographed and whimsically distinct, the *Seventh* invites us to compare human diversity with material diversity, and the formal qualities of found people with those of found objects. (The margins of the stage, crowded with objects already discarded or not yet employed, present a visual corollary to this unseen huddle of human difference.)

Their particular outfits and hairstyles, peculiarities of bearing or gait, degrees of proficiency or discomfort with the task of performance, scrupulous blankness or unconcealed irony, are as unpredictable and deserving of attention as the routines they perform. Indeed, as the spectacle progresses, it's hard to know where to look. Should we be appraising the objects or the people disposing them, and is it liberating or discomfiting to find yourself considering the material qualities of the bodies and the activities of the objects (rather than vice versa)?

As the *Seventh Spectacle* illustrates, Sherman's manipulations are designed for perishability. They vanish from memory so quickly precisely because they're so extravagantly detailed. They're shoved from the mind by the immediate challenges posed by their successors. Every moment in one of his spectacles is so dense with possible meanings that spectators must simultaneously furiously interpret, trying desperately to grasp the onrushing images, and emphatically abandon them, endeavoring to catch an early hold on what's about to appear, a heightened version of the perceptual arbitrage we practice in every moment of conscious life. His tiny TV-tray stage points to a still-smaller (but actually infinitely larger) theater, the mind's stage, on which the drama of experience unfolds, measured in perceptual instants. His radically distilled idioms pack more potential meanings into time than any other theater I've ever seen. He keeps spectators in a perpetual state of surprise, interrupting their relations with the ordinary. It's precisely this sort of interruption that Philip Fisher has argued is the necessary precondition for wonder,[17] and for that matter, of reenchantment.

This process is made exponentially more difficult, and the manipulations made more ephemeral, by the fact that humdrum objects are doing unaccustomed things and moving in unaccustomed ways. Sherman dissolves everyday use value to point out objects' hidden linguistic and semiotic exchange values. His things romp across the categories of habit that keep them docile. The performances' structuring by associative links between objects, perceptual and linguistic, mimics the aleatory nature of consciousness, which is also incalculably influenced by its situation among objects. In every moment of waking life, Sherman suggests, we are accepting and rejecting, focusing and ignoring, situating and resituating ourselves amid a sea of things that are both inside us and outside us. If beginningless thought and endless seeing are the human predicament, how can we isolate the intervals where perception ends and thought begins, how can we separate exterior and interior worlds, even when most conceptions of the self depend on beginning with such a discernible frontier?

Mundane Magic

Sherman's pieces have a vital relationship to both still life and collage. He assembles concatenations of mundane objects chosen for their compositional relations rather than any real-world affinities. But however revelatory the juxtaposition of objects might be, he isn't content to let them stay permanently counterpoised. The added complications of time and mnemonic failure further unsettle his rapidly dissolving structures. As he proved later in life with occasional sculptural commissions for various galleries and outdoor installations, any one of his manipulations contains the germ of an artistic idea worth freezing and preserving as a finished artwork. But because Sherman's roving practice privileges ideation over application, inspiration over execution, he mostly allowed his gestures to remain gestures, ephemeral performances of thought-in-motion.

Watching one of Sherman's routines—collages-on-the-wing, motile combines—it's as if a Rauschenberg piece were suddenly to erupt into motion, coalescing and dissolving before our eyes. Analogous to the way Rauschenberg's hybrid works muddle two- and three-dimensional vision—representations that smear into the actual everyday objects represented, a painting of a bed running into an actual bed—Sherman's vignettes blur the borders of spectators' perceptions. He's interested in the liminal intervals where nouns are transmuted into verbs, visual stimuli into mental pictures, objects into representations, concepts into concretions (and vice versa). His handling of the objects is eminently tactile, but they're deployed in such a way as to suggest images, words, and concepts as much as they do their own material properties. They coalesce into ideas before dissolving again into junk. They're both there before us, as familiar bric-a-brac, and strangely absent, as Sherman isolates them from their usual places as nodal points in webs of everyday object relations, or easy-to-ignore consumer detritus, and pulls them into new configurations based on linguistic affinities, formal qualities, or fantastical flights.

In the *First Spectacle* (1975), for example, one manipulation involves draping a scarf rakishly round his neck, fanning empty ice-cube trays around his feet, and subtly miming ice-skating. The series of actions instantly connotes "skating," but then you wonder why this should be so. Ice-cube trays are used to make ice, to be sure, but they're also mass-produced plastic knickknacks that, in themselves, aren't really icy at all. They're not cold, not made of water, not naturally occurring.

In this single gesture, Sherman raises a host of questions about the way our ever-processing brains link the disparate figments of the world together. Is ice-skating always waiting in the wings when we fill the ice-cube tray? If so, what a great deal of drama and incident we repress when we instrumentalize an object. For Sherman, it's almost as if the truly remarkable effort lies not in devising new theatrical uses for all the stifled things that lie inert around us, but rather in muting them and confining them to their conventional uses at all. To employ an ice-cube tray only for making ice means squelching all its other potent associations.

Brooks McNamara, in a *TDR* essay from 1976, notes the surface resemblance of the spectacles to the hustle of a street magician proffering shell games or sleight of hand. At that time, Sherman did take several of the spectacles outdoors, adding the chance element of accidental spectatorship to pieces that already somehow suggest that audiences have happened upon thoughts in progress.[18] *3 Mercer Street*, a 1975 experimental film by Jaime Davidovitch, amplifies this eavesdropped quality of Sherman's work. In it, the camera pans in slow, dizzy circles around the white walls of a Soho gallery space. In one corner of the room, Sherman is performing one of his spectacles, and the camera finds and abandons him, over and over again, without indulging the spectator's desire to linger and find out what he's up to. His already ephemeral routines are made doubly so, distilled to a blur of eye-catching, and eye-frustrating, motion.

But concealment and misdirection were never Sherman's methods of choice. He never hides a thing. As McNamara puts it, Sherman "rejects the secrecy of conjuring, preferring to concentrate on showing the form of the trick while also demonstrating that the trick itself is explainable."[19] (A recent exhibit of Sherman's work, curated by his longtime collaborator Yolanda Hawkins, was called "Nothing Up My Sleeve.") Sherman made the distinction clear for McNamara in their interview by saying that the "only real magic" is to "discover what you think is magic isn't. I believe that stage magic makes the natural world outside—the dull world we live in—uninteresting by comparison. But, on the contrary, I think that the dull, the mundane are very interesting in their own right."[20]

In other words, the conjuring Sherman was actually interested in was more elemental and more profound: the ability of perception and consciousness to make and remake worlds in every sensate moment, screening the vast plenitude of the material world into foreground and background, sense and non-sense, visible and invisible, meaning and non-meaning, habit and exception. For Sherman, the real magic lies in the mysterious alchemy by which objects cross from exterior to interior worlds, the way the eye takes objects and translates them into mental images. Just as our thoughts arise from a crowded perceptual field, ineffably shaped by the busy stage from which they arose, so too do Sherman's pieces emerge from his inert piles of objects, disturbed from humble invisibility into sudden life.

The proscenium arrangement of Sherman's pieces is deceptive. It would be more useful to think of spectators and Sherman as performing analogous activities on two sides of the objects he manipulates, the common objects of their contemplation. He is revisiting object-sentences at the speed at which he initially thought them; the audience is encountering his thoughts. Though at first viewing Sherman's pieces might seem dauntingly hermetic, it's this spurning of easy intimacy that actually makes them profoundly sociable. He refuses to impose his own interpretations on spectators, to slow down an "important" manipulation and freight it with sententious surplus symbolism, or speed up others to imply mounting suspense or climactic simmering. He's interested in creating intervals of common thinking, a shared activity that admits the impossibility of two subjective beings ever truly sharing the same experience, while still allowing for radically different subjectivities to contemplate the same objects at the same time. This, for Sherman, is as close as we can get to a common reality, to a communal experience that doesn't intrude on an individual's unique measure of distance from the world or from others.

Sherman's ritually deployed objects, his precise dispositions of costume and stage, together with his interest in transmuting material objects so that words become solid, and concepts become corporeal, suggest a Catholic mass as much as they do a magician's ruses. And indeed, "communion" is an idea Sherman often returns to in his diaries, a wished-for union with the everyday world, a surmounting of the separation between subjectivity and objectivity, words and things. (Recall Sherman's plangent artistic imperative, quoted above, to confront finality in order to reinfuse everyday experience with sacral power, clothing it in "heavenly raiment.")

The transubstantiation of the host, he suggests by analogy, is the primeval act of consciousness: word become flesh become word become flesh, in endless oscillation. Without too much exaggeration, we can think of the spectacles as secular ceremonies of communion, joining thought and action, ideation and materiality, spectators and performer. Moving at the pace of thought, choreographing objects known to all, Sherman conducted symphonies of shared cognition, during which it was possible to imagine that dozens of people could think together about and with common objects, and, while doing so, think common thoughts. His pieces collapse mimesis and poesis, inviting a participatory making of meaning that disappears as quickly as it's made. The spectacles posit intersubjectivity, public thinking-together—a simultaneous effort, if not an identical process—as a form of communion for a world irremediably refracted into individual selves.[21]

As many thinkers, Andrew Sofer eloquent among them, have argued, a stage object constantly oscillates between registers as an actual object and a represented object.[22] In Sherman's spectacles, the syncopation of theatrical perception becomes a figure for the oscillations of thought. In daily life, too, objects are both material things and abstract things, functioning as parts of speech, concepts, ideas, and so on. A kind of rupture is always present in our relationship to things, Sherman suggests. They are there before us in their stubbornly material but also perceptually elusive thingness, but they are also with us as preexisting categories and concepts, and, even more strangely, as the doppelgangers of double-functioning words, the shadowy semantic surplus accumulated by exchanges of arbitrary signifiers. They're animistic totems of associative meaning, actors in the daily dramas of thought and language.

The choreography of Sherman's performances, in turn, suggests the recursive logic of his linguistic experiments. His desire to create eloquent manipulations can't truly be separated from his quest, often reiterated in his diaries, to compose beautiful sentences. Sherman was in the habit of writing short koan-like poetic texts that amplify linguistic slippages into semiotic whirlpools. The enigmatic aphorisms are the literary equivalents of his object manipulations. They proffer both too much and too little meaning at once, their emphasis shifting rapidly from formal properties of language to descriptive ones and back again. "He changed into a sweater and wore himself out"; "Bright as the light is, it is not as bright as it was before this sentence diminished it."[23] In the latter example, the light is diminished by description, by its translation from phenomenon to representation, but also by the falling cadence of the sentence itself. Sherman simultaneously describes and undoes the description, thereby suggesting that our every attempt to translate primary experience into the shopworn ready-made containers of language is doomed to failure. Thought that is legible as language is both the record and the ruin of experience, carried away by language's furious undertow.

At one point in the *Fifteenth Spectacle*, Sherman carefully sets up three clear plastic rhomboid cylinders on his table-stage. The middle one is filled partway with uninflated white balloons; the other two are empty. Repeating the same basic sequence several times, he spritzes a dollop of white shaving cream into one of the empty cylinders and draws a disposable razor methodically across their surfaces. (He then pops an inflated balloon, perhaps to suggest the irrevocable change in state from "unshaved" to "shaved.") Though the foam is contained within the object—inside instead of outside—and their blemishless walls proffer nothing to trim, a spectator's humming brain, determined to piece things together, nevertheless will likely leap to the action of "shaving" (in the piece's final witty flourish, Sherman applies aftershave to his own face).

Indeed, geometric objects are endowed with "faces" by the English language. But what does it mean to call something a face when the object in question has not one, but four, none possessing the individuating features that are the hallmark of a human face? What does it mean to our understanding of human faces to say that a clear plastic rhomboid has them too? This brief, telling manipulation reminds us that when we say a geometric shape has a "face," we are making an analogy that brings us closer to the thing before us, humanizing it, but also, in that same cognitive swoop, estranges us from it, because its faces and our faces have almost nothing to do with each other. Does anthropomorphosis humanize the objects around us, Sherman seems to ask, or disperse the very notion of humanity among them? For him, language is constantly pulling us closer to the world and shoving it away, a vertiginous attraction-repulsion latent in every conscious moment. (Similarly, in the *First Spectacle* he invites spectators from the audience to come onstage and tie him up—with neckties. In the *Twelfth*, he "combs" through a text with a large comb. His manipulations reveal the semantic pressure points at which homonyms or puns crack language, uncovering vertiginous abysses of uncertainty.)

Looked at a different way, though, this same push-pull motion means that language is not a purely abstract or intellectual quantity. If words have their tangible correlates, they are, in this limited sense at least, both in and of the material world, not simply arbitrary signifiers but immanent aspects as well. And because thought and language are worldly in this way, we can join with them and each other. Worldly words can be shared between minds.

In one of his so-called book reviews, inspired by Frances Yates's *The Art of Memory*, Sherman praises an art of "not remembering" that "deserves to be practiced as much as playing the piano."[24] In typical Sherman fashion, these occasional pieces weren't sober essays, but playful, subjective variations on the theme of his reading, charting the idiosyncratic intellectual flights the books prompted in him. Yates's book is a meditation on the Renaissance-era practices of enhanced memory whereby mnemonic virtuosos would construct mental theaters to house stored knowledge, stocking the shelves of an imaginary library with ideas clothed by objects. Sherman's theater of the mind posits the necessity of the opposite: clothing objects in new ideas so as to make spectators forget their usual costuming, and even the whole habitual world that precludes the possibility of a new one.

This is what the philosopher Jennifer Anna Gosetti-Ferencei calls the "ecstatic quotidian," the latent transformative possibilities that inhere in the unexamined humdrumness of everyday experience.[25] Undoing habitual relations with objects has the potential to undo the social world built on the armature of such relations. The fact that we don't notice objects contains the potentiality that we can notice them hyperintensely. Their innocuousness is the precondition of their singularity.

A World Equal in All Its Parts

In recent years, Sherman has been re-embraced by the visual art world, heralded as a seminal performance artist, and made the subject of three New York gallery retrospectives in the last decade and several abroad. Theater history, however, continues to neglect him, despite Sherman's important enmeshment in the experimental theater scene of the 1970s, and his lifelong engagement with the means and intellectual repertoire of the theater considered more generally.

Arnold Aronson, in his history of the American avant-garde theater, devotes a few paragraphs to Sherman, mostly digesting the analyses of Trudy Scott and Brooks McNamara, under the heading of "conceptual performance," alongside Laurie Anderson.[26] But he barely touches the breadth of Sherman's performance work, citing only one spectacle, and the theatrical portrait pieces from the 1980s, and his categorization removes Sherman from his more vital relationship to contemporaries like Charles Ludlam and Richard Foreman. Sherman acted in productions at Ludlam's Ridiculous Theater and Foreman's Ontological-Hysteric Theater. He performed the initial public showings of the *First Spectacle* on the set for Foreman's *Pandering to the Masses: A Misrepresentation*, in which he was a cast member. (Foreman reciprocated by performing in the *Second Spectacle*, along with Ontological stalwart Kate Manheim, Stefan Brecht, and Sherman himself.) In a teasingly brief catalog essay for a recent retrospective of Sherman's work, Babette Mangolte hints at the relationship between the "task-based efficiency" Foreman demanded of his performers and the evolution of Sherman's own performing persona, his version of neutral, a version more unprepossessing than stonily defiant:

> In Foreman's theater of images, a neutral expression and an unblinking gaze were the skills of the performer whose stone face had to be emptied of any affect. The performers were chosen for their abilities to impose the intensity of their presence, and staring straight into the spectator's eyes was an important part of it.
>
> In Stuart Sherman's solo work, the apparent selflessness of the performer bore some similarity to the Ontological-Hysteric school of gestures but without the intense gaze that was prevalent in Foreman's plays.[27]

As resolutely visual as the other artists Bonnie Marranca would group under the category of "Theatre of Images,"[28] Foreman and Robert Wilson prominently among them, Sherman's investigations of perception are almost the categorical inverse of Wilson's. They're small, whereas Wilson's 1970s performances were large; they're short, where Wilson's were long; and they are intimately tied to visible aspects of the everyday, whereas Wilson's belated realizations of the promise of a surrealist theater favored dream images and warping perspectives. (The two artists have a common interest in the vagaries of language.)

But Sherman also shares important characteristics with the other artists I consider in this study, concerns that link him to the longer genealogy of the American theater of the everyday. Like Thornton Wilder, his pieces turn the expectations and practices of realism inside out, reversing the priority of foreground and background. Also like Wilder, he uses theatrical spectatorships as a metaphor for human perception, making perception itself the main drama of his theater—and the inevitable loss of vivid experience its implicit tragedy. He submits the self's borders to blurring scrutiny, staging the theater of experience. Like Nature Theater of Oklahoma, his epic forms point to the still-larger project of redeeming all of everyday experience for art, to the utopian prospect of a world seen as beautiful in all its aspects.

Sherman measured his distance from the theater throughout his career. In the 1980s he composed several pieces, less profoundly concerned with the mysteries of everyday cognition, and so of less interest to me here, that were devoted to Sophocles, Strindberg, Goethe, Brecht, and Chekhov. His *Chekhov Spectacle* distills the playwright's entire oeuvre to a tea party and a falling tree. But these more obvious engagements with theater history are only part of a larger, running, dialogue with the mores of theatrical representation—and their wider implications—that continued throughout his life.

In several of the spectacles Sherman toys with the properties of props, deploying objects with almost fetishistic theatrical importance such as swords and pistols. Simply brandishing a revolver, he suggests, implies bubbling drama-to-come, the climactic fulfillment of Chekhov's famous imperative that a gun glimpsed onstage must eventually be fired. With such potent signifiers available, who needs actual plot complications? Similarly, by simply announcing the names of a host of famous literary and historical figures, then stepping forward, and applying the nominal "costume" of a top hat, the performers in the *Second Spectacle* stand in for these characters—inviting spectators to fill in the blanks by imagining that important person's persona and biography and inventing reasons why he or she might be there.

Sherman's theater violates the traditional realist contract with quotidian stage objects, turning realism inside out. ("I see myself as a metaphysical realist," he once puckishly pronounced.)[29] In most performances, such objects—set dressing—ratify the texture of the onstage fiction before ceding priority and place to human actors, the necessary background to realist drama's foreground. Realism both trades on and represses its bargain with metonymy. Though a part is standing for an implied whole, this part is understood to be a precisely schematic section, not a symbol. Stage realism must always rely on metonymy, the proverbial kitchen sink, but it must also pretend that it's not dependent on the logic of symbolism. As Bert States so eloquently puts it: "Metonymy and synecdoche, as we find them on the realistic stage, are devices for reducing states, or qualities, or attributes, or whole entities like societies, to visible things in which they somehow inhere."[30]

The *Second Spectacle* contains a sequence devoted to refracting the realist logic of carefully selected parts adding up to a representative whole. In it, the performers carefully set up a tableau representing a domestic scene: an ironing board, clothes, a stool, and Kate Manheim sitting and reading the paper. Sherman's voice suddenly breaks into the scene, proclaiming that the scene is "wrong" and needs to be fixed. The performers promptly flip the tableau, so that every object switches sides, almost as if we're now seeing it from the other direction, though its alignment is still oriented frontally, within the same picture plane. We're forced to ask what it could possibly mean for such a scene—instantly, comfortably recognizable—to be incorrectly composed.

The routine considers the assembly of such a rote domestic scene as an epistemological act. How is it that so few objects can stand for so much? And what does it mean for the scene to be "wrong," to need to be readjusted? And how can it be "right," in that case, if simply reversed? (In a later section of this chapter, I'll discuss another manipulation that engages still more sharply with the blinkered normativity embodied by such domestic scenes.) Sherman's theater, though it engages with the realist tools of synecdoche and metonymy, is interested in expansion, not reduction, the dilation of other possible worlds based on the same objects, the spinning-out of chains of linguistic and visual association, rather than the compression of existing worlds to a few representative objects.

The literary theorist Bill Brown's helpful distinction between the transparency of objects and the unruliness of things provides another way to think about this conceptual reversal (his ideas have informed my use of these words throughout this chapter). He describes the object relations of everyday life in terms that are uncannily similar to States's analysis of the object-logic of realist representation. Brown argues that, in the everyday run of events, we look "through objects (to see what they disclose about history, society, nature, or culture—above all, what they disclose about us)." In other words, we can make them a meaningful but inert environment, a tissue of facts, the fit surround to our more compelling human dramas. But, he argues, "we begin to confront the thingness of objects when they stop working for us," when they no longer simply lie still and mean, or perform their rote functions. When such an interruption occurs, we're forced to confront the ways in which they work *on* us, as well us for us. As Brown puts it, "the thing really names less an object than a particular subject-object relation."[31]

Sherman's reversal of perspectives in the *Second Spectacle* dramatizes just such an interruption. Suddenly, we can no longer simply look through the assembled objects to a cozy domestic scene. We must look *at* them. And by doing so, we must consider who the real actors in the scene are. Are they the human beings, ironing and reading the paper, or are they the newspaper and the iron, compelling the human beings to wield them in particular choreographies?

Here I draw on the ideas of the performance theorist and historian of material culture Robin Bernstein, who has animated thing theory's insights, transforming them into tools for performance historiography. She argues that objects submit to us, the subjects, allowing us to act upon them and with them, conscripting them to utility. Things, a more restive category, act on us, scripting our behavior. Her invitation to the historian is to "dance" with things, to allow oneself to fall under their spell in order to recover some fraction of the manifold ways they may have shaped the thoughts, feelings, and behaviors of our ancestors. (Bernstein's main examples, perniciously ideological alphabet books and photo booth settings, are seemingly inert objects that prompt charged performances of racial otherness or draw readers into participating in fantasies of racial domination.)[32]

Sherman's entire body of work could be described as dancing with things, and his manipulations suggest that Bernstein's categories are a constantly fluctuating accompaniment to any of our daily interactions with material stuff. At first glance, his pieces seem to be about deft manipulation, about human ingenuity and mastery of objects. But they're equally about the ways things use and manipulate us. Their thingness resides in their ability to affect thought and perception. In this, Sherman anticipates Bill Brown's definition of thingness as what is "excessive" about objects:

> what exceeds their mere materialization as objects or their mere utilization as objects—their force as a sensuous presence or as a metaphysical presence, the magic by which objects become values, fetishes, idols, and totems.[33]

In Sherman's pieces, objects suddenly assert themselves as things, and, as they do, they insist that perhaps they always were, except that we were working hard to keep them in the subjugation of objecthood, and were eliding universes of associative meaning to focus myopically on instrumental utility. Sherman devises new scripts for objects we think we know, but he also allows them to devise new scripts for him, making them not just objects, but subjects. He permits them to escape their usual categories, and to subvert habitual arrangements. You could even say that Sherman posits thinking as a kind of duet with things—thing-king, if the pun can be excused.

Sherman was fond of literally staging his inversion of realism's object-contract. Instead of encoding stage objects with outside realities, shrinking the wider world to material symptoms, he blurs the distinctions between his own body and the theatrical objects he deploys, or even the physical stage itself. This is a stage materialism far removed from the values of realism. He devotes large segments of the *First Spectacle* to carefully inventorying the fictive environment of the set for Foreman's *Pandering to the Masses*, in which he was performing at the time, as a real place, with doors and cabinets, walls and floor, halls and hidden recesses, subverting its theatricality, interacting with it as a massive found object. He opens and closes cupboards and curtains, measures the theater's circumference by audibly trudging around, throws a small object offstage and goes to fetch it, runs into the audience to place it on the seats. (Similarly, in the *Second Spectacle*, Kate Manheim opens and closes the loft space's real window and adjusts its air conditioner.) He takes spaces devoted to representation, to standing in for other places and times, continually disavowing where and what they actually are, and returns them to themselves—rooms of some certain dimensions, filled with certain kinds of furniture, certain useful equipment.

While doing so, he also treats his own body as a stage, making use of it as an object, and a set of formal possibilities, in much the same way as he does the actual theater. He is literally making a spectacle of himself. Adapting his own body to the spatial and material qualities of the theater itself, he allows these properties to script his actions. In a manipulation that occurs late in the *First Spectacle*, Sherman, rolls of tape in hand, lies down on a sloping declivity center-stage, matching its v-shape with his own figure, and marks a careful outline around himself. Thus spiked, like stage furniture, he shouts an anguished "Help!" while seemingly trapped by his taped contours. Leaving in place the tracing, a rough approximation of a human figure, with a discomfiting similarity to a chalk outline and a more than passing resemblance to the stick drawings in Sherman's visual art, he stands up and begins to retape the borders of the image, the scraggly cartoon getting sloppier and sloppier.

The implications of the routine are deeply ambivalent. It flattens Sherman's eloquent performing body into first a stage property to be precisely anchored to its coordinates, and then to the barest abstraction of a pictograph. Yet, when the new image's borders are traduced by sloppy taping, you feel the violation keenly. The anthropomorphic image somehow attracts empathy in its fleeting moments of integrity. Sherman's body is "killed" by its reduction to a glyph, but this symbol can be killed, too. He passes from body to object to image to body to object again in eerie sequence.

An analogous manipulation from the *Fifteenth Spectacle* returns to this theme. Wrapping a leather belt around his TV table crosswise, dividing its surface into identical quadrants, Sherman then buttons up his shirt and tucks it in, showing us that he is wearing an identical belt. One after another, he produces two swatches of red fabric, holding them up to his shirt to show that they are of an identical hue, and then lays them across the upper two quadrants, above the belt. He repeats this gesture with two black swatches, comparing them to his pants, before laying them across the table's bottom two quarters. He has put a "shirt" and "pants" on his table, creating a geometrical abstraction of his own figure. The belt not only holds up his pants: it also upholds the uncanny fiction of the image as his double. It's obviously not him, but it's not entirely not him, either. Alternating between shuffling the swatches and undoing his own belt, accompanied by an impish shimmy, he reorients the tabletop figure. Is it standing up? Lying down? He dances with himself as a thing, juxtaposing his own figural integrity as a body with that of the sculptural assemblage he has just created. Sherman merges with his stage, blurring the line between performer and theater, positing performance as a blending of stage and actor, occasion and entity.

Another manipulation from the same spectacle examines the violence inherent in sublimating bodies into abstractions. Taking out a plastic gun and a plastic model heart, he does up the buttons on his shirt while announcing the title of the routine, "Button Down Death." Pointing the gun at his chest, he rattles the trigger a few times. He then places five round stickers on his shirt, the "bullet holes." After shooting the holes once again, chasing effect with cause, he takes the stickers off his shirt and affixes them to the model heart, continuing the imaginary bullets' trajectory inward, while further abstracting this fictive wounding. He now proceeds to stick the sticker-bullet holes on the gun itself, collapsing cause and effect, action and agent, before placing them on a strip of red cloth, matching his shirt. Bullet holes—body-holes—have become buttonholes. The wounds, extreme acts of violence, irrevocable interruptions of the continuity of everyday life, by any measure dramatic, have been eerily reabsorbed into Sherman's jaunty stage persona. The real violence, he suggests, was committed in each successive conceptual leap from concrete cause to abstract effect. What's the difference, Sherman inquires, between cutting holes in cloth to make buttonholes and shooting holes in flesh with bullets? Obviously, a great deal. But when considered from such a position of radical formalist detachment, both operations share certain important characteristics.

This is another variant of Sherman's interest in communion-through-art. He integrates himself with the material world onstage, both literally and in the thoughts of his spectators, who are complicit in smearing human form into abstract imagery. Staging himself as an object, as artistic material, he opens a shockingly de-anthropomorphized perspective by means of a rigorous attempt to think through a mode of artmaking that does not privilege human apartness from the material world (though this is only possible by appealing to human aesthetic sense). This form of communion circles around from the opposite end of the aesthetic spectrum. Instead of using objects to materialize thoughts, he attempts to join with the material world by emphasizing his own categorical similarities with objects. ("I judge the world to be equal in all its parts,"[34] he once said, a battle cry for radical aesthetic democracy, one akin to the artistic principles espoused by Thornton Wilder and Lee Strasberg.)

Sherman's performances dramatize the rhetorical figures by which artists and thinkers confer aspects of personhood on the material world. Reaching down into his suitcase, he apostrophizes, addressing objects in their unrecognized splendor, lifting them out of obscurity. Setting them onstage and into motion, he anthropomorphizes them, or examines our propensity to do the same, imbuing them with animist vitality. He employs prosopopeia, speaking through seemingly inert things; he personifies, putting stilled objects into complex choreographies, granting them agency. A large ethical concern looms behind these investigations. If we must consider things afresh, as not so apart from our selves and our thoughts, if we must examine the manifold ways things can be like people, then we must also contemplate the opposite proposition. How do we treat people like things? How do we transform them into objects in our daily dramas?[35]

Material Democracy

The spectacles' combination of visual superabundance and extreme perishability has prompted two conflicting kinds of critical response from commentators attempting to reckon with Sherman's work. Some observers, like Brooks McNamara and Trudy Scott, both marvelous thinkers about Sherman, succumb to the lure of transcription in their accounts. Their essays segregate description from interpretation, putting elegant expostulations of Sherman's work, rendered in general terms, alongside meticulous inventories of the materials deployed in one particular spectacle, with almost no moment-by-moment attention to the experience of what it was like to watch these objects make their metamorphoses. Though invaluable as performance documentation, the microscopic level of detail leads to eye-defeating supercrowding on the page, making the performances appear more forbiddingly dense than they are. It's as if all the guests at a party were simply listed in order as a narrative of the entire evening.

At the other extreme, Berenice Reynaud's "Stuart Sherman: Object Ritual," written for the influential journal *October* during the first blush of the poststructuralist moment, is practically all macrocosm, spinning abstractions far removed from Sherman's humble stage. Such divagations forget the first principle of Sherman's spectacles, which is that our thoughts are never free from the material world that surrounds us, however much we might like to imagine that they are. His pieces certainly invite abstraction. You could even say they're about abstraction, as a mental and perceptual process, but they also rebuff it, maintaining that cognition arises from the tangible world's insistent presence, not despite it.

Throughout this chapter, I've attempted to wend my way between these two extremes, offering a vivid accounting of the examples from which I draw my analysis so as to show the evidence that undergirds my formulations, while also allowing description and interpretation to intermingle. To do otherwise when reading Sherman is to negotiate in bad faith. His nearly wordless work can too easily stand mute on the page. I recognize, of course, that any such description is already an interpretation, a retrospective translation into language of experiences explicitly intended to defeat such transpositions. To see Sherman's spectacles is to struggle, and fail, to describe them. But the failure is productive. The failure is the point.

It's worth spending a little time with Reynaud's argument, both because it's the longest critical article published about Sherman to date and because it's a revealing study in strong reading. Reynaud's ideas are enormously suggestive, but they also foreclose many possibilities. Powerful as they are, it's worth reconsidering many of her assertions. Exploring the counterarguments helps to bring Sherman's work into sharper focus.

To start with, Reynaud's ideological premises (post-Marxist, post-Freudian) lead her to assume that because Sherman occasionally employs mass-produced objects—plastic kitsch—among many other sorts of things (tools, food, winsome homemade collages and drawings), he's making the same kind of "critique of the object" that a certain kind of European leftist might make. His work, in her view, amounts to a despairing indictment of postindustrial capitalism's vitiation of the inherent value of objects in favor of "gestures." In the meaning-desert of the late 1970s, she argues, not only has exchange value replaced use value, but the "signifying value" of objects has also "been transferred from the object to the manipulation of those objects."[36] Metastatic commodity fetishism has both alienated the labor that produces objects and depreciated their very ability to *mean* anything.

This is a debatable idea in a number of ways. Isn't a substantial part of what objects "mean" for us based on what we can do with them, on actions and gestures, whether we're talking about a piece of plastic kitsch or a lovingly handcrafted tool? But it's perhaps most significant in its anti-theatrical premises. Like Rousseau, Reynaud sees a fall into theatricality as symptomatic of cultural corruption. Objects have become actors performing the roles of objects. In this light, representation can only be abstracting, dehumanizing, secondary—bad, in every way possible—and Reynaud bluntly states that "Sherman's performances do not depict anything; they have no representational content."[37] But what if, as Sherman's work avers, representation and theatricality are the strong forces of human consciousness, surrogating the object for the word and the word for the object, showing nouns performing as verbs, verbs arrested into nouns? What if, in other words, the object-world is always already theatrical? And what if the human histories that objects index are not simply those of occluded labor, but also their potential as material for thought and perception, a nimbus of semantic and cognitive possibility?

Since Sherman's objects mustn't represent, they must instead nullify representation. Reynaud sets up a fascinating contrast between the dehumanizing repetitions of the assembly line and the (by implication) re-humanizing effects of Sherman's discovery of variations within "productive chains of action." She suggests that Sherman's performances make spectators laugh in the same way that Chaplin's *Modern Times* does:

> If the laugh excited by one of Sherman's performances ironically deprecates the "cheap artifacts" he uses, it is perhaps this ironic negation that constitutes the subject of a film like *Modern Times* or one of Sherman's performances, and may be the source of its pleasure.[38]

For Reynaud, Sherman's performances have the power to "negate" objects. In fact, she seems obsessed with seeing objects "negated" by the performances.[39] (At times, the antimodern cast of her argument brings her perilously close to primitivism. Her positive example of an object-based exchange that "sets up a relation between two subjectivities" is a Native American potlatch ceremony.)[40] There's some object-snobbery at work here, a lingering trace of the aesthete's disdain for kitsch. For Reynaud, the detritus of American consumer culture can only be fit material for artistic investigation if the purpose of the work is to negate "the cheap disposable simulacrum of real" that it represents.[41] But in Sherman's case, recognizing the ubiquity of mass-produced knickknacks in daily life, or what she revealingly calls "cheap artifacts," is not identical to anguish about authenticity lost.

The spectacles' reveling delight in color, form, and movement surely also testifies to Sherman's nearly boundless enthusiasm for these humble citizens of American material democracy. Although Reynaud astutely acknowledges Sherman's place in a modern art tradition of employing found materials, including disposable consumer junk, that runs from dada and surrealism to Cage and Rauschenberg, she doesn't consider that, as Andy Warhol (another link on the chain) once pithily put it, making art about such ignoble objects can be a way to enjoy them. Neither does she consider that the effort to make art out of what she calls "the inchoate and unexplored space of postindustrial consumer capitalism" can be a profoundly democratic exercise intended to renew both the everyday world and art itself, conducted with zeal for opening new territory.[42] (As Jay Hoberman slyly points out in a recent essay, Sherman's manipulations bear a more-than-passing resemblance to the "gadget demonstrations" that had become mainstays of 1970s daytime television programming, gleeful mixtures of ingenuity and commerce, virtuosity and blandishment.)[43]

Reification, the "transformation of thought into substance,"[44] as Bill Brown elegantly defines it, is for Sherman not just an ideological operation, but a basic mechanism of human consciousness, and its multivalent operation can testify as much to the recuperation of our relationship to the material world as to our alienation from it. This becomes especially important in light of Brown's observation that

> the history of modernity, propelled both by capital and instrumental reason, is the history of proscribing objects from attaining the status of things, proscribing any value but that of use or exchange, secularizing the object's animation by restricting it to *commodity* fetishism alone.[45]

Arguments like Reynaud's perpetuate this vitiation of things by narrowly considering Sherman's objects in negative terms. Whether resisting or helplessly reinscribing the regime of commodity fetishism, they are still defined in relation to it. But what if Sherman seeks to reenchant what Brown calls "modernity's disenchanted world of objects"[46] by reminding his spectators of the manifold other lives that objects have for us in language, imagination, and ideation?

Two routines from the *Eleventh Spectacle: The Erotic* (1979) do much to separate Sherman's more flexible conceptions of both desire and postindustrial material culture from Reynaud's sometimes-limiting views. In both, he uses mass-produced, often plastic odds and ends to create vivid models scrutinizing powerful, complex feelings. Both are clearly representational, without being reifying in the straitening manner Reynaud abhors. Selected for their formal properties and signifying power, his "cheap artifacts" aren't negated by the pieces, but absorbed as one aspect of a layered argument. And if a cheap plastic globe can stand as easily for the idea of a world as the word itself—as it will shortly, in the first of my examples—perhaps that's as much a commentary on the ease with which we make such conceptual substitutions, and the overworn words within which we transport ideas across the frontier between thought and language, as it is about the degradation of material culture's signifying aura. The cheapness of Sherman's objects points to the cheapness of our words.

In one of these routines, Sherman stages the binding power of the desire for a home. Unrolling a long piece of black electrical tape, he lays it across his tray-table, sticky side up. Taking out a deck of cards, he deals eight cards at intervals along the tape. Next, he produces a pitch pipe and blows a series of notes as he carefully places small objects on the cards: a tiny plastic chair, a fake nose, a little table, and a wind-up fish, among other mismatched metonyms. Spilling the articles off the cards, he wraps the taped cards around his neck, necklace-like, while heaping the little objects into a pile. Rolling a tiny plastic globe around the assembled objects, he measures the song lines of a domestic planet.

The routine encapsulates the complex route by which a haphazardly collected assemblage of objects, large and small, becomes a home, and so the foundation for a world. Despite inevitable aleatory influences (the cards)—none of us deliberately selects every possession—a fragile impression of harmony (the pitch pipe) can nevertheless be sustained. And that harmony can be the grounding for a stable conception of self (the tape), which depends on the adhesive force of need. The arbitrariness, the randomness, the fragility of this assemblage does not obviate its power, and the material bathos of Sherman's cast-off objects only enhances this poignancy. Such a home can create an illusion of stability that denies time. Sherman produces a pocket watch, and masks its face with that same binding tape. But, of course, this temporary refuge from entropy is eminently susceptible to it, and the seemingly permanent household can dissolve at any moment. We put our faith in such agglomerations of objects to buttress continuity. Though such arrangements feel durable, that's a wishful product of our own need.

The routine clearly traffics in representation, not of the pernicious alienated commodity variety, but the everyday linguistic-conceptual kind. It demands to be read outwards as symbolic, microcosmic, but also acquires meaning precisely because such inconsequential objects are being asked to bear the weight of so much conceptual and emotional freight, just as our larger but ultimately no less unequal material codependents do.

In another routine from the same spectacle, Sherman transforms the tribulations of a glass piggy bank into an allegory of the imprisoning effects of capitalism's urge to competitive success. Blinded by a little curtain at each step, the piggy follows a trail of coins, to the dictates of a tiny traffic light, which turns out to be painted on the obverse of a dollar bill. The bill then becomes the road on which the piggy travels, accumulating a meager bundle of coins, which then becomes another moving target, as the glass critter strives to hold on to its accumulated capital. Only when its savings are lost, tossed off the precipitous cliff of Sherman's table-stage, can the piggy defeat its false consciousness, sweeping the dollar traffic light away triumphantly. This is obviously a critique of late capitalism's colonization of desire, but it is one achieved in cooperation with representation, and the possibility of interpretive meaning to be derived from it.

At the heart of Reynaud's argument is a Derridean-Lacanian notion that "in Sherman's work, the object of repression, that which is continuously revealed as the central obsession of all his manipulations is writing, writing as forbidden bliss." She goes on to say that

> it becomes clear that the repressed writing has nevertheless continued to assert itself, masked though triumphant, yet without its usual means of expression: letters, words, phonemes, a piece of paper; these things remain only as isolated symptoms. Then, passing from neurotic repression to perversion, this writing appropriates "unnatural objects," the theoretically infinite collection of cheap artifacts whose constitution and use are unlimited, unlike the grammatical and linguistic laws which determine the juggling of words.[47]

Reynaud scrutinizes Sherman's performance like a psychoanalyst scanning for etiology. For her, Sherman's artwork is a symptomatic presentation of unconscious currents. And she arrives here at an illuminating conclusion. The disparity between the infinite possibilities of the object-world and the closed systems of language, despite the seeming vastness of the imagination's reach, a reach limited by language's grasp, is a key paradox in Sherman's work. We're accustomed to thinking of the clutter of everyday life as the constrained territory and to think of language and thought, the supposedly free terrain of imagination, as the unbounded regions, but Sherman's work reverses these terms. ("There is an idea for every object," Reynaud quotes Sherman as saying, a notion that points to the boundlessness of thinking-through-objects and the boundedness of hemming those ideas into words.)[48]

Calling the performances a "swerve through the realm of objects taken in order to bypass writing," she argues that the "use of purchased objects"—again, it's worth taking note of the taint of capitalism—"preexisting in space enables Sherman to avoid the unbearable gesture of subjectivity inherent in writing"

> in which to all appearances one's words are drawn from oneself, from one's most intimate recesses (even though these words only pass through us, they have nonetheless penetrated us, and undergone the action of our own chemistry in an almost physical sense), making the most natural metaphor for writing the emission of bodily excreta: come or shit.[49]

Here, I must depart from Reynaud's reading. The idea that words and thoughts come from some secret sacred place deep inside ourselves, instead of from the friction of consciousness on the flux of the world (and vice versa), is precisely the assumption that Sherman's spectacles engage and refute. It's the subject of much of his work, not its latent content. For him, subjectivity, and the writing that attempts to contain it or convey it, arises *from* the material world, not in spite of it. Writing isn't the repressed other of his performing world, but is waveringly present, moving in and out of view—a reminder of the way language structures our relationships with objects, but also of the ways objects condition our understanding of language. His objects aren't inert but bristling with meaning, at once linguistic and prelinguistic. There are no unnatural objects for our omnivorous minds.

Far from being free of representation, I'd argue, Sherman's pieces are almost too full of it. Every sequence of objects indexes manifold possibilities, exploding in the mind, before being succeeded by other, equally rich image-chains, object-sentences, cues to associative flights. Sherman refuses to ratify any one level of signification because everyday consciousness doesn't, either. Viewers are welcome, indeed compelled, to oscillate between parsing metaphors and paying close attention to the present performance reality, piecing together a story or watching objects as blunt presences, imagining the piece to be "about" Sherman or about themselves. "Meanings are infinite," he once pithily put it, "I vow to intend them. Unintended meanings are welcome, if invited—i.e. made plausible and/or inevitable by your actual intentions."[50]

Reynaud is a case in point. Eager to free his work of the politically suspect taint of representation, she falls instead into meta-representation. Sherman's work symbolizes the state of material culture in the postindustrial age; the vexed status of writing in Western metaphysics; the struggle of the unconscious to force its thrashing to the surface of consciousness; the patriarchal order's perpetual denial of pleasure. It embodies and so "proves" the ideas of Lacan, Baudrillard, and other thinkers.

I'll argue for a different interpretation of Sherman's nonstop flirting with language. No one was more aware of his vexed relationship with writing than Sherman himself. His diaries are a constant litany of battle with the limits of language, and his constant struggle to improve his writing only appears more heroic in light of his clear-eyed view of language's hard limits. But the spectacles—winsome, poignant, scrupulous, but never pathological or obsessive—don't render this struggle as repression and perversion. Rather, they attempt to document the very texture of consciousness itself, as perception slips into thought and then into language, and then back again: ecstasy and communion, communion and ecstasy.

Correspondences

The fliers for Sherman's performances frequently featured a head-on portrait of the artist wearing large black eyeglasses, a visual pun on the "spectacles" they advertised, but also a microcosm of Sherman's methods. (The title comes from Sherman's wry admission that by doing the solo performances at all, he was making a spectacle of himself.) The image trades on the linguistic peculiarity that the same word means both an aid to sight, an object that frames and corrects vision, and performances best appreciated with the eyes. But it also suggests that the purpose of Sherman's pieces lay somewhere in between these two meanings, that the theatrical performances were designed to help spectators see anew, and that they were intimately concerned with the ways that everyday objects (like a pair of spectacles) index ideas. In such pictures, the photographed spectacles that Sherman wears sometimes conceal his actual eyes, creating a mask of sight. One iteration shows Sherman's eyes obscured by the word "eye." You couldn't ask for a more perfect encapsulation of his tempestuous love-hate relationship with language's refractory power, helping us see, but also blinding us.

A key manipulation from the *Eleventh Spectacle* animates this suggestive constellation of imagery. It's no accident that this routine comes from a piece subtitled "The Erotic" and devoted to examining the motive force of desire, broadly conceived. The trick begins with a round toy eyeball mounted on a long spike, perhaps a knitting needle. Sherman passes another toy eyeball, this one mounted on a magnet, over the first, one blind eye "looking" at the other. He then meets the inanimate gaze of the two dummy eyes with his own, seeing eyes. This brief object-sentence unfolds a simple comparison with profound implications. On the one hand, our eyes, objects set in our heads, are a mechanical apparatus for trapping light. On the other, the images they capture and broadcast to our brains are the very fuel of subjectivity, the substance of individual outlook.

Sherman then goes on to cover one of his eyes with half a pair of those trademark black spectacles, the lens covered over with the word "eye" in large black letters. Taking the blinder off, he impales it on the spike and surveys the arrangement with the magnet-eye. He repeats this sequence with the other half of the spectacles, this one covered over with the corner of a picture frame. In this phase of the routine, Sherman plays with the perceptual paradoxes hinted at above, that language both helps us see and obscures experience behind a veil of preexisting meanings, and that our own particular vantage points are at once the foundations of selfhood, and the prescriptive framing we can never escape. We can never know what it would be like to see from a different pair of eyes. (He follows this sequence by putting on both pieces of the spectacles, completely obscuring his eyes behind language and vantage.)

The final section of the manipulation circles around the erotics of perception as a penetrating and penetrative act. On a literal level, light rebounding from the objects we see does, in fact, enter our bodies through our eyes, and images enter our brains as the translation of this input. But, as Sherman spikes his two blindfolds, language and worldview, he also seems to suggest that true seeing requires piercing these barriers to sight, pushing peepholes into the accrued crusts of habit, language, and representation that mediate everyday experience. The routine concludes with Sherman holding the point of his needle in tense tandem with a toy eyeball, an image of imminent violation, before turning his eyes, real and fake, and the spike toward the audience. Sherman ends the manipulation, and the spectacle (it's the last routine in the piece), by reminding his spectators that by dint of the last forty minutes or so of performance, he and his ideas, having punctured the veils of apperception, are already "inside" them, but also that their eyes, perhaps honed sharper than before, have seen (and will see) more penetratingly because of this penetration. This is a playfully queer erotics, one that hints at the more avowedly queer work Sherman would make later in his career. He suggests that topping and bottoming, penetrated and being penetrated, giving and taking, are oscillating dynamics built into both artistic and everyday experience. For Sherman, perception itself is a queer act, always full of subversively uncontainable potential.

If his spectacles demonstrate how what we see gets inside us, they also examine how perception and thought take place as much "out there" in the world as they do "in here" in our brains. The visual anthropologist Michael Taussig argues that in the moment of perception, the very phenomenon that, in the classical Cartesian model, sets up a chasm between the observing subject and the observed object, also undoes it. Some part of ourselves is always outside ourselves in the moment of perception, leaping to scan the object seen, confusing visuality with tactility, inferring sound from action. Tactility, the synesthetic shadow of touch, complicates sight. Our thoughts are as much about our sensory apparatus leaping outside itself to brush the grain of reality as they are about mastering it with the dominating force of reason inside the safe precincts of the mind.[51]

Gosetti-Ferencei, in her study of phenomenological thinking in modern art and literature, develops a similar line of argument when she discusses the blurring of the self's borders that transpires in the instant of perception. Perceived images, she suggests, are not simple copies or renderings, mental mimesis, but a "correspondence between things and the gaze in its recess toward the seer." Visual qualities such as light, color, and depth are "there only because they awaken an echo in our bodies." Such images, then, are "not tracings or copyings of the world; they are overlappings of the seeing and the seen, the 'inside and outside of the mind.'"[52] Language, too, brings consciousness into frictional relation with the world, as objects at hand ineffably influence objects in speech (and vice versa). These, too, are forms of communion, temporary meldings-together of self and world.

And here is a profound paradox. As we come closer to the world by taking it in, asserting our presence as spectators, we also slip further away from what we understand to be ourselves. Every encounter between the senses and the world, each assertion of our subjective perceptions, also contains the potential for ecstatic removal from the self. Thus, by attempting to think with objects, Sherman stages this immanent but often undernoticed phenomenon of consciousness's embrace of the outside world. Communion and ecstasy, ecstasy and communion, are partners in a constant pas de deux. For Sherman, metaphor is not simply a literary correspondence but the record of consciousness touching the world. (Like the double-meaning spectacles, books are lodestones for Sherman, material objects made of language that contain and concretize ideas and help us see.) This is Sherman's version of reenchantment, the transformative recognition that we are not as apart from the world as we imagine, that all our abstractions can also render us more concrete, that our minds are always reaching out to touch the world they attempt to describe. To find such enchantments, Sherman suggests, we need only acknowledge the strangeness of our minds, and realize that the more we try to think ourselves out of the material world, the more we discover ourselves within it again.

Because Sherman's work is so intimately concerned with leaping back and forth across the porous borders between perceiving subject and perceived objects, my suggestion here is that phenomenology's enriched attention to thought and perception as bodily processes arising from our situatedness within the everyday world makes it a more flexible interpretive paradigm for Sherman's work than the repression-perversion dynamics of late psychoanalysis or the commodity-fetish fetishism of post-Marxism. To my mind, thinkers like Heidegger, Merleau-Ponty, Bachelard, and Taussig—and their invaluable interpreters, like Gosetti-Ferencei—are more apt guides to Sherman's experiential philosophizing.

In his essay on Cézanne, Merleau-Ponty makes the elemental observation that our brains do not simply impose order on the chaos of the world from some Cartesian point outside it. Rather, our sifting of the world arises from that same welter of objects, which precedes and surrounds us. Our thoughts are always among the things of the world, figures on a shifting ground, not held apart from them. As he puts it: "We live in the midst of man-made objects, among tools, in houses, streets, cities, and most of the time we see them only through the human actions which put them to use. We become used to thinking that all this exists necessarily and unshakably." What he goes on to argue about Cézanne could just as easily be said, perhaps more forcefully, about Sherman. The painter's work "suspends these habits of thought and reveals the base of inhuman nature upon which man has installed himself."[53]

Sherman's journals from the 1970s, the time he was beginning to work on the spectacles, preserve a transcribed passage from Claude Lévi-Strauss's *The Savage Mind* about the place of ritual objects in "primitive" cultures, a passage that testifies to Sherman's preoccupation with the constitutive function of humble things in our own supposedly less fetish-obsessed society: "it could even be said that being in their place is what makes them sacred, for if they were to be taken out of their place, even in thought, the entire order of the universe would be destroyed."[54]

You could describe Sherman's entire artistic project over decades of spectacles as taking objects out of their places, removing them from their usual positions in the world, and in language, before returning them, subtly changed. Interpretations of Sherman's work usually neglect the vitally important moment-before, and moment-after, in any given routine, intervals of preparation and recovery that remained remarkably consistent throughout his decades-long work on the spectacles. At the margins of each manipulation, the moment when Sherman plucks an object, often after much unhurried rummaging around, from the anomie of a cluttered suitcase or haphazard pile splayed at his feet, and animates it with sudden, singular meanings, dramatizes this project of unmaking and remaking the habitual world, one ice-cube tray or disposable razor at a time. His heaps, the "base of inhuman nature," to employ Merleau-Ponty's phrase—are at once figures of chaos without meaning, absolute difference that renders all meaning null, and images of habit-dulled invisibility, objects unseen because unnoticed. (Gosetti-Ferencei talks about an idea of the everyday, common to modernist thinkers and artists alike, as "fallen," exiled from grace, both because ordinary life has been voided of theological immanence and because daily automatism dulls us to so much of experience. But this idea also implies that the everyday contains the germ of its own redemption.)[55]

The "realism" of everyday consciousness, in which by necessity we forget our surroundings in order to stage the dramas of experience, is inverted, too. Here, such humble bit players vividly assert themselves before disappearing once more into the heap. Sherman takes a process so primary to our daily perceptions that it is necessarily invisible—the screening and sorting of objects into a stable backdrop so that we can place ourselves among them and act—and makes it the main drama of his theater. His pieces unknit our visual field by showing how the eye leaps from analogy to analogy, piecing together a stable surround from unmanageable surfeit. Instead of these received ways of making sense, he posits others founded on chromatic properties or material affinities.

For example, a manipulation from the *Fifteenth Spectacle* with the punning title "Green Yarn" unspools a disconcerting visual narrative about the ways, abetted by language, we separate and classify with our eyes. Taking a ball of green yarn and an orange from his suitcase, he places them next to each other on the table, creating a temporary still life. Taping the end of the yarn to the orange, he rapidly winds it around the fruit until the orange—the hue and also the fruit—is completely masked by the green cord. As he does this, he reveals that the center of the original ball of green yarn was a green apple. Is an orange still an orange when it's no longer orange? And conversely, if color confers identity, does a green apple become somehow an orange if, as Sherman does next, it's covered with orange tape? Is the apple now an orange, and the orange an apple? By literalizing the cliché of comparing apples and oranges, a phrase usually employed to indicate that no such comparison is advisable or even possible, Sherman shows that there are perfectly valid reasons to make such a likening. He avers that, in actuality, on perceptual evidence, there is as much compelling data with which to compare apples and oranges as there is not to do so, implying, as he does, that many such seemingly sturdy conceptual commonplaces are built on experiential sand.

The next phase of the manipulation further denatures the hapless fruits as Sherman interrogates their other characteristic formal properties, passing them through a piece of cardboard through which circular holes have been cut, leaving each object sitting on a circular coaster. He then removes the two shrouded fruits, turning the cardboard discs over to reveal yellow undersides, upon which he places two lemons. The orange and apple have swapped identities, and have then both been transformed, by visual syllogisms, into lemons. (You could say he's making perceptual lemonade from language's lemons.)

The last part of the routine puts a more sinister spin on this imagistic punning. Retrieving a pair of white gloves and some sheets of white paper, Sherman covers his hands and places one of them on one of the blank leaves. With a white pencil, he draws an invisibly white outline on the white page, and his hand seems almost to disappear, phased out by perceptual blurring. It's hidden by the glove, doubled by the unseeable but eerily present tracing.

A later manipulation from the *Fifteenth*, called "Color Theory, A Finger Exercise," continues this line of inquiry. Sherman begins by cutting zigzags into a piece of white paper with a pair of green scissors. While holding up the jagged shape that results, he produces an exact duplicate in green paper, which he then cuts with yellow scissors, prompting the appearance of a yellow doppelganger, and so on through the spectrum, each color diminishing in size, until nothing is left but a small red speck, which Sherman tears up and discards. This prismatic diminution parses our propensity to sort and classify, subdividing the world so carefully as to almost annihilate it.

Breaking the Codes

The kinds of objects Sherman usually selected for his manipulations often belong to the category that Martin Heidegger termed "ready-at-hand," objects that cry out for human manipulation and mastery, components in everyday world-making, habitually overlooked because they are seemingly inconsequential without human use. Glossing one of the philosopher's more concrete examples, Gosetti-Ferencei points out that a hammer, for example, is

> there in respect to our need for it to work on this or that sort of project. Hardly noticed, the hammer belongs to a system of references by which it points to other things: the hammer, cut to fit [the human body] indicates the nail, and points to the wood and the forest from where it came, the house that is to be built, the people who will live there, and so on. Because of this nexus, which in part makes up a world, this equipment encounters us as a totality; things belong to the world according to their arrangement alongside and significance for other things . . . In Heidegger's terms, the hammer is ready-at hand . . . as we are about to use it, pick it up, set it down; only when it breaks is it . . . *present-at-hand,* encountering us, unusually announcing itself as a problem.[56]

In Heidegger's conception, even the most familiar objects have a mysterious aspect. Objects never really exist for us in their true quiddity because we see them obscurely through screens of language and use. In this sense, they are always mediated.[57] They're hidden from us not only because, on a literal level, we can never see them in their full cubist dimensionality, from all sides at once, but also because they inevitably arrive embedded in ramifying circles of use and meaning: the hammer–the nail–the board–the tree–the forest, and so on.

In other words, the hammer can only really be seen for itself when it can no longer perform the functions that typify it. It only becomes a hammer when it can't be a hammer anymore. By separating everyday objects from their systems of reference, making them problems instead of means, present in his hands instead of ready at ours, Sherman disrupts the webs of meaning, the implied worlds, within which these objects constitute fixed points, pointing to the possibility of other possible human worlds undergirded by different constellations of objects.

Perhaps not even coincidentally, given Sherman's voracious reading, one of the most remarkable manipulations in the *Fifteenth Spectacle* involves a Heideggerian hammer. Producing the box for an oversized set of playing cards, Sherman quickly draws six regular-sized cards from the mismatched enclosure, fanning them out into a hand, their backs to the audience, poker style, while glancing suspiciously over their tops. As he coyly reveals the cards, it becomes evident that they are blazoned not with numbers or suits but with large alphabetic characters. Putting his cards on the table, he deals himself the hand "H-A-M-M-E-R." Returning to the box, he shakes out six segments of an actual hammer cut into pieces, and places them carefully on the cards, one section to each letter. He then produces an intact hammer and holding it above the sundered one, begins to affix the letter-cards to nails attached to its head, spiking them so that the letters "H-A-M-M-E-R" collapse into a single unit and the signifying word is mashed into the signified object.

He then joins together the hammer segments lying on the table into a seemingly undivided object, a temporary simulacrum. The distinction between the pieces of the hammer and the letters that make up the word and concept of a "hammer" couldn't be clearer or more disorienting. The letters, with which we happily subdivide the idea of a hammer, each have recombinative potential and discrete identities as alphabet characters. The riven parts of the actual hammer have no corresponding value except as amputated chunks of a now useless object. If the word "hammer" truly represents the object known as a hammer, then the pieces of the hammer—the handle divided in chunks, the severed head—must be comparable to the components of the word: H-A-M-M-E-R. But of course they aren't, and to divide either object and word so far is to dissolve both meaning and use.

The rest of the manipulation drives this point home—writing about Sherman's work makes you particularly conscious of your own metaphors—as Sherman goes on to "shuffle" both the letter-cards and the hammer fragments once again. Playing both parts in an imaginary game, he fans out the cards at each end of the TV-table like a savvy cardsharp, hiding his hands from us, and then throws pieces of the hammer into the center of the table, making his bets with the dead currency of the now-useless object.

We gamble on language to convey our meanings, both to others and ourselves. But, Sherman suggests, it's a sucker's bet. The house always wins. The cards remind us that the world's seemingly infinite meanings can only be expressed with combinations of those twenty-six familiar characters. (There are twice as many cards in the box as there are letters in the alphabet.) We all play the game of subjectivity with the same soiled, thumb-worn deck. Language, the most seemingly orderly of human systems, is actually deeply chaotic, made of random assortments of fixed characters, unlike the things it fixes with meanings, which can only ever be what they are, and which would be ruined if subjected to the same rules of cutting and reshuffling that govern language. (Recall the spoiled hammer, unable to survive its reduction to more elemental units.)

Having anted up all the parts, he pockets them. Spilling a bunch of nails out of his original box, he uses the spikes to affix the letters "H-A-M-M-E-R" together once more, re-creating with language the ruined object that he just threw away, slyly "nailing" together a "hammer." He then lays letter cards saying "N-A-I-L-S" over the preceding set, places the full "deck" on the table, and places the hammer segments to either side of the cards, so that the image of an actual hammer is interrupted midway by the cards, now invisible, of course, denoting both nouns and verbs, objects and actions.

The words "Hammer" and "Nail," in one of those peculiarities of the English language that becomes stranger the more you think about it, can describe both the tools themselves and the gestures associated with them, inert objects and productive activities. Sherman graphs the transitive hiatus in which a noun—staid, stationary—becomes a verb, vital and busy, and an object suddenly becomes an actor. The hammer hammers, nailing the nails, and the nails are nailed. The moment of his performance surrogates the linguistic shift into the present participle, staging the theatricality of language itself. He has chopped up the concept of hammering nails in the same way he subdivided the actual hammer. What would you call the syntactical elements of a thought? Could they be cognemes?

This strange ideational collage encapsulates the universe of ambiguities and slippages, the leaps from concrete activity to conceptual abstraction and back again, that attend even the very simple project of hammering a few nails. Wavering in and out of materiality, the routine shifts from Sherman's deft manipulating hands to "hands" of cards; from the fanned cards, to equally arbitrary combinations of letters, to the words those aleatory combinations nonetheless somehow denote; back to the objects those words name but perhaps also vitiate; to the linguistic threshold at which nouns become verbs (and vice versa); from the object at hand to the more abstract concepts and categories that name it and place it amid the everyday world, and back again. The routine charts the wavering way that consciousness slips in and out of contact with the tangible world. Concluding the manipulation with a droll flourish, Sherman brandishes his intact hammer above the interrupted concept-hammer on the table, slowly miming the action of hammering four times, while intoning "Bang!" and holding a small sign in his other hand that says "Bang."

In this manipulation, and others like it, Sherman stages a quintessential paradox of language. It creates objects by naming them, thereby giving them reality and meaningful existence, and placing them within the world. But, by doing so, in the same moment, it destroys their particularity. This singular object, with particular material properties, with a unique history of use, is suddenly only one hammer among many hammers, a tool among tools, forever bracketed off from other potential affinities or prospective categories. Graphing an object onto language's coordinates means sacrificing some part of its material existence, just as hammering the roundness of a thought through language's square holes means surrendering its primordial perceptual fullness.

Sherman subtly points out that the hammer and nails have an elemental status in both language and practice. They're fixed points in a semantic system and a link in the chains of meaning-through-use that undergird our shared reality. If language is an arbitrary system in which each word only has meaning in relation to the others, Sherman suggests that the building blocks of everyday material reality share a similar interdependence. Remove a hammer from the hierarchy of object relations and whole spheres of activity might collapse. In this sense, objects are words in the lexicon of the everyday world.

Other Visions, Other Worlds

It's here that the queerness of Sherman's theater resides. He was one of the artists for whom Stefan Brecht, an occasional performer in the spectacles, and the first audience for the first one, devised the category of "Queer Theatre" in his unfinished book of that title.[58] By directing attention to how we screen objects and meanings, include and exclude, abject and valorize, Sherman is also considering what bodies, identities, and practices we choose to ignore or elide. Though much of his work might seem hermetic or apolitically formalist, his few forays into an explicitly socially engaged practice suggest the political underpinnings of his less obviously argumentative work. In his world of objects, utilitarian norms—aesthetic, perceptual, functional—keep things confined, stifle their possibilities, smother them with habit.

Sherman's surviving notes for his *Queer Spectacle* (1994), spectacle eighteen, and one of his last performance works, indicate that the manipulations centered on objects charged with meaning for his life and memories as a gay man: a phone, a jockstrap, a zipper, a frankfurter. (On a draft of the announcement preserved with Sherman's papers at New York University, Sherman handwrote the word "PERSONAL" in capitals onto a typewritten sentence indicating that the spectacle would reflect his "experience as a gay man.")[59] Not only does the recipe for the piece imply that it will resituate "straight" or supposedly inert objects as icons of queerness. The jockstrap, sigil of jock-hetero athleticism, becomes a charged sexual signifier, while the neutral communication apparatus of the telephone becomes an erotic fetish heralding sexual encounters. It reminds us, to employ Bernstein's terms once again, that if such things can script queer actions, they contain worlds that more normative uses deliberately ignore.

Conversely, Sherman's *Eleventh Spectacle: The Erotic* contains a routine that anatomizes the constraints of gendered domesticity. Positioning the king and queen from a chess set on miniature chessboards, each surrounded by an array of tiny houseplants—constrained natural verdancy—he sets up a miniature kitchen table between them. Spilling the pieces off the boards, he reveals images of stereotypically "male" and "female" silhouettes on their obverse sides, the sort that might gender a restroom.

Gathering all the little plants on the overturned kitchen table, he covers this domestic tumult with the miniature chessboards and positions the king and queen to "play." The social rules that determine "male" and "female" identities and govern the expression of "male" and "female" desire, Sherman suggests, are at once as arbitrary and as immutable as the rules of chess, a tightly proscriptive grammar that stunts biological pith, much as potting a plant hobbles its growth. (The well-worn patterns of an old relationship add a further layer of regulation to the model kitchen.) To underline the point, Sherman audibly narrates a few chess moves: "Queen to Rook 5."

Turning over the "kitchen's" tiled floor, a cardboard sheet decorated with a binary black-white pattern, Sherman reveals an image of blooming flora violently flourishing beneath: the primal urge, rude nature. He gazes puckishly at his audience through a square aperture amid the fronds, before setting down over the table and chess figures the jungle scene, the wildness that civilization has regulated since time immemorial. Sherman lays two leaves, fig leaves perhaps, on top of the table, the untrammeled jungle becoming a momentary picture of the Garden of Eden, the flourishing of desire before shame began to trim its foliage.

Returning the players to their original positions, amid the imprisoned plants, Sherman calls the game: "Stalemate." Sherman renders the hetero-battle of the sexes as an exhausted, compulsory game of worn-out moves, stale mates, mating stalely. His audience is left to imagine all the libidinal possibilities excluded from normative realities.

This and similar examples show Sherman's intellectual and political affinities with the eloquent object performances being devised by feminist artists during the 1960s and 1970s, performances that sought to unpick the ideological assumptions invested in domestic totems. We might think of Lucinda Childs's 1964 solo piece *Carnation*, in which she reimagines ordinary objects—hair curlers, sponges, a colander—as fanciful costume elements, garbing herself as an alien creature. Childs stages an appearance as strange as the gendered stratifications that prescribe cleaning or cooking or taking out the trash as women's work, one hinting at wellsprings of domestic alienation, culminating in her sequential assaults on a plastic bag.[60] Martha Rosler, in her 1975 video performance *Semiotics of the Kitchen*, in which she stands at a kitchen island reminiscent of Sherman's tabletop stage, performs the seditious persona of what she calls an "anti–Julia Child," replacing "the domesticated 'meaning' of tools with a lexicon of rage and frustration."[61] Reciting a litany of kitchen implements in alphabetical order—apron for "A"; fork for "F"—she vehemently demonstrates the gestures those scriptive things prescribe, furiously beating at empty air or brutally stabbing outwards with a fork. As she does, she describes the vocabulary of household oppression, detaching the movements from their instrumental functions to isolate them as a carceral choreography, detailing how these tools hold women's physical lives hostage to their domestic demands.

As the performance goes on, though, she begins to sever objects from the alphabet. The last sequence of letters—UVWXYZ—is indicated by violent gestures, freed from conventional usage, building to a furious, knife-slashed "Z" that suggests the promise of insurrection. But this belligerent conclusion is belied by the video's last image, in which Rosler steps away with an insouciant shrug, as if to remark on the profoundly arbitrary methods by which we align bodies with gender identities, and so with social roles. Both Childs and Rosler, then, like Sherman, point to the groundless but stultifying grammar of everyday reality, a set of given associations as arbitrary as language, and as ready to be deconstructed and imagined anew.[62]

Quantum Realities

Sherman was fascinated by the elementary particles of human experience. In his pieces he frequently sings scales, spells words, takes objects apart and puts them together in new ways. By doing so, he shows that the very elements that allow us to create feelings of wholeness—the meanings bestowed by words, the worlds of use implied by objects, the harmonies behind sounds—destroy, even as they create. Language fragments reality, only to reassemble it according to its own rules; objects structure what we can and can't do; music orders sounds. The smallness of his performing objects suggests other world-building elements: letters, sounds, words, visual affinities like color and shape. (Recall the manipulation about home I described above.)

He's equally preoccupied with humdrum things that model wider realities. How often do we really think about the immensity of the world when we encounter a tiny globe, the power of a jetliner when we see a toy plane, the oddness of the human bite mechanism, which is simultaneously a machine for pulverizing nutrients and the apparatus of speech, when we come across a clattering pair of novelty dentures? For Sherman, it's as though we reduce these sublime facts to miniature forms and disperse them throughout quotidian life so as not to have to contemplate them in their true imponderability. These fetish objects obscure reality's more troubling dimensions. The tiny symbols make larger, stranger immensities manageable, thinkable.

"Travel Piece," the last manipulation in the *Fifteenth Spectacle*, makes these invisible leaps eloquently tangible. Taking a tiny plastic globe from his pocket, Sherman spins it, and places his finger on the corresponding spot on the world map he has set up on the table. Both these images represent the world, but one is round and a fraction of the size of the other, which is flat. Yet we have no trouble seeing each as a figure for the known world, which is actually so large we can't even truly picture its diversity.

Taking a plastic caliper from the suitcase, Sherman begins to measure imaginary distances across the map, huge journeys encompassed by tiny increments. Turning the map over to reveal a blank black underside, he repeats the measurements, reminding spectators that those huge symbolic movements were simply inches of progress across a piece of paper. Still, these tiny intervals suggest the trace of the global crisscrossings they represented only seconds before. As though to remind us of the disjunction between those wide immensities and the miniscule movements that can denote them on a map, Sherman then models the missing term in these imaginative fluctuations. Turning the table on its side, he first measures lengths of its side with the calipers—those global journeys traversed only precisely this much of the table's length!—and then walks jauntily in place for a moment to recall the true human measurement of distance: the step.

Having brought us to the zero-degree measurement of travel, the distance we can span in a single stride, Sherman hurtles out to abstraction again. He replaces the map, and remeasures distances that now seem both more concrete (because of how closely we have considered how big the space described by the calipers truly is) and more airily fantastical (because of how easily we make the leap back to modeled hugeness we still can't truly consider). Placing the blanked globe on the blanked map, he spins the globe and then spins himself, executing a winsome pirouette. As he does, Sherman reminds us that at both very large and very small magnitudes, human perception converges. Our microcosms—globes, maps, and other such models—allow us to imagine the sublime, but they also prevent us from ever truly contemplating its vastness, since we can easily supplant it with a more comestible alternative. We spin the globe and the globe spins us.

Sherman's games with scale point to the odd convergences of human apperception. We can only see smallness by enlarging it, whether literally, in a microscope or with a camera, or more commonly, by amplifying minute objects with linguistic description or sustained attention. Gazing at an object intently enlarges it to the size of our own minds. Placing an object into a sentence rescales it to the importance of the idea expressed. By the same token, we can only contemplate the truly gigantic—the world, the universe, the mysteries of the body—by reducing such sublimities to perceptible scale. This happens literally, in the simple sense that words containing big ideas are not necessarily more immense than words containing small ones. They move across the stage of consciousness or the page at about the size of other words. But this reduction also happens physically. Our eyes make big sights little, reduce enormous vistas to fields that can be surveyed by our small eyes. The smaller the object we scrutinize, the bigger it must become; the bigger the object we attempt to survey, the smaller it gets. Looked at this way, nothing could be larger than Sherman's bric-a-brac, suggesting as it does both the boundlessness of perception and the constrictedness of language.

As Gaston Bachelard once wrote of the way imagination slips, almost inadvertently, from small to large as soon as we fix our attention onto a miniature world, "right away images begin to abound, then grow, then escape. Large issues from small, not through the logical law of a dialectics of contraries, but thanks to liberation from all obligations of dimensions, a liberation that is a special characteristic of the activity of the imagination." As Bachelard points out, and Sherman's spectacles illustrate, the more we focus our attention on a small thing, the more detail we see and remark upon, the more we allow association and metaphor to do their work of aligning interior and exterior worlds, the larger this small thing becomes, and the more imaginative space it occupies: "Thus the miniscule, a narrow gate, opens up an entire world. The details of a thing can be the sign of a new world, which, like all worlds, contains the attributes of greatness."[63] Sherman's nutshells bound infinite space. (In this sense, all of Sherman's spectacles are a study in the enlarging and transforming power of sustained attention, multiplying meanings from humble substrates.) Here is another through-the-looking-glass variation on

Sherman's ideal of artistic communion. We can disappear into contemplation of a small object that becomes as large as we are capable of thinking it.

Another way to say this is to note that in the very moment we identify an object as "ordinary," it ceases to be so. The more we look at an everyday object, the less everyday it becomes. Ludwig Wittgenstein once asked what "the ordinary" feels like, his point being that we only notice something ordinary when it has ceased to be ordinary (recall Heidegger's broken hammer). In his fascinating study of the aesthetics of wonder, Philip Fisher expands upon this insight:

> To characterize wonder we are forced to look at its alternative, the qualities of the ordinary, and paradoxically what we end up saying is that there cannot be any experience of the ordinary. . . . The ordinary is what is there when there are no experiences going on. It is the necessary optics within which there can be such a thing as an experience, but which cannot itself be seen.[64]

Treacherous Images

Sherman picks up where Magritte left off. In perhaps his most famous painting the artist indicts the "treachery of images." A painting of a pipe is not a pipe—it's a representation of a pipe. Sherman spins this ontological examination still further. For him, even material objects themselves are frequently not themselves. They can easily be made to stand in for whole categories of objects. They can be obscured by their relationships to words or their visual harmonies with other objects. Even an actual pipe can never be just a pipe, because it's also a "pipe." Our double- and triple-dealing minds make objects into images and images into words and words into objects, playing language off reality and reality off language.

This is one way to interpret Sherman's propensity for deploying cutouts in his performances, cartoonish cardboard images of objects as well as the negative space of silhouettes cut from a sheet of paper or cardboard. These representations occupy a strange midpoint between objects in life and representations of objects in language. Substituting a cardboard cutout of a necktie for the cloth article, as Sherman does repeatedly during one whimsical sequence in the *Twelfth Spectacle*, is absurd. But he thereby reminds us that we make no less remarkable substitutions in our minds all the time, by surrogating the object with the word, or by severing it from other objects like it that may share other commonalities unrecognized by language's blunt categories (other cloth items of the same color, other things that dangle, and so on). The cardboard necktie cannot perform the sartorial functions of a real necktie, but it is instantly recognizable by its form as some kind of "necktie."

Similarly, by passing material objects through cutout silhouettes of their outlines, Sherman reminds us that we enact similar operations in consciousness all the time, forcing material objects at hand through preexisting, abstract categories. Language itself is a "cutout," a system of arbitrary signifiers whose flimsy partiality is revealed when they're snipped away from the other arbitrary signifiers. It's also the instrument that does the cutting out. Language is both paper doll and scissors. Sherman puts ontological states into competitive flux, fake versus real, cutouts versus models versus the thing itself. (Even more grotesque, Sherman performs similar substitutions with costume shop body parts: outlandish plastic ears, noses, hands, feet. He puts "ears" over his ears, "hands" over his hands, false feet next to his shoes.)

Sherman's spectacles search for a middle term between reality and thought, staging the hazy in-between states when experience is no longer sensation, but has yet to become objectified (or communicable) as language, the still-molten moment before sensation rushes into the channels cut by habit. In one manipulation from the *Twelfth Spectacle (Language),* Sherman parses the many invisible mediations of language involved in a simple telephone conversation. Beginning by placing a rotary phone dial over his mouth, he holds up a cardboard sheet decorated with two rotary arrays of alphabetic characters. Placing a telephone handset nearby, he begins to punch letters out of the sheet, strewing the loose characters around the handset, thereby transforming the rotary arrays into dials. Unscrewing the handset's earpiece, he fills the cavity with the letter-tiles from the table, and then raises the language-stuffed device to his ear. He then carefully spells the salutation "Hello!" by jauntily tugging a thread run from the handset's earpiece to its mouthpiece, one pull per letter: H-E-L-L-O.

The routine charts the movement of speech as it crosses from inarticulate impulse submitted to the arbitrary regulations of language, to vocalization amplified and articulated by the mechanisms of the body, to vibration materially registered in the telephone apparatus, to aural signals picked up by the interlocutor's ears, subsequently translated back into mental representations (now in another brain). Language has literally crossed from mind to mind through the intermediary of an object, passing from abstract to concrete to abstract again, a figure for the action of the spectacles themselves. Lingering on words or letters as sounds, Sherman considers the materiality of speech. Rolling over the contours of a word, tracing its passage through the mechanical apparatus of the body, he makes words as solid, as object-like as they can be—even as he dematerializes objects by treating them like words.

Redistributing the Sensible: Aesthetic Democracy and Possible Worlds

The philosopher Jacques Rancière has coined an elegant phrase, the "distribution of the sensible,"[65] to describe the ways in which epistemic paradigms overlap with individual human knowledge and perception to govern what ideas, identities, or social formations become legible—meaningful—at a given historical moment, the hidden currents governing the process of making sense. Sherman's spectacles aim to redistribute the sensible by hand and eye, working from first principles and material substrates, to imagine other ways of making sense, other modes of seeing, other potential configurations for the multitude of human-made and human-manipulated objects that populate our daily lives. Envisioning and testing new possibilities for our material codependents, Sherman works to expand the hidden vocabulary of experience.

If the spectacles' multiplicity, the hundreds of manipulations transpiring at dozens of venues across hours of performance and decades of work, can be suggested by a single gesture, or a single image, it is Sherman reaching into his suitcase and removing some small object from its accustomed place, at once overlooked and absolutely fundamental, precipitating the collapse of whole worlds—of language, of vision, of habit, of use—and setting a blank stage on which new ones might grow. For Sherman, as for Thornton Wilder before him, the littlest thing is more than big enough.

Chapter 4

✦

Dancing to the Cosmic Murmur

Nature Theater of Oklahoma's Poetics of the Everyday

Today Only and Never Again

In the eerie final chapter of Franz Kafka's novel *Amerika*, his hapless hero figure, Karl Rossmann, having fled Europe under duress and endured many picaresque adventures, encounters a strange advertisement, proffering a tantalizing promise of democratic welcome to the weary expatriate:

> The Oklahoma Theatre will engage members for its company today at Clayton race-course from six o'clock in the morning until midnight. The great Theatre of Oklahoma calls you! Today only and never again! If you miss your chance now you miss it forever! If you think of your future you are one of us! Everyone is welcome! If you want to be an artist, join our company! Our Theatre can find employment for everyone, a place for everyone! If you decide on an engagement we congratulate you here and now! But hurry, so that you get in before midnight! At twelve o'clock the doors will be shut and never opened again! Down with those who do not believe in us! Up, and to Clayton![1]

This passage is quoted in full on the website of the New York theater company Nature Theater of Oklahoma. Led by creative and life partners Kelly Copper and Pavol Liska, the company takes its name from the mysterious organization that lures Karl from his solitary wanderings. The advertisement is a succinct statement of their similarly democratic aesthetic program. In their work of the last decade, the company has mined theatrical material from seemingly unlikely sources, resolutely flaunting traditional borders between art and life, the aesthetic and unaesthetic. Nature Theater revels in the ums and uhs of ordinary conversation, the strange figments of mnemonically reconstructed narrative, the surprising gracefulness of quotidian movements closely scrutinized. They've admitted performers who lack the saleable virtues of the professional actor but replace them with the felicities of the amateur: enthusiasm, unvarnished idiosyncrasies, gawky charm. They've endeavored to absorb the typical difficulties of making art—day jobs, lack of rehearsal space—into the artworks themselves, thereby alchemizing mundane working hours or frustrating restrictions into creative material.

Like Kafka, Nature Theater has found strangeness in the ordinary, and ordinariness in the strange. The way the one-letter difference in Kafka's title kicks the idea of the country askew, slyly indicating that the author's America was a country of the mind—he never made it there, but savored its myths from afar—is also suggestive of Nature Theater's project. Defamiliarizing the molecular stuff of everyday American life, they've been creating their own "Amerika."

The urgency of Kafka's original notice—pay attention now, or it will be too late, you'll miss it—also corresponds to the company's deeply felt belief, inherited from John Cage, that art is happening all around us, all the time. ("It's the biggest theater in the world," says Fanny in Kafka's version, "there are almost no limits on it.")[2] For Nature Theater the question is not just how we attend to the aesthetic events that we do bracket in such an exalted way, but how we can bear to let all the others, which we can't help but neglect, slip away. If art is happening all around us, all the time, then we're doomed to miss out on much of it.

Looked at another way, what would it mean to see it all, to manage to transfix each instant of evanescent beauty as it appears and perishes? What kind of godlike sight could give every vanishing perception a full measure of contemplation or fully register the sparks of quotidian creativity involved in something as seemingly simple as structuring a line of conversation or taking a walk? What would it be like to see everything as art? This vision of the aesthetic sublime haunts the company's work, surfacing in the closing passages of pieces like *No Dice* or *Romeo and Juliet* as a fleeting moment of enriched perception, a moment when we see the design of the whole and also see how our own personal perceptions have been integral to creating it.

This twofold mode of seeing—aspiring to see everything, and haunted by the inevitability of losing most of it to memory's vagaries and consciousness's vicissitudes—suggests why theater, the quintessentially ephemeral art, must be the company's medium. It explains the tension between fixity and flux, between loss and preservation, recorded permanence and theatrical perishability, which underlies much of their work. It's the key to what I'm calling the company's poetics of the everyday, a set of aesthetic principles founded on the paradoxes of everyday experience itself. Maurice Blanchot phrases the problem of the everyday's elusiveness this way, a definition that illuminates Nature Theater's preoccupations: "Whatever its other aspects, the everyday has this essential trait: it allows no hold. It escapes."[3]

With the exception of *Poetics*, Nature Theater's everyday pieces have all been based on recorded interviews conducted with acquaintances and friends. The company makes use of recording both to harvest the ephemeral aspects of everyday speech and to shift focus to the sounds we usually tune out. For Nature Theater, the figure of the recording apparatus suggests the kind of unrestricted perception that attends to details usually tuned out by habit. The tape recorder hears everything. Fully formed words and preverbal stutters are given equal attention; conversational false starts have as much weight as polished sentences.

But the affinities between Kafka's mysterious Oklahoma Theatre and the company's work don't stop at mere inspiration. His chapter's narrative contains a kind of microcosm of their theatrical methods as well. When Karl arrives at the Oklahoma's recruiting station, he encounters an awesome spectacle. In front of the entrance to the racecourse, across a gigantic platform, hundreds of women garbed like angels in long flowing white robes, mounted on pedestals, stand blowing long trumpets in a clamorous chorus redolent of the Last Judgment. The daunting scope of this apocalyptic vision is quickly undercut by the revelation of the slapdash methods used to construct it. The trumpeters don't blow in harmony but according to whim. The disparity between the massive ornate costumes and the puny performers within becomes comical upon close examination. The celestial musicians are just workers doing their jobs. In fact, Karl finds that he knows one of them, Fanny, from earlier adventures, and she cheerfully steps down from her pedestal to take a break and chat. She lets Karl try her trumpet, and he finds that the ecumenical instrument, though "roughly fashioned," is capable of "almost any refinement of expression."[4]

This vision of the theater as a cosmic *gesamtkunstwerk*, a truly total work of art, albeit one performed by cheerful amateurs, is countered in the chapter's final passages by a theater of a very different kind. Having been engaged by the Oklahoma's division of technicians—the all-embracing institution has departments for every trade and level of expertise—Karl is on the train, heading deeper into the unknown spaces of the American wilderness. He glances out the window, past the hum of chatting travelers and the mundane pastimes—card-playing, smoking—with which they are whiling away the trip and is struck by the sublime immensity of the landscapes outside. The chapter (and the novel) close on a transfixed moment of awed perception:

> Masses of blue-black rock rose in sheer wedges to the railway line; even craning one's neck out of the window, one could not see their summits; narrow, gloomy, jagged valleys opened out and one tried to follow with a pointing finger the direction in which they lost themselves; broad mountain streams appeared, rolling in great waves down on to the foothills and drawing with them a thousand foaming wavelets, plunging underneath the bridges over which the train rushed; and they were so near that the breath of coldness rising from them chilled the skin of one's face.[5]

Here, we are made to understand, is the true "nature theater" of Oklahoma, the grand stage to which the tatty pageants constructed by human beings cannot compare. Some commentators have suggested that Kafka's manuscript was, in fact, unfinished, that he intended Karl's adventures to continue past the epic train ride. But for my purposes, his chapter's design couldn't be more perfect and clear. We go from a manifestly artificial spectacle with the most hubristic of artistic ambitions, to a far more awe-inducing sight framed by nothing but the instant of human perception straining to contain the majesty of the world. Moreover, the chapter's architecture suggests that the former has primed Karl to see the latter. Art has prepared the way for a deepened view of life, theater has helped him, and through him, helped the reader, to behold nature, the wider stage outside. The constant background noise of quotidian existence links these scenes of theater. The routines of organized labor underwrote the grandiose spectacle. Karl must look up from the murmur of everyday life to catch the beauty outside. He must *notice* the eye-reeling majesty challenging every glance.

Both these figures—the humdrum routine that sustains art-making, suddenly uncovered within the artwork itself, and the sudden look with fresh eyes that catches daily life unawares, startling it into revealing its situation within a vaster surround—are recurrent preoccupations in Nature Theater's work and building blocks in its dramaturgy. Performers frequently squint with winsome surprise at the lines they've just uttered, or look askance at their own gestures, aghast at the strangeness of some utterly unremarkable syllable or movement, foreshadowing in moment-by-moment microstructure the epiphanies of revelatory estrangement their pieces seek to induce in spectators.

There are biographical affinities with Kafka's novel as well: Pavol Liska came to the United States by himself from Slovakia at the age of eighteen and spent his first year in Oklahoma. As Kelly Copper recounts, in a fittingly Kafkaesque coincidence, Liska lived "across the street from where that first postal worker went postal and shot up the whole post office."[6] When we first met, Liska elaborated on the stance of productive distance his status as an outsider inside grants him:

> I feel like I'm able to see things that you can't see because to me it's all exotic, to me it's all material, and I never take anything for granted. To me it's also fascinating, because coming from the outside . . . America is still the land of unlimited opportunities, it is a mythological country.[7]

In a foundation story almost too apt to be believed, Copper and Liska met in a class on dada art and performance at Dartmouth College. In fact, aside from one other student, they *were* the class. (In an interview with writer-director Young Jean Lee, they gleefully recall terrorizing their professor with dada-inspired interruptions, determined to have a dada class, and not simply a class about dada.)[8] The insouciant anti-movement that made the notion of the "ready-made" part of the twentieth-century artistic vocabulary, testing aesthetic limits with attributed urinals and snow shovels, dada is an important artistic ancestor of the duo's work. Copper and Liska are the inheritors of a genealogy that passes from Marcel Duchamp to John Cage, by way of Judson Dance Theater and other pioneering artists of the 1960s. As in theater, so in life. Since theirs is a domestic as well as a creative partnership, Copper and Liska's artistic and everyday lives are uniquely bound up in each other. As Copper explains to Lee in their interview, the couple works all the time. When they were first making performances, they'd frequently rehearse pieces in their old studio apartment on Saint Mark's Place in New York's East Village. The rolling chairs in *Poetics* were a solution to worries about the noise caused by dancing on wood floors at night. The result is that, as Copper puts it, they can't tell which one of them came up with what idea for which piece.

Like the above-mentioned artists, Nature Theater is dedicated to redrawing the borders between art and life based on acts of perception, not inherited aesthetic criteria. As Liska once explained to me, tracing the company's aesthetic program:

> It's all related to the everyday, the mundane, the things that are around us. The restriction in *Poetics* was that there should be no language, and so if you have no language, but you still are interested in what's around you—human life minus talking, what do you get? You have the way people move when you're not trying to be creative. Then, the next show *No Dice* was language: what language is around us? How do you capture it, harvest it? And so we used recordings. But it's the same move. In *Poetics,* movements that are around us every day. In *No Dice,* the language that is around us every day. And then the question left over was: story-telling and stories and why do we tell them, and how are they actually used in our daily life? You know, it wasn't that we were trying to tell the best story, we couldn't care less about *Romeo and Juliet* or *Rambo.* What we cared about is how is it useful in daily life, and what do people use it for? . . . The stories that are ever-present, imprinted on our consciousness—there must be some use for them. So we were trying to figure that out. And *Life and Times . . .* the project after *Romeo and Juliet,* is taking that to the extreme. It's just somebody's life—it's a story, but it's not everybody's story, it's just somebody's life from birth to age 34. But all of those projects are connected by interest or curiosity about what we do every single day that we don't see or pay attention to.

For the duo, this project of making art from the materials of everyday life is a quintessentially American one, with deep roots in the philosophy of the transcendentalists. In her eloquent introduction to the published text of Nature Theater's *Romeo and Juliet*, Karinne Keithley links their work to Emerson's dictum that the American scholar must embrace "the common, the familiar, the low."[9] But their art is also a response to the straitened economic circumstances of progressive theater-making in idea-rich but cash-poor New York City. Nature Theater has toured frequently in Europe. At various points, the creation of their epic piece *The Life and Times* was funded by an Austrian theater. In a particularly ironic piece of programming, the first installment of the project, singing the sorrows and pleasures of a very American childhood, was featured in Berlin's Theatertreffen festival as one of the ten best *German* productions of the year.

Even as the company's work moved closer to the alluring America of its aesthetic imagination, practicalities took it further away. Being put in the strange position of ambassador for American culture abroad prompted a great deal of brain-searching about what it really means to make American art. Liska elaborates:

> What does it mean to be an American artist? So it's not a patriotic or limiting description, but it has more to do with what the transcendentalist poets were doing when they were asking themselves what is American literature? . . . I think we're trying to get under the surface of what does that mean to be making work in America, and what kind of work can only be made in America.

"There's no high culture in America," Liska adds, mischievously, "so in a way, we have to invent it. We use low culture ingredients, but ultimately we have the highest ambitions." For Nature Theater, the other side of America's benign neglect of its artists is that there are still rich seams of unexploited experience waiting for the right artist-surveyor to locate them and stake a claim:

> LISKA: What's more important about America to me is the stuff that happens in the Midwest. Or, you know, where does one look for gold? Aesthetic gold. . . . I think there's just vast areas of aesthetics that haven't been even approached. I know they're there, but to me they are exactly where there is no culture or support of art. In Oklahoma City, tell us about it! Or Milwaukee or somewhere in Nebraska or something. . . . So, we're looking for a grant to go travel through the Midwest and—
>
> COPPER:—mine for aesthetic gold. I remember reading this book by Marjorie Perloff, *The Vienna Paradox*, where she talks about being a Viennese person dropped into American culture and just seeing it really clearly. And . . . she makes a pretty good case for . . . America being the only place . . . where the everyday can be considered an

> art, because culture and life are such separate things. Like culture is so high and life is so not cultured, but here you have people like John Cage or like Gertrude Stein or people who are really mining those materials of daily life and for whom daily life absolutely has to be—the art has to be vital, useful . . . You know, that whole Puritan thing that it has to be useful, it has to be practical, it has to educate, it has to inform. So it's the frustrating end of the everyday half of the art having to be everyday or workaday. And the other side of it that, is that there can be five different degrees of art starting with everyday life and ending with high art, you know? So that was interesting to me that she pegged that as an American thing, because I never really thought about it before.

While chafing against narrow, instrumental definitions of useful art, a belief in art's practicality and everyday helpfulness does buttress Nature Theater's work, the larger aim of which is a kind of continual perceptual fine-tuning that enriches spectators' appreciation of the world around them. (Without stooping to pat biographical explanations for aesthetic obsessions, it's not irrelevant to mention that Liska has described himself in interviews as a reformed alcoholic and his furious addiction to artmaking as an essential substitute for drinking in combating depression. He needs to see the redeeming beauty in daily life as much as anyone else.)

But, as Liska explained to me, the group's innovative creative process just prepares the ground for the real work that happens in the space between the stage and the seats:

> We are really only concerned with the audience. Whatever happens to me, whatever happens onstage is secondary. Whatever happens onstage is just an excuse to get a group of people in the room. And that's when the real work begins. . . . That's why it's always necessary for Kelly and I to be at the shows—the work, the real work, begins when the audience starts to come in.

When I asked about the group's metaphorical use of the dramatic theater's most hoary conventions and sensational clichés—mysterious late-act entrances and sudden exits, melodramatic gasps and wide-eyed stares, outlandish costumes and trumped-up accents—Liska described them as, essentially, bait, suggesting that the company employs shopworn tropes in order to lure audiences into attending to complex artistic structures:

> For me, it's a way of addressing a context in which we work and also keeping the attention of the audience and finding a way to trick them into actually paying attention to what we want them to pay attention to. Sometimes it's a trick of just like, no, don't worry, it's

> just like you thought it was going to be! It has the proscenium there, there's masking, comedy, tragedy, that's—so far so good, you understand? Nothing strange is going on! No! People have come on with costumes, . . . just like you expected, new person enters two-thirds into the first act, just like you wanted it, right? . . . For me, it's a way of meeting people halfway so that some type of communication happens. And also, on the other hand, finding pleasure, just pure, genuine pleasure, in theater, not fighting against it. This is the form, this is the art form we have chosen, there are a lot of great things about it, you know?

Whether willfully naive or cautiously humanistic, Nature Theater's aesthetic of the everyday does assume that most human beings are united by certain commonalities: the need for stories as meaningful packagings of consciousness, the effort to communicate interior experience with the imperfect tools of language, bodies whose unnoticed grace is worthy of celebration. This makes their theater postdramatic—but certainly not in the sense of an absolute break or departure from received dramatic conventions. Rather, they relish such ready-made experiential shapes, deploying them as vital perceptual shorthand or a wellspring of metaphor. Their pieces continually measure the distance between drift and delineation, both onstage and off, between provisional structures and inevitable loss, clarified experience and mnemonic oblivion.

Nature Theater of Oklahoma has proceeded with its artistic program of panning for what Copper calls "aesthetic gold" in the uncharted territories of American everydayness with the systematic thoroughness and unbridled ambition of a nineteenth-century prospector. It's no accident that Liska speaks of "capturing," "harvesting," or "mining" everyday language and movement. The company is exploiting a renewable natural resource. Beginning by investigating the offhand grace of ordinary movement in *Poetics*, continuing by examining the ingenuity of daily speech in *No Dice*, they went on to consider the uses of well-known stories in the highbrow/lowbrow diptych of *Rambo Solo* and *Romeo and Juliet*. The group's latest series of pieces, *The Life and Times*, still touring until very recently, though finally coming to a close as the company moves on to new aesthetic terrain, synthesizes these concerns by retelling the oral biography of one of Liska and Copper's friends, relayed in an epic multipart series of phone calls, as a nine-episode operatic, theatrical, and filmic epic, one of the most ambitious projects undertaken by downtown theater artists in recent memory. In this chapter, I'll trace this line of aesthetic investigation through a selection of the company's pieces, from everyday movement transformed in *Poetics*, to everyday talk in *No Dice*, to found narrative in *Romeo and Juliet*, and the culmination of these experiments in the first part of *The Life and Times*. Like Stuart Sherman before them, Nature Theater's theater of the everyday is the product of years of continuous artistic research, as much one mammoth ever-expanding performance piece as it is a series of discrete works.

Nature Theater's basic premise that inchoate art exists all around us, waiting for the right revelatory moment of perception, recalls John Dewey's notion of consummation. As we've already seen, Dewey's democratic aesthetic theory posits that a moment of startling, revelatory perception bracketed off from daily life can linger as memorably in the mind as any painting—art is experience, and experience can be art. Art in its more commonly recognized manifestations models this kind of enriched perception, but doesn't exist apart from it. The point is that the experience, whether of making, or beholding, attains what Dewey calls "consummation," in which it arrives at a shapely structure, an organic form based on the realization of its own internal qualities. Like Nature Theater, he posits a spectrum running between life and art, with many moments of dialectical exchange.[10]

Dewey's idea of consummation provides a useful way to illuminate Nature Theater's propensity for revelatory endings to their pieces, moments in which the total design of the piece becomes manifest, when the meanings of what spectators have already experienced retroactively shifts, when they collaboratively rewrite the piece. These sequences, which demand active imaginative participation, model the kind of aesthetic consciousness that transforms everyday events or phenomena into art. They deliberately counter the pessimistic notion that the everyday must inevitably elude such examination. Here is Blanchot again:

> The everyday . . . belongs to insignificance, and the insignificant is without truth, without reality, without secret, but perhaps also the site of all possible signification. The everyday escapes. This makes its strangeness—the familiar showing itself (but already dispersing) in the guise of the astonishing. It is the unperceived, first in the sense that one has always looked past it; nor can it be introduced into a whole or "reviewed," that is to say, enclosed within a panoramic vision; for, by another trait, the everyday is what we never see for a first time, but only see again, having always already seen it by an illusion that is, as it happens, constitutive of the everyday.[11]

Nature Theater's consummating pieces attempt to challenge this sense of the everyday as unperceived and unperceivable, creating fleeting glimpses of panoramic visions capable of reviewing vast swathes of perished experience, and perhaps of allowing spectators to see some of it as if for the first time, in violation of the already-seen-ness that Blanchot so ably describes.

The ramifications of this process bedevil habitual divisions between text and performance, experience and memory. Diana Taylor makes a well-known distinction between the archive and the repertoire. The first of these terms refers to the hardy modes of preserving experience on which we are accustomed to founding the edifices of history and literary culture: documents and literary texts primarily, but also seals, inscriptions, and other sturdy modes of mark-making. The fragile modes of human expression that fall into the gaps between these categories, such as oral storytelling, or the embodied knowledge of dance traditions, or, by extension, even more perishable quantities like the torrents of linguistic invention expended in everyday conversation, or the happy accident of a casual movement apprehended in transit, make up the repertoire, the massive troves of evanescent experience lost to time—as ephemeral as theatrical performance itself. The idea of the repertoire ultimately gestures to an immense, irremediable absence in our understanding of past lives and past cultures, the thoughts, feelings, and words of the billions and billions that went before us.[12]

Nature Theater of Oklahoma's artistic methods deliberately confuse these two terms, making archives from the repertoire, and repertoire from the archive.[13] By means of transcribed audio recordings of conversations between Liska and friends or acquaintances, the company transforms ephemeral utterances into theatrical text, preserving a scrupulous record of chat, down to placeholder sounds and stuttering half-pronunciations that should, in the normal course of things, disappear forever. By rigorously choreographing seemingly offhand movement patterns, they introduce order into accident. Conversely, in retelling canonical dramas or well-known pulp fiction narratives according to the faulty recollections of an interview subject divagating from memory, the company unsettles familiar stories, reminding us that the received and codified version of a text isn't necessarily the one we carry with us in our fallible memory banks. We ultimately forget whole swathes of these stories, or use a personal version for our own ends. In turn, these retellings prompt the uneasy realization that our experiences of art, the first encounter of text and consciousness, are as perishable and unrecoverable as the bulk of our sensations of daily life.

Like the artists I've considered in previous chapters, the company's pieces reverse the usual practices of the mainline American realist theater. Instead of rendering formalized dramatic text made to seem "spontaneous" and "natural" through the studious application of fumbling, stuttering, and uncertain phrasings worked up in the rehearsal room, Nature Theater formalizes spontaneous speech, approaching each recorded hesitancy or malapropism with the seriousness and gravity due the lines of a literary classic. Like the most passionate of Method actors, the company looks for glimmers of artistic truth in the nonsignifying "noise" of speech and behavior—the tics and stammers, ums and uhs—but to vastly different ends. Rather than bestowing the patina of extemporaneous utterance on preexisting text, they transform those hallmarks of spontaneous expression into performance texts. (Also unlike the scriptophiliac mainstream, text, in the sense of a written script, is usually one of the last elements of a production to appear, the record of a piece, rather than its blueprint.)

With its use of precise archival technologies, transcripts, and microscopic attention to notating the answers of interview subjects, Nature Theater's practices suggest those of documentary art, the oral histories popularized by Studs Terkel, perhaps, or especially the prismatic documentary plays of Anna Deavere Smith, Rimini Protokoll's "theater of experts," or the British school of so-called verbatim theater that flourished in the aftermath of 9/11. Recorded testimony is transformed into theatrical texts ratified by real-world origins. But even when Nature Theater's pieces have an ostensible subject—Shakespeare's *Romeo and Juliet*, say—they are not primarily concerned with collecting personal testimony *about* something: a particular historical event, social milieu, or political group. Rather, Nature Theater creates documentary theater that documents the processes of thought itself as it struggles into verbal form. Their pieces narrate narration, capture consciousness's attempts to create transmittable containers for experience or reconstitute a slippery memory, and observe the choreography of words swarming to make meaning.

The company's performance techniques are designed to maintain the spontaneity of this cognitive coalescing. The words to the pieces, too halting and digressive to be easily memorized anyway, are frequently fed to the performers through earpieces. They're thus joining text to gesture and enunciation in time with the recording's flowing stream of consciousness, not enacting a learned score. They're rediscovering the recording's felicities as we encounter them for the first time, and estranging them with mock astonishment.

It is the human capacity for communication that performs first and foremost in the company's work. Their recordings retain the strivings of human minds working to explain themselves. To borrow Walt Whitman's description of the fecund instabilities and innovations of American slanging, Nature Theater is fascinated by "the froth and specks"[14] cast up by everyday talk, surface evidence of the deep submarine movements of consciousness. Unlike Deavere Smith, who precisely mimics the physical idiosyncrasies and vocal quirks of her interviewees to convey more aptly a sense of documentary fidelity to historical specificity, Nature Theater painstakingly reproduces similar tics to achieve allegorical generality.

In this way, closer precedents for their work are the films of Andy Warhol or some of the recording experiments of John Cage, preserving whatever unforeseen and felicitous events the apparatus records, making these aleatory happenings into the unpredictable substance of the artwork. A recent side project for the company has been a painstaking handmade re-creation of Warhol's epic of everyday perception, *Empire*, which trained a camera on the Empire State Building for eight unflinching hours. Nature Theater crowdsourced a hand-drawn cartoon version, inviting prospective collaborators to contribute a few cels. As Cage once put it, "I found that I liked noises even more than I liked intervals. I liked noises just as much as I had liked single sounds. Noises, too, had been discriminated against; and being American, having been trained to be sentimental, I fought for noises."[15] Nature Theater's democratic aesthetic, like Cage's, sticks up for noise, for the accidental, offhand, casual, and half-articulated; for the usually ignored or smoothed-away underdogs of speech and gesture—the material usually considered outside of sense, and outside of art. For Copper and Liska, the ums and ahs are evidence of cognitive labor, revelatory gestures.

The recordings are, of course, edited. Copper, who is also a visual artist, used to make collages of found images, mainly film stills from old home movies, scavenged at flea markets. Her manipulation of the recorded conversations is a similar activity. In an interview with the writer Amber Reed, she describes cutting and splicing the recordings to make "holes," gaps or fissures for spectators to fill in. By doing so, she believes she is being faithful to the hermeneutics, more than the specific content, of everyday conversation: "It's not like when we speak, we make sense necessarily—it's just that the other person translates for us or fills in our blanks."[16] She transfers the role of conversational interlocutor, originally filled by her or Liska, on to the audience.

While watching a Nature Theater piece, we are, in a sense, reprising Copper or Liska's job on the phone, drawing the speakers out with our sustained attention, filling in the empty spaces in the talk with our own imaginative resources, collaboratively writing the dialogue. The uncanny intimacy of phone conversation, its quasi-confessional seclusion separating disclosure from visual scrutiny while closing great distances between speakers, resembles the paradoxical admixture of proximity and anonymity that characterizes a theatrical performance. Theater invites intense, potentially transformative experiences that are designed to be shared by many strangers but will be preserved mostly in personal memory. It promises a direct line of communication from stage to audience and back, connecting performers and spectators, unacquainted to begin with, but becoming progressively more familiar to each other throughout the evening in ways that both preserve privacy and invite intimacy. Theater vaults conventional social barriers to touch intimate truths. At its best, theater is where a group of strangers have profound, deeply private experiences at the same time, and then never see each other again.

If the recordings freeze the wafting drift of conversation, allowing the company to grasp at the branching complexities of everyday talk, the physical life of Nature Theater's productions is pitched to disappearance. Aleatory techniques produce ephemeral alignments of word and gesture, or facial expression and thought, that may never be repeated in even the doubling-with-a-difference mode that a more conventional rehearsal process might produce. In Nature Theater's *Romeo and Juliet*, from a box at the lip of the stage, a prompter cues gestural combinations loosely derived from nineteenth-century acting manuals. In the first part of *The Life and Times*, performers mimic the facial expressions of audience members at that evening's performance, creating a real-time contrast, a feedback loop, between the production's reanimation of piecemeal memories and the perishable present of experience, shared by that evening's serendipitous combination of spectators and performers.[17] Fixity and flux again: the recordings remain, the archived record of ephemeral talk. The gestures vanish: the evanescent combinations have a shorter expiration date than even the usual brief life span of a theatrical flourish.

These aleatory choreographies capture, in an estranging mode, something like the improvisations of everyday communication. We all draw every day on an idiosyncratic trove of words and gestures, at once personal and inherited, our own and common to many. The chance operations also allude to the happenstance of everyday perception: our constantly forgotten thoughts and feelings and our equally fleeting movements, the transitory stuff of everyday experience, arise in cooperation with the unforeseeable stimuli of an average day.

Discussing John Ashbery's poems in her wonderful study of what she calls "everyday poetics" in American poetry, Siobhan Phillips describes the way pronouns shift fluidly in his work between general and personal, "I" and "You," creating what she calls "ordinary and impersonal autobiography."[18] She goes on to suggest that

> his conversational poems make their way only by joining with others in a collective sense of improvisatory decisiveness . . . In this, Ashbery's self-definition seems genuinely democratic; it assumes a group of individuals united by common time. In this, too, his self-expression seems genuinely egalitarian; it aspires to a general relevance driven by common creativity.[19]

Nature Theater's work, too, aspires to a general relevance driven by common creativity. Whether considering the improvisations of quotidian movement, the rich broth of everyday conversation, the creative deployment of ready-made narratives, or the dramatic arc of a nondescript biography, Nature Theater assumes that human beings are united by the basic fact that they're committing creative acts all the time, most of which slip away unnoticed.[20]

This form of experiential humanism is manifested in their pieces by the ways actors unexpectedly and fluidly trade personas and passages of dialogue; by the way that such new or reassigned voices are never introduced or explained in any conventional manner; by the fact that their interview subjects, the "characters" being temporarily embodied, are never named or described. The assumption is that any one of us could have said these things, or things like them. The point is not the particulars of what is said, but the act of trying to say them, the record of extemporaneous conversational ingenuity or real-time mnemonic archaeology, the general relevance of human beings' common creativity.

Nature Theater's work haunts the shifting margin between art and life, partially undoing the difference between the two terms, even as they continue to reassert the importance of an aesthetic realm marked off from everyday experience. For them, art functions as an essential pole in dialectical exchange, an outside reference point, a source of experiential tools—like dramatic conventions—and useful metaphors, containers for experience. The importance of dialectically crossing and recrossing the shifting borders between art and life is literally staged in Nature Theater's pieces when, as frequently occurs in their work, performers move back and forth from stage to audience, and it is also staged perceptually, as we are forced to readjust our evaluation of the aesthetic or nonaesthetic properties of a household gesture, a normally overlooked demi-word (like "like") or a line of everyday talk.

Manifest Destiny: *Poetics: A Ballet Brut*

Poetics: a ballet brut, the group's first piece, which began as Liska's final M.F.A. directing project at Columbia University and was later performed at Riverside Church in New York City in 2006 and then at the 2008 Under the Radar Festival, can be profitably considered in light of Nature Theater's sweeping aspiration to a kind of aesthetic manifest destiny, heading, like Karl riding Kafka's speeding train, ever deeper into America's strange, uncharted zones.[21] Announcing, manifesto-like, the company's vast territorial ambitions, the hour-long dance theater piece stages simultaneously, along crossing vectors, the takeover of the aesthetic space of the theater by movements grabbed from the run of everyday life, and the widening of that aesthetic space to encompass the theater's workaday zones, as well as the privileged podium of the stage. By the time the piece is over, dancing has colonized the auditorium, the technicians' booth, even the hallways outside the auditorium, with the implication that this process will continue as spectators filter back into the world outside, their eyes (and perhaps their bodies, too) primed by the piece to register grace in unusual locales. Even as the stage grows more expansive, taking in the hidden utilitarian places normally unnoticed in performance, *Poetics*' choreographies enact a dialectical exchange between artistic and inartistic movement, represented, as the piece's title suggests, by ballet's geometric silhouettes, at one pole, and the pedestrian business of drinking a cup of take-out coffee or shifting listlessly in an office chair, at the other.

When, precisely, does one kind of movement shade into the other? When does a series of movements become choreography, and an utterly banal and forgettable gesture cross the border into the realm of art? When does simple movement become dance? What are the added elements that prompt this shift in registers? Is it unison, or the presence of catchy music to accompany the movement, or is it the number of performers onstage? *Poetics* toys with all these variables, adding and taking away, until the line between life and art, between moving and dancing, has shifted decisively. These questions make *Poetics* a poetics. In a manner prefiguring their later use of ready-made materials, Liska and Copper began with nothing—no textual blueprint, no preexisting narrative—except their performers' bodies, aleatory choreographic techniques, and the aesthetic space of the theater itself, with its attendant expectations. The piece flirts with conventional narrative, or rather with spectators' ability to construct narrative out of spatial relationships and gestural evidence. Narrative is an act of perception, the piece reminds us, continually revised and updated as we watch. We construct provisional containers for the evidence before us, renovating them or discarding them as necessary. In Nature Theater's work, narrative and storytelling are subjects, not objects, media but not necessarily messages.

The stories *Poetics* tells are really about form: about space, qualities of movement, and the modes of seeing that create distinctions between them. *Poetics* compels spectators to move constantly between perceptual registers: between the kinds of seeing we do when we look at art, as opposed to the more mundane glances that notice less or tune away the world to make it manageable to look at. This is perhaps its most intricate form of choreography, a dance of enriched sight.

Spectators enter the theater through a side entrance down an alley. When we arrive, we're not sure where we are: a rehearsal room, somewhere backstage, or a small black-box theater. All we can see is a narrow slice of stage running before closed curtains. As *Poetics* begins, the architecture of seeing and performing seems to follow the most conventional proscenium pattern possible. The audience looks on as the four company members enter, one after another, stopping to adopt nondescript poses at staggered intervals along the stage's forced-flat pictorial plane. Dressed in thrift shop T-shirts and sneakers, bringing along messenger bags and take-out coffee cups, they look as though they could be waiting for a bus. One stands, arms crossed. Another clasps his hands behind his head in an attitude of display. They acknowledge each other's efforts, and the presence of the audience with preverbal noises and facial expressions that hint at communication but don't resolve into legible attitudes: throat-clearing, dry chuckles, grunts of apprehension, snorts of derision.

Soon, the lachrymose piano and flute strains of "All By Myself" swell up, to accompany this study in being by oneself or being with others. Of course, none of them is really by themselves, as their frequent and frank glances at spectators make clear. The performers pause to stand together in opposed pairs, or abruptly walk offstage, only to reenter to the accompaniment of some momentous-sounding sentimental swelling in the score. They're still doing the same old movements, but the music makes them seem outrageously significant, positively pregnant with meaning. Throughout the piece, we're given many opportunities to meditate on the power of musical accompaniment to create dance out of gestural dross, transforming sequences of steps performed haphazardly by performers standing alongside each other into groovy unison numbers.

Soon, the happenstance of the first passage changes to more organized choreographic routine. "You Should Be Dancing" urges a throbbing disco beat as the performers settle into a group rendition of their earlier solo efforts. But the implication of using these humdrum moves to make the dance is that maybe you already are dancing, much of the time, without really knowing it. The piece's score is like someone's party playlist of bouncy dance music favorites about dancing, full of various exhortations to get up and shake it—get on the scene, do your thing, don't stop till you get enough, she's the dancing queen, you can dance if you want to. With its cheerily blatant recorded accompaniments, and atmosphere of can-do amateurish gumption, *Poetics* looks at times like a karaoke ballet.

Suddenly a strange pell-mell sequence erupts, seeming to mock the very idea of narrative choreography with semiotic superabundance. Jogging with enthusiasm, one performer frenziedly gesticulates oblique pantomimic signs. She is trying to convey some kind of story we can't penetrate: cradling an imaginary baby, groping her chest, pointing emphatically away from herself, resting upthrust fingers on her forehead to signify horns. Next to the ordinary movements that have preceded this outburst, her antics seem altogether too symbolic. They're packed with so many private meanings it becomes almost as hard to ascribe artistic meaning to them as it ordinarily would be to impute aesthetic significance to everyday actions like drinking coffee from a take-out cup or clearing one's throat. This series becomes a leitmotif in the piece, passed between performers, interrupting more colloquial movements with the promise of some kind of mythic story waiting to be realized. In light of the occasional *Swan Lake* references that pepper the piece's teasing conversation with ballet, some of the overwrought gestures—horns on head, cradled baby, frantic pointing—seem almost to allude to another tragic animal story about to be told through narrative dance (*seem*, of course, being the operative term).

Meanwhile, we've been helplessly constructing provisional stories almost in spite of ourselves in response to spatial arrangements, the groupings and regroupings of the performers. But the piece is more about spectators' ability to see such momentous patterns in arrangements of gestures and dispositions of space than any one of those possible patterns. Even more important, it articulates the company's expansionist artistic plans.

The performer continues the series, now seated in an office chair, as the curtains are raised to reveal the deep red square of the stage, and, beyond, the shadowy rows of another auditorium, standing empty. Suddenly, we realize we're sitting on the stage of a much larger theater. This is the first of the piece's many territorial expansions. Having discovered choreographic togetherness, the performers are laying claim to the stage. (Periodically, one performer rolls off the stage into the inky unknown with a startled yelp, marking its borders.)

An essential part of *Poetics* is the reconsideration of simple movement phrases from multiple angles and in multiple combinations of performers and gestures. One series from this next section begins with a performer crossing and uncrossing his legs while seated in a wheeled office chair, shifting to rest a foot on the opposite knee, moving through attitudes of repose with as much seriousness of purpose as a ballerina working through pointe positions. The movements are vaguely reminiscent of the shifting and shuffling we spectators are doing in our own seats. This sequence repeats in myriad configurations—standing, sitting, reclining, with music, without, as solo, as duet—as though daring spectators to spot the exact moment it transforms from monotony to meaning. At one point the scale of the choreography shrinks radically to just the performers' hands. Laying on the stage, they reprise the crossing-uncrossing leg movements with their fingers, making tiny dancers of their digits. Later, it forms the basis for boisterous *Riverdance*-style hopping and stepping. Here again is *Poetics* as a poetics: the movements passed back and forth between performers stage a gestural version of the invitation to contemplate common creativity that Siobhan Phillips finds in John Ashbery's poetry. We all dance through our days doing personal versions of choreographies like these, at once entirely particular to ourselves and almost archetypal in their generality.

Midway through, a performer comes downstage and adopts a public-speaking stance, as though he is the *raisonneur* figure come to tell us what the piece is about. "Blah blah blah," he says, "Yadda yadda yadda," punctuating nonsense syllables with the emphatic hand motions of a practiced politician. In a sense, this *is* what the piece is about. Its choreographies are transforming the "noise" of everyday movement, the constant play of gesture and expression habitually tuned out into a background hum and signifying nothing, into music. It's making sense of non-sense by looking at it in a new way.

Poetics teases with balletic structure. It has solos (one for each performer at various intervals in the piece) and duets, trios and unison full-company dances, swooning stage crosses. One performer, long-haired, tattooed, handlebar-moustached, more biker than ballerina, rips his shirt off and grimly works through some ballet positions, leaping and jete-ing with fierce resolve, mixing the classical steps with the office-chair vocabulary from before, then traveling headlong across the stage, arms flung back like the wings of a dying swan, running into the winds of fate. Juxtaposing this parodic ballet stage-crossing with a similar diagonal trajectory achieved by furiously propelling a wheeled office chair provokes serious consideration of what, exactly, we are moved by when contemplating such gestures. Is it the intrinsically aesthetic properties of ballet's stock phrases set into clockwork motion, or simply the sight of sudden and swift movement at an opportune moment? Similarly, when a performer raises his arms into a balletic arrangement while seated in that prosaic chair, does it spoil the gracefulness of the pose or prod us into seeing it afresh?

We're constantly reminded of the performers as bodies at work. They take breaks to guzzle sporty energy drinks. Midway through, headset-wearing technicians come out with fresh thrift shop T-shirts to replace their sweaty predecessors (how often do we see ballerinas perspire?). While James Brown's strutting "Super Bad" blasts from the speakers, they take off their shirts to display tattoos, chest hair, sports bras, slight paunchiness or gym-trained bulk. We are very far from ballet's eugenic ideals of bodily perfection. Instead, we're encouraged to see the aesthetic merits of untrained bodies incandescent with the desire to dance, working hard to hit their marks.

The piece's third movement shifts from staging everyday public gestures to private ones: tossing and turning in sleep (to the haunting strains of Hawaiian slide guitar); caressing an intimate acquaintance's face; pairing off for inaudible, intimate chats; leaning in for a kiss; or reassuringly squeezing a shoulder. Having already mined outdoor and workplace behavior, the piece moves "indoors." We've observed the ways in which the space between bodies can create unbidden narratives; we now contemplate those bodies making contact. This shift in emphasis prompts closer attention to the mixed private-public dynamics of both theatrical performance and theatrical spectatorship. We might recall Thornton Wilder's creative use of a similar structure in his early plays. Although seated together, constituting an improvised and temporary community united by a common object of attention, *Poetics*'s audience also resounds with the hum of many individual minds creating private versions of the experience of watching the piece. The performers are exhibiting public versions of private gestures that usually pass unnoticed, or are performed for a distracted audience of one; spectators are busily constructing a private narrative in a public place.

After carrying out several renditions of this sequence, the company filters from the stage into the audience, picking out particular spectators to caress, squeeze, or amicably peck on the cheek. The encounters are consensual and friendly, seemingly unhurried and conducted with no aim beyond making contact. Audience members don't have to respond in any particular way, and no particular action is demanded of them. The exercise renders tangible the unspoken intimacy of theatrical encounter. Though we haven't really been introduced to the performers, we'll spend the piece's duration looking at them unabashedly. Our anonymous glances are integral to their project. This violation of the already porous border between stage and house, art and life—the company is making a claim on us, annexing the audience to the piece—prefigures the dialectical fantasia of *Poetics*'s showboating finale, in which spectators and performers, stage and house get permanently confused.

After a final, full-company rendition of the lively stepping-and-hopping dance from before, and a winsome solo dance recapitulating the piece's accumulated trove of movements—smoking a cigarette, explaining, cradling the baby, a little scruffy ballet—the curtains close, and then open again to display a giant chorus of performers, perhaps forty or so, who we've never seen before. They're cheerful young people in casual outfits, bopping through versions of earlier dances with big Broadway grins on their faces, backed by strobing lights. In defiance of the piece's scrappy do-it-yourself aesthetic, we now have an unapologetically huge production number, the simple choreography augmented by light, sound, and the sheer number of bodies suddenly onstage. The performers scamper back to join in the general hullabaloo, prompting raucous audience participation, the clapping and cheering rendered more meaningful by earlier investigations of the mutual necessity of spectators and stage.

After the curtains blink again, the stage is moodily blue-lit and flooded by dry ice, as befits a climactic passage in some romantic ballet, with a ballerina, resplendent in pink tutu and slippers, tripping lightly across it. Traveling on pointe, she begins to perform a version of the company's homespun routines, applying horns to her head, pointing suddenly away, transposing their rough-hewn enthusiasms into the geometric grammar of classical ballet. This sequence should look more like "dance" than anything we've seen till now, a perfected version of the steps beyond the reach of Nature Theater's unstudied cavorting. The lines are clean and straight; the performer's long-limbed, well-tutored body executes precise choreography with virtuosic ease; she's appropriately costumed, and the onstage atmospherics suggest mystery and exaltation. But somehow, now that we've been seduced by Nature Theater's amateurish charms, by passionate enthusiasm and cultivated idiosyncrasy, the ballerina's efforts look somehow less artful than what came before, too hidebound by convention, too impersonal, too cold. Her methods impose art on spectators from outside by way of tradition and expectation rather than allowing them to freshly apply such definitions themselves.

When the curtains part once more, the huge chorus of supernumeraries that graced the stage moments before is seated in duplicate banks of seats across the way. What seemed at the outset to be a proscenium stage was always a platform between two auditoriums. From their chairs, mirroring the arrangement of *Poetics*'s actual spectators, they perform a dance based on spectator behaviors, like shifting in place and grooving constrainedly to the music, and on more extreme kinds of fan activity cribbed from sports or rock concerts, like doing the wave and hoisting their shirts to flash the stage, all in time to the throbbing disco score. Meanwhile, the ballerina is still skipping across the stage and, mixing ballet with *brut*, is now subjecting her classical technique to the score's bouncing bass lines. This sequence reminds spectators that they too have been performing this whole time, acting the roles of attentive watchers.

The choreography of spectatorship becomes worthy of consideration in its own right. Though an integral part of the performance, which has been sustained by the continued attention of its audience members, their quiet labors have been carried out almost invisibly, as they almost always are at conventional theatrical performances. But now, looking out at the chorus, our joyful double, dancing their appreciation for the ballerina's efforts, spectators are given a moment to appreciate afresh their own role in creating the performance, and the subtle ways in which their own quotidian movements—leaning in to focus on the choreographic patterns onstage, crossing and uncrossing legs, shifting subtly in unconscious unison with fellow spectators sitting beside them—are as worthy of renewed appraisal as those freshly burnished by Nature Theater's dances. The performance has actually been a duet danced between stage and auditorium.

In this and other moments of gleeful spectacle, *Poetics* also announces an amicable but necessary intellectual break with the group of artists whose innovating efforts haunt *Poetics*'s quotidian choreographies, the Judson Church Dancers. Choreographers like Steve Paxton and Yvonne Rainer deliberately adopted pedestrian movement partly in order to strip away sensationalism from dance spectatorship: to stop audience members from looking for the high points, radical extensions, and classically harmonious bodily feats characteristic of both ballet and Martha Graham. Their art became, at least in Rainer's case, private-in-public, carried on despite or with the audience rather than for it. Nature Theater pursues the opposite strategy, transforming mundane steps into outrageous spectacle in order to, paradoxically, preserve their mundanity, while simultaneously lending them a (hopefully lasting) highlighting halo of strangeness. The idea is that once you've seen *Poetics* you'll never look at somebody drinking from a take-out coffee cup the same way again—and that you'll look for longer when you do.

Once more the curtains close, and when they snap open, stage and house have been vacated, but outside the auditorium, in the backstage areas beyond, hallways coldly washed by institutional fluorescents are bursting with movement. The company leaps and gambols past open doors, a blur of joyful agitation. The technicians too are visibly bopping in the control booth. Having spread from stage to seats, dance has now left the theater proper and is lighting up areas normally reserved for the invisible labor of theater-making, where cues are called, entrances awaited. And by implication, perhaps its wildfire movement will continue further, carried out into the world by departing spectators. (And by Nature Theater's future work, the prospecting efforts of which are foretold by *Poetics*'s unstoppable expansionism.) The winking motion of the curtain in these final passages suggests the minute perceptual realignments we make all the time as our eyelids close and open, interrupting and re-creating our sense of the world many times each minute.

In the piece's resplendent conclusion, the core company members and scene-swelling extras unite onstage to form an exultant chorus, performing a massive unison version of a simple box step derived from earlier sequences. The dance isn't particularly challenging. The scene's spectacular appeal derives from the range of bodies—sizes, shapes, hues, hairstyles—arrayed onstage. Each performs the steps according to his or her ability. The image provides a glimpse of how Nature Theater sees the world, everyone dancing, all the time, if only we could notice.

Dancing to the Cosmic Murmur: John Cage, Richard Foreman, and *No Dice*

If *Poetics* was a manifesto, announcing and embodying with its territorial claims Nature Theater's mandate of aesthetic expansionism, *No Dice* (2007) put those principles into enlarged practice.[22] One way to think about the piece is as an extended session of aesthetic shadowboxing between two conflicting artistic principles governing how one makes art out of everyday experience and the divagations of everyday consciousness, embodied by two of the figures Liska and Copper have called their most important artistic predecessors, John Cage, and Richard Foreman. Liska worked with Foreman during his early years in New York City. Let's call these two principles the continuous present (inherited from Gertrude Stein) and the Zen gaze. *No Dice* employs both, pitting them against each other, before joyfully torquing the terms of the debate. Seeing this process in sequence helps to preserve the piece's sudden transformations of shape and meaning, an integral part of its purpose and dramaturgy. In my account I'll attempt to preserve this element of surprise, striving to capture what it was like to be startled out of complacent viewing habits, engendered by both theatrical and day-to-day perceptual conventions, by *No Dice*.

Upon entering the performance space for *No Dice*, a renovated former indoor playground on White Street in lower Manhattan, you get in line for a sandwich, prepared on the spot by Copper and Liska. They offer a choice between peanut butter and jelly and ham and cheese, nursery food for a nursery setting. Signs enjoining adults to stay off the equipment, remnants of the room's old purpose, still adorn the walls. The free meal is a welcome surprise to audience members plainly rushing from work. The show begins at 6:30 p.m., in deference to its four-hour duration. The Financial District site was specially adapted for *No Dice*. The show is a brief aesthetic blip in the building's commercial life, an aberration between renters. The program provides a real estate agent's telephone number in case a spectator is moved to move in. Even before the performance begins, life and art have been jostled into an unstable relation. Continuing *Poetics*'s policy of aesthetic expansionism, the piece is taking place in nontheatrical environs, in a neighborhood dedicated to hard-edged commerce, and at a time that rubs up against the pressures of the working day. Moreover, here are the piece's creators, visibly part of the event, hard at work making and serving their audience members' dinners (while hawking T-shirts and other Nature Theater knickknacks). But all this, of course, is very much the point. *No Dice* is about the dynamic interplay, and mutual interpenetration, of art and everyday life, and the various ways one sustains the other.

The pastel-hued stage for *No Dice*, its play school colors repurposed as corporate blandness, is subdivided loosely into planes of "art" and "life." Upstage, fluorescent lights blanch office cubicles; downstage, a tatty hand-painted proscenium arch holds a makeshift curtain, garish cardboard comedy and tragedy masks leering from above. The actors begin upstage, popping their heads up from behind cubicle walls as they commence reciting *No Dice*'s looping, halting, ambling text. Throughout the piece, they wander between the set's embodied principles, a constant visual counterpoint to the script's thematic zigzagging.

At first Richard Foreman's influence looms, seemingly a defining presence. The principal performers look like the kind of kitsch archetypes-cum-hermetic emblems that populate his fevered stages. One wears Hasidic sidecurls and a pirate's hat, declaiming his lines in enthusiastic but erroneous Jamaican patois. A second, clad in khaki shorts, sleeveless shirt, and cowboy hat, resembles Australian rough trade but speaks with an accent that wanders the greater United Kingdom. The third is a perpetually surprised pixie in black fishnets and bustier, wincing and simpering in parody-French cadences. Two other mostly silent performers—powdered wig and sunglasses; mouse ears and cape—stalk the margins of the stage, playing snatches of accompanying music alternately boisterous and hip–hop-inflected and schlockily Vincent Price-sinister. It is as though the central figures from a Foreman play have fled his omnipresent supervision and wandered further downtown, taking the script with them, but leaving behind the director's bellicose apparatus of interference—the buzzers, the perspectival string-lines, and the harsh sound effects—behind. At this point, the spectator can't help but receive the piece's stumbling text as Foremanesque attempts to ambush language while it isn't looking, sidestepping structure with opposing impulses. (It turns out to be something else altogether, but we're not quite there yet.) There is no overbearing deity-voice blaring on intercom in *No Dice*, but there is a theological dynamic. The actors all wear earpieces, the text is coming from elsewhere, and the performers are mouthpieces for some absent presence.

The three main performers congregate in pairs or trios to converse at cross-purposes about deliberately banal subjects: filling in time request forms for Walmart, feeling guilty about occupying a day job in real estate, making the rounds as a voice-over actor, Mel Gibson's great roles, the inability to avoid drinking to excess: "I wanna—you know . . . / I just— / I think that's the drinking—is— / that's the prob— / biggest problem I have with / DRINKING is that it / gives you a break. / (*pause. Breath.*) / And I don't necessarily need a / break from THINKING . . . / (*pause*) / -or even feeling! / . . . I just need a- / need to have LITTLE breaks!"[23]

But though certain passages return, passed back and forth between the performers, the play's language mostly treads water. It's trapped in the continuous present by a contradictory acting style that treats excruciatingly quotidian routine with bemused astonishment and humdrum small talk with exaggerated sorrow. The piece's digressive movement score counterpoises the work-talk with groovy little dances, and frivolous exchanges with abstruse gestural figures (hands cinching an imaginary belt, thumbs jabbing the sky disco-style, tugging an invisible bell-pull). The payoffs are mostly moment-to-moment, an uproariously quizzical glance, an abrupt and comically unmotivated exit, a felicitous dissonance between word and gesture.

The preoccupations of the text are Foremanesque as well, repeatedly returning to the difficulties of telling narrative (or, by extension, making a play). A passage in which one actor asks another to tell a story, only to see the attempt fail, is a leitmotif traded between voices:

> ANNE: (*pause*): You know any good stories?
> (ZACK *enters*)
> BOBBY:(*pause*) I don't know . . . (*pause*) Stories about what?
> ANNE: Anything. (pause). Make—somethin'—
> BOBBY: Well . . .
> ANNE:—tell me a story! Or make one up.
> BOBBY: Ha ha! A fictional—?
> ANNE: A-amuse me.
> BOBBY:—story?
> ANNE: Yeah. Amuse me.
> Bobby: Oh God. (*pause*) Well there was that thing in—about—the party . . . ? This story isn't going to go anywhere! Gha!
> ANNE: Ha!
> BOBBY: Ha! Nevermind. Ha ha ha ha ha! Terrible story.
> ANNE: Which one?
> BOBBY: Ahhh ghhh. No! It's awful. Uh. (*pause*) Um . . . (*pause*) NO! I don't know any goddamn stories!
> ANNE: Uh huh.[24]

These capsized efforts at communication, coupled with *No Dice*'s own apparently meandering formlessness, seem to be making points about the imprisoning effect of consciousness, the inadequacy of language, and the ultimate foolishness of any artfully constructed narrative.

Another refrain, in which one performer haltingly consoles another, also sounds pitched to its own failure, stuffed with bromides and anodyne statements of generic optimism. Late in the piece, the actors move into the audience and deliver it to particular spectators in gentle, consoling tones, and its meaning will be very different.

> BOBBY: Well . . . good to talk to you! / I—I'm—I'm sh-sorry that, um . . . (*breath*) / things are not rosy at your workplace. / (*pause*) / But I know that if you / you know, I mean . . . / I-I think . . . you got (*pause*) / GREAT STUFF— / ahead of you. You know I / mean, I think if you—if you— / you should just GO for / it!–you know? / You should just— / follow that. (*pause*) / I think your in-instinct

is right. / (*pause*) / And—and—and seems like you're (*breath*) / stepping on the right. . . . (*pause*) / ROAD. (*pause*) / —you know? / Just—if you—you know— / putting yourself in the way / of . . . / (*big breath*) / somethin' / (*pause*) So something's / gonna . . . / HAPPEN! . . . I THINK GOOD THINGS ARE / A' COMIN'! / (*big pause*) / You know, I mean like— / you know, the beginning of the / MILLENNIUM . . . / things are . . . / bound to . . . TURN AROUND! / And I feel like there's a lot of— / lot of good WORK being / done . . . and a lot of / —GOOD ENERGY. . . . and . . . maybe . . . I'm just more / NAÏVE and—and / (*breath*)— / and STUPID-? / Pfft!—and— / UNINFORMED? / And that's why I may—maybe / OPTIMISTIC? / You know, but I-I feel- I feel / good things are (*pause*) / You know . . . if you . . .

ZACK: Well, they're definitely out / there—it's just a matter of . . .

BOBBY: Yeah.

ZACK: —how you work your way toward them.

BOBBY: Yeah. (*pause*) / Well—I think— / I think we're working our way towards each other . . . So let's get together and eat / some hot dogs or / something.[25]

From time to time, the ghost of a conventional plotline exerts pressure on the stage, only to fade away again. Near the end of the first act, a mysterious new character, Kelly Copper in luxuriant green, makes a grand, protracted, entrance while talking about the desire to make a grand, protracted, entrance to an expectant audience:

> ONE PICTURE . . . I always think about . . . is some UNBELIEVABLE—TOTALLY STEREOTYPICAL—SEXY DIVA ENTRÉE—ONSTAGE! . . . I love like, you know—PERFORMANCES on stage just have these sort of . . . LEADING. . . . like they LEADING toward something . . . there's gonna be a CHARACTER that's gonna COME and . . . I LOVE that EXPECTATION! . . . as an AUDIENCE? . . . Like "Oh my gosh! What's going on!?" . . . then you KNOW he's gonna arrive, and he FINALLY ARRIVES!—and it's like "OHHH! My goodness!" You know? . . . I'm saying that's the . . . EASIEST THING! an actor can do. If everything has been PREPARED for you . . . ! You don't have to do ANYTHING—just . . . ENTER AS GOOD as you CAN ! . . . You ALREADY favorite . . . It's almost like . . . if we can IMAGINE that . . . the person would just have to come on stage and LEAVE, and he would be the star of the play![26]

She promptly exits, having simultaneously achieved and explained her dramatic function. Similarly, right after intermission the performers begin discussing some terrible event that has just transpired:

ANNE: Did you get that email from Matt?
ZACK: (*speaking again with Irish accent*) Yeah! That's horrible!
ANNE: Isn't that weird?
ZACK: (*big breath*) It's so . . . That's so strange.[27]

We never learn what has happened (or, for that matter, who Matt is).

At intervals throughout the piece, one of the musicians, clad in sinister black, stalks around the stage to creepy thriller music, a melodrama villain without a virginal damsel to persecute. With all of these incidents Nature Theater excites conventional theatrical expectations to point to their persistent power as experiential deep structure. We all spend our days devising dramas to dignify our daily round of strutting and fretting, casting the villains that oppose us, enlarging our triumphs and painting mishaps with tragic grandeur. These eruptions of drama are also an early indication of the way that the creaky well-made plot of the tacky dinner theater mystery discussed in parts of the text is providing a shadow armature for *No Dice*, explaining the performers' outlandish costumes and accents.

Now comes a reversal as profound as any Sophocles could arrange. In the closing moments of *No Dice*, a scene of recognition transpires that, with an almost Aristotelian thoroughness, retroactively transforms the spectator's entire experience of the piece. The landscape shifts and reorders itself as though, having trekked through scrub and undergrowth for three hours, we have emerged onto a promontory, and now, from a distance, can see the contours of the terrain we have traveled. Disparate features merge into a suddenly legible image.

The lights go down, and on a screen pushed downstage by one of the performers, we see the projected transcript of a recorded conversation between Liska and actor Anne Gridley's mother. They discuss her second visit to a scrappy South Dakota dinner theater, the one, we realize, whose kitschy amateurishness has been a recurring feature in *No Dice*'s looping text. The first time, the performers floundered; this time, she says, the play was much different:

> they MANAGED the accents. . . . one of them used—even managed to have a cockney accent! And . . . that—that—was APPROPRIATE! . . .'cause he was a taxi driver. . . . so . . . It worked! It—it just—everything WORKED! . . . And I'm very excited about this—this little group that—you know, really work hard and struggle, and PERFORM and—you know are trying to build a new theater . . .[28]

Just as the struggling troupe's wretched first effort has given way to something more accomplished and theatrical, so too does the Nature Theater's play begin to mutate from a witty, ironic, Foremanesque meditation on consciousness—clothed in camp, performed in an eddying continuous present—into a higher unity, drawing together all the piece's raveled verbal threads in a stunning moment of aesthetic alchemy. We realize that recorded conversations like this one have formed the entire text of the piece: more than a hundred hours of discussions between Nature Theater members, and with relatives, friends, and colleagues (including Richard Foreman, as the introduction to the published script of *No Dice* stipulates).[29] What sounded like ironic pastiche is actually archival preservation. Rather than making a postmodern pessimist statement about prefabricated culture speaking through people, the piece has been mining verbal ingenuity from habitual speech.

In this, Nature Theater resembles the great collector hermit of the American avant-garde, Jack Smith. Just as Smith accumulated cultural debris in his loft, saving perishable kitsch from disappearance, *No Dice* preserves huge heaps of verbal detritus. The number of words, spoken or merely thought, banal or beautiful, used and discarded in a single conversation, the narrative ingenuity that goes into following a line of talk or ordering the scattershot sensory messiness of a day's perception are fantastic quantities for the Nature Theater, worthy of preservation. Ideational kitsch is piled alongside lapidary flashes of insight. Like Smith, they practice an aesthetic of aggregation, grains adding up into a heap. At one point, the speakers discuss a webcam poised over Times Square, registering the constant traffic across New York's most caffeinated stage. The cam's unbiased stare, gazing at whatever crosses its lens, its elevated perspective estranging the doings of the tiny figures moving below, seeing them as individual sounds in a constant murmur of activity, all suggest Nature Theater's own project, using technology's democratic ear to catch the murmurings of everyday thought normally tuned out or left to evaporate. The piece is full of references to technologies of recording: the cam, the films that the voices discuss trying out for, and of course, the conversation-in-progress itself.

The wacky costumes and goofy accents adopted by Nature Theater's performers derive directly from the South Dakota troupe's outlandish efforts, as do the recurring vestiges of melodramatic plot that have stalked the periphery of the piece. And now, we see that we too have just spent the evening at a piece of dinner theater, erasing the difference between the temporary community cemented with a meal at a tacky dive theater in Worthing, South Dakota, and that created by an experimental theater company that makes sandwiches in downtown New York. The discussions of office work minutiae and the vicissitudes of the actor's life are not simply satirical indictments of corporate ennui or show business banality, but documents from the company's life while making the piece, recording the sacrifices of time and creativity that were necessary to earn space for artistic work. Nature Theater incorporated all the day job hours that sustained them during *No Dice*'s creation into the total story the piece tells, redeeming those hours from waste in the process.[30] The frivolous gestures that accompanied dull workplace conversation look less like Foreman-style complication of signification and more like attempts to enliven deadening routine, a playful retrospective act of artistic embellishment. Liska: "The limitations of making theatre are what made me quit theatre five years ago and the limitations are what made me come back to it. . . . I wanted to figure out how to deal with everything as material and not obstacles—to use everything as creative material."[31]

At this point, Richard Foreman is countered by John Cage. What looked like irony and extreme subjectivity, the solipsistic fancies of the company, is objective and earnest, rooted in the ideas of others. A show that seemed irretrievably inward-looking has been turned inside out; everything inside is, in fact, only a frame for realities from "outside." Art's subjectivity must be tempered with objective methods, the piece suggests, if it is to communicate, rather than remain the vehicle of an endless archaeology of the self.

Both *No Dice* and *Poetics* were choreographed using chance operations. *Poetics* was based on numerical patterns determined by rolling dice. Each face on the die indicated a particular gesture, and a second roll decided which limb would perform it. A dreidel determined the duration of sequences and the spatial placement of actors.[32] The word-stuffed *No Dice*, as its title suggests, abandoned this method for three-fourths of a pack of playing cards, each suit representing a different trove of physical vocabulary: one derived from a DVD of magic tricks, one inspired by disco dancing, and one based on the sign language employed by Liska's Slovak-speaking mother to communicate a story to his English speaking-cast.[33] Sounding very much like Cage, Liska has said that this aleatory dramaturgy allowed the company to get out of the way of its own work: "Everybody is learning from it as opposed to everybody arguing . . . You're fighting with a force that's outside of you."[34] This flickering semaphore—vagrant signifiers unloosed from their signifieds—also serves as an insistent reminder of the miracle of everyday talk, of how many disparate gestures, words, and meanings must line up to achieve a single precarious instant of communication. But the piece's dialectic is not as simple as Cagean reframed reality surpassing Foreman-style interior drama.

As the conversation progresses, and Teresa reveals how excited she is to hear "how well *No Dice* has gone,"[35] how surprised she is that so many of her words have been used, the piece's even larger aims suddenly leap into view. Liska tells her that "You wrote half of our play!" and Teresa admits that she "REALLY FELT (*very long pause*) VERY FLATTERED."[36] *No Dice* has been an alchemical exercise in the refinement of everyday creativity into art. The company gives new meaning to Richard Schechner's definition of performance as "twice-restored behavior."[37] They are returning ephemeral mundane experience, smelted by art to a poetic brilliance, to the world, and giving that experience back to its original authors—brighter, clearer than before, its previously invisible glories suddenly apparent.

Two passages from earlier in the piece erupt back into the mind:

> BOBBY: . . . We don't hear ourselves. / We just talk, and—and / things . . . things go unrecorded. / The—the creativity . . . that we— / that we . . . uh . . . USE! (*pause*) to— / To let's say to talk right now / or to . . . LATER or . . . ! / Or the conversation that we / have . . . / It all goes unnoticed and / unrecorded. / We don't—We don't consider / it—! / It's not part of— / We take it for granted! / We don't—we don't make / anything out of it. / And then . . . how can we / transform this . . . / universal cosmic murmur . . . ?! / This—this uh—(*pause*) / STREAM of constant— / into-into-so that we can / notice it!? / So that when . . . after you see—(*breath*) . . .
>
> ANNE: —to feel that connection!
>
> BOBBY: Yeah!–to the connection, / to the—to the—to the— / how can you—? / How can you then go / through. . . . / through your day . . . hearing music constantly?[38]

And:

> BOBBY: That's what the storyteller is / for. / because some—uh, the— / there— / there's a whole population of people / who / (*pause*) / who can't do that, but need / it to be done . . . ! / Who need that sort of— / they need that in their lives! / And so . . . there is a group of people, / a CLASS of people / . . . who exist to do things for people that they— / that people cannot do for themselves . . .[39]

The total event of the piece itself is the primordially theatrical story that *No Dice* is telling, a group of performers getting together to transform the fragilely meaningful words and experiences of others into art, to accomplish something for them that they cannot do themselves. But this change in the show's molecular structure is achieved primarily within the minds of the spectators, who also become, in turn, storytellers in their own right, transforming the raw stuff of lived consciousness into exquisitely complex artistic form. It is the human facility for making artistic shapes, finding meaningful containers for experience, that *No Dice* ultimately celebrates, and Nature Theater pays its audience the great compliment of assuming they can accomplish the imaginative task of rebuilding the entire architecture of the piece they have just seen.

Paradoxically, it is at *No Dice*'s most "Cagean" moment—that is, as recorded speech from the outside world is allowed to speak directly for itself within the frame of the piece—that *No Dice* also shows itself most clearly as a highly wrought aesthetic entity. Here, then, is Nature Theater's artistic answer to John Cage. Cage's central premise was that "daily life is excellent and that art introduces us to it and to its excellence the more it begins to be like it."[40] But Cage's Olympian detachment implicitly advocated acceptance of the world as beautiful in its received shape. The difference between art and life was simply a matter of perception, opening the former's frame to allow the latter in. The Nature Theater holds to the first half of Cage's maxim, while differing with the second. To Liska and Copper, daily existence is indeed chock-full of tiny acts of creativity, minute artworks in their own right: shared witticisms; sudden, ephemeral aphorisms; the graceful operation of a mundane movement; or, even more elementally, the invisible mental currents that allow us to locate a word for a meaning, or to communicate the desire to dance from nerves to muscles. For them, as for him, the task of art is to gradually acclimate our eyes to the world's immanent beauties. Like Cage, Nature Theater is working in the gap between art and life, but their method of perceptual training is more dialectical, not all-embracing and Buddhist, a constant push-pull between the allure of structure and the messy cognitive surplus of feelings, ideas, experience that always exceeds it. Stories are necessary to make experience meaningful, but no one story is capacious enough. Climaxes, beginnings, middles, and ends are always provisional, but, according to Nature Theater, they are necessary ways of structuring experience. Liska once explained his artistic perspective as a cycle of three terms, the first two Cagean, the last a distinct departure: "What I look for is three things: How much of the world around you do you perceive? How capable are you to let the world you perceive change you? And then: How do you change the world? It's a cycle of these three things."[41]

No Dice points a rebuking finger at jaded downtown theatergoers, chastising them for allowing once-liberating habits of seeing to ossify into routine. You thought you knew how to see this, Nature Theater chides, but you don't. We have been watching as if at a Richard Foreman piece, attentive to the unfolding moment, anticipating the imminent collapse and disappearance of any coagulating narrative, expecting the mitotic creation of new lines of dissociated creativity. (And we haven't been disappointed: *No Dice* seduces by seeming to employ such ironic techniques of spectatorial exasperation.) Trained to accept the presence of interpretive blind spots—Foreman's lumberjacks and kabbalistic glyphs—we haven't allowed telling details to accumulate, instead assigning impenetrably hermetic significance to the silly costumes, the estranging gestures, the stumbling dialogue. All the cues suggesting an irony-washed Foreman epigone were there, and we took the bait.

What we should have been doing, the spectatorial labor the piece was actually demanding, was something else entirely: following patterns with analytic alertness, reading structural links between parallel tracks, creating and rejecting forms that might have encompassed the show's variegated offerings. In other words: writing the story of the piece. Too quick to assume that the text was a mishmash of ready-made linguistic trash, a media mélange, we glanced past the emerging shape of a coherent whole until such blinkered watching was no longer possible. Enjoyably lost among the trees, we are flabbergasted by the abrupt appearance of a forest. Copper and Liska's purpose for *No Dice*'s afterlife in the mind is precisely opposite to Foreman's ethos. Instead of an hour-long immersion in consciousness's divagations and false starts, leaving behind nothing but perceptual traces and cognitive questions, Nature Theater is after the lasting memory of a fleeting moment of sublime artistic order, a romantic intuition of cosmic unity, a consummation. Liska and Copper are not naïfs: the piece does not conclude that there really is such a transcendent order, just that the human facility for making artistic shapes can offer a nourishing, but necessarily fugitive, glimpse of what such an empyrean picture might be like. Their utopia is firmly bounded by the mind. And here another, more venerable predecessor announces himself. Thornton Wilder's description of *Our Town* as "an attempt to find a value beyond all price for the smallest events in our daily life"[42] works equally well to encapsulate Copper and Liska's artistic endeavor.

The final sequence of *No Dice* reprises its entire aesthetic process in miniature. During their telephone conversation, Liska asks Teresa: "What kind of dance would you choreograph for yourself?"[43] Teresa hems and haws, suddenly abashed, explaining that she couldn't make a dance for someone able-bodied. She uses a wheelchair. But it turns out she is an avid dancer in daily life, with a regular partner, Jared, who makes up for her constrained movements with wild, ecstatic high-kicking: "He—ah—has his own . . / UNBRIDLED, / CRAZY . . . / slightly PSYCHOTIC moves! / (*pause*) / He LOVES to dance!"[44] Teresa's dance partner has been a part of the play all along. Discussions of his drinking problem, and thwarted attempts at writing, have formed the text of several earlier scenes.

Now the recorded voices fade away, drowned by raucous music, and the Nature Theater actors reappear, scrubbed of accents and bizarre accouterments. They proceed to stage the dance that Teresa described to Liska: her balletic arm movements, her partner's joyful leaps. Until now in the piece we have seen actors standing in for absent voices, channeling recorded speech too circuitous and stilted ever to memorize, and so master, by any conventional standard of embodiment, and, in the epilogue, we have heard recorded voices made present by electronic playback or projected transcript, but not granted the authority of corporeality. But at this moment, bodies and choreography blissfully line up, and the actors take possession of the stage with a wild display of gleefully slipshod dancing. They stage an impossibly liberated version of Jared and Teresa's duet, freeing both from life's limitations to the plane of art, dancing to the cosmic murmur. (In a final complication of the piece's already dizzying two-way trafficking across the porous border between art and life, sometime later Jared himself joined the company for a while to tour with *No Dice*, playing the strange Batman-like caped figure.)[45]

Nature Theater's landscape drama is a form of pastoral, retreating into the authenticity of documented everyday speech and thought to find a redeeming second glance that dignifies both. The transformation we all seek, the difference beyond difference, to recall Boris Groys's phrase, was always there, we simply needed to be reminded how to find it. *No Dice's* coruscating artistic complexity allows it, paradoxically, to return to the simplest of theatrical truths: the wonder of perished behavior re-presented, the defiant pleasure of the dance. The arrangement of *No Dice*'s stage—we look past art to see life—is Nature Theater's answer to Richard Foreman's crisscrossed sight lines. Stories are not a barrier to experience, but its necessary prerequisite. Every life is an epic: loose, baggy, accommodating flashes of drama along with intervals of interminable waiting. It is our ability to make contingent structure out of experience's continuous present, rather than our surrender to its endless vagabond potential, that allows us our fugitive moments of connection. Looking back at the moment when Nature Theater crossed the boundary between their world and ours, their simple gift of affirmation, saying that things will improve, that there is an end to shape our means, no longer feels like risible naivete, but the fullest consolation art can bring.

Too Like the Lightning: *Nature Theater of Oklahoma's Romeo and Juliet*

In another century, and another America, as Lawrence Levine reminds us in his *Highbrow/Lowbrow*, Shakespeare was part of daily life and mass entertainment, kept on the family bookshelf alongside the Bible (perhaps the only two books most households possessed), staged in theaters alongside more demotic attractions like acrobats and popular singers. For early-nineteenth-century Americans, Shakespeare was popular culture, a source of melodramatic thrills, a fount of practical wisdom.[46] After the traumatic schism of the Astor Place riots, Levine goes on to explain, Shakespeare was gradually annexed to literary culture, an elite taste rather than a plebeian author.[47] But thanks to compulsory reading, movies, and perhaps the odd trip to an outdoor Shakespeare festival, picnic in hand, or even a visit to a regional theater, the plays remain a part of most Americans' imaginative repertoire, however blurred by foggy reminiscence, mixed up with movie versions, or tainted by unhappy scholastic associations.

Nature Theater of Oklahoma's Romeo and Juliet began with questions that might in fact be unsurprising to the nineteenth-century peruser of Shakespeare for homiletic advice or diversionary purposes. How do Shakespeare's plays, those aristocrats of the literary canon, actually fit into quotidian consciousness, into everyday life? What do people retain from their high school or college encounters with his *Romeo and Juliet*? What remains of poetry and theatrical incident after the initial rush of experience fades, and the particularities of image, metaphor, and rhythm—not to mention the sonorities of the verse vocalized, the sensual alignments of play and players—are filed down by time and forgetfulness to a handful of unevenly recollected plot points? To provide answers, Liska and Copper asked a group of friends and acquaintances to tell the story of *Romeo and Juliet* from memory over the phone.

The piece's setting, too, makes explicit reference to the nineteenth-century era of popular American Shakespeare, the time of Forrest and Booth. Looking like an illustration from a book about old-time theater, the simple platform has painted across it the planks of an itinerant booth-stage, suggesting the makeshift efforts of touring barnstormers, with a bright blue proscenium and curtain daubed behind. The resemblance to nineteenth-century traveling showpeople goes beyond mere visuals; Copper delights in describing how the set folds up to fit into a single bag. European theaters, used to the technical demands of munificently funded auteur directors, frequently anxiously inquire when the company's equipment is going to actually arrive. (When we spoke, she intimated that she considers ragtag downtown troupes like Nature Theater to be the true heirs of the nineteenth century's vagabond show people.) Footlights line the lip of the stage, casting looming melodramatic silhouettes behind the actors, flattening their figures into pictorial relief. A prompter's box sits prominently in the foreground. The performers, too, are clothed to satisfy cliché: a pair of young ingénues, clad in storybook-Shakespeare outfits. The young man wears tighter-than-tight classical actors' tights, a fluffy ruff-thing at his collar, and pointy buckled shoes. The young woman wears a long, flowing blue dress, a princess awaiting her champion.

The duo declaims sentence fragments, abandoned clauses, conversational tics, and place-filling semi-words in the stentorian, somewhat Anglo tones of the snooty classically trained actor. Aspirated "w" sounds abound; extra syllables are tacked on in surprising places. This mode of delivery, as distant from everyday drawls and stammers as could be imagined, is here used to pronounce quotidian phrasings and fragments, simultaneously estranging those speech patterns so we can hear them with new ears and poking fun at the high-art pretensions of such rarefied speaking techniques.

Conversely, as was the case with *Poetics*'s sly choreographic comparisons between classical ballet and Nature Theater's own demotic dancing, the substitution of spontaneous extemporizing for the galloping step of Shakespeare's pentameter allows us to appreciate the serendipitous rhythms of everyday speech—the surprising halts or divagations, the improvised iambs ("I know / That's all I know"),[48] trochees and spondees.

The costumes and parodic mode of delivery heighten the contrast between our recollected concept of Shakespeare's poetic virtuosity and the scrupulously reproduced stammering being declaimed before us. "Um" gets as much emphasis as whatever vestiges of pentameter surface from the memorial murk. Savoring the subverbal syllables, Nature Theater's performers subtly point out that many of the sonorous qualities we associate with the finest performances of classical verse can be found in everyday language too. Do we love Shakespeare's words for themselves, or do we just love round, singing vowels, and sharp, amplified consonants? As George Hunka has remarked, the various interviewees' flawed memorial reconstructions of *Romeo and Juliet*'s plot suggest the imperfect reassemblies from memory by venal actors that led, in Shakespeare's time, to bad quartos and competing versions of the play.[49]

Perhaps predictably, what most people seem to retain are the by-products of the play's plot, its sex, violence, and moments of comic relief, its epic swordfights, funny secondary characters, hormonal yearnings, and baroque double suicide. And they hang their memories on the ever-present pairing of Romeo and Juliet. Nature Theater's two-handed staging reflects the fact that most of the accounts distill the play's large cast into a duet, occasionally swelled by passersby like the Nurse or Friar Laurence. What disappears, except in flashes or stunted figments, is the texture of the play, its poetry, the elusive thing that animates the play's action, not just the meaning of the words but their sounds, their sounds together, the present-moment pairing of language and incident. The speakers apologize for their foggy recollections, and express guilt at not remembering the dramatic icon better after having studied it at university or in the high school classroom. This causes spectators, too, to mull over the gaps in our own recollections of the play, perhaps prompting astonishment at how much of a story we think we know intimately is actually missing from our minds.

Most poignantly, many of the speakers struggle to convey the play's love poetry, the gorgeous lines that vouchsafe the cosmic scope of the lovers' passion: "There's a lot of tenderness in the— / In the—in the love scenes. / (*pause*) / And— / You know, that's what makes it so / heartbreaking!"[50] They recall the occasions of the play's poetic flights, like the lovers' first glimpse of each other at the Capulet ball or the balcony scene, but can't capture the substance and expression of those scenes:

> I remember there's some kind of love scene with the balcony? Where he's saying—He's saying this stuff about
> "The moon doesn't compare to—YOUR beauty . . ."
> And all this gooey stuff. Ha ha!
> The—"That thou her maid art far more fair than she!" (I remember that part!) But um—And: "What light through—?" "What light—?" "But light—! What DAWN! Through yonder window breaks! It is the EAST! And Juliet is the SUN! Or the MOON!"
> Heh heh! I can't remember which one it is![51]

They remember the Queen Mab speech but can't recall who delivers it or why. They remember snatches of exegesis, riffs on the play's class dynamics borrowed from some dimly recalled class discussion, or bits of secondhand theater lore, like the antics of a famously inept actor, whose death scenes became occasions for hilarity, despite (or perhaps because of) his striving to make them tragic.

One interlocutor speculates, juxtaposing the literary sublime with the pop culture ridiculous to comic effect, about the purpose of stories of thwarted desire like *Romeo and Juliet*—or the star-crossed exploits of Anna Nicole Smith. Transcending the run of everyday existence, such tragic narratives give us containers to share experience, they're: "an EASY WAY to like—Talk about culture. And other—Things. Like—We have like—ALLLLL this SHIT! To TALK ABOUT! In—Our—LIVES!" Otherwise, the speaker goes on, "we just like FUCKING—! Like—I don't know . . . Uh watch—watch—Um. YOUTUBE!"[52]

Their memories are also frequently filtered through pop culture renditions of the play: a well-meaning teacher who showed the Baz Luhrmann movie version, making sure to fast-forward through the sex scenes; the ubiquitous *West Side Story*. In the aggregate, the competing versions of the story provide an eccentric vernacular history of Romeo and Juliet's traffic through American culture in recent decades. In W. B. Worthen's wry phrase, the piece is a "contact narrative."[53]

Paradoxically, though, Nature Theater's roundabout retelling cuts straight to the quick of Shakespeare's own preoccupations. The piece progresses as a series of lonely soliloquies, delivered alternately by Bobby Johanson and Anne Gridley, culminating in a much-expected, much wished-for duet. We can't help but hope the lonely performers will "meet" at the end. This love story about theatrical expectations foregrounds other pairings implicit in the piece: the seduction of the various anonymous narrators by Liska and Copper, speakers and listeners, as they coaxed them into telling the warped, idiosyncratic versions of Shakespeare's plot that form the basis of the piece. The quintessentially romantic story the speakers narrate highlights the erotic charge of everyday conversation, the to-and-fro satisfaction of the desire to hear and know by the urge to speak, to locate words for elusive meanings. Then there is Nature Theater's own seduction by Shakespeare, consumed with the desire to make us hear the poetry afresh and separate the play's inimitable beauties from its carapace of accumulated clichés, and their taboo-bending ravishment of Shakespeare's revered verse with their own low-prose renderings. The piece's full title—*Nature Theater of Oklahoma's Romeo and Juliet*—points to this playful desire to master, to take possession of the original. (If we follow the traditional Elizabethan linguistic hierarchies, whereby the high-born speak highfalutin verse and the commoners talk blunt, earthy prose, then Nature Theater's stammerers occupy some kind of sub-commoner station.)

Periodically, between sequences, a performer dressed as a giant chicken, luridly hued in sports-mascot yellow and red, struggles out of the prompter's box and spends a few moments engaged in a strange personal dance. The moves are, by turns, oddly sensual and endearingly goofy-gawky, conducted in time to a tune heard only by the bird. Besides being a weird visual joke, the lowest kind of low comedy, something from a collegiate football game, interposed as a ridiculous contrast to the sublime idea of Shakespeare (look at this funny bird!), the sequence introduces an odd imponderable interval of pure spectacle. Nothing about either Shakespeare's play or Nature

Theater's piece has really prepared us for this avian koan except, later in the piece, its earlier appearances, and so we must figure out what to do with this strange riddle. It's the sort of weirdly indelible moment that an interviewee asked by some future theater artist to retell Nature Theater's piece from memory might dwell on: "And then this chicken appeared and . . ." This creates another moment of good-natured competition with the Bard (see, we can invent a theatrical gimmick as memorable as anything from Shakespeare!). The incident is likely to stay with Nature Theater's audience, carried along in the memory banks, perhaps becoming the sort of image that returns unbidden to interrupt an average day. The chicken also suggests the diversionary entertainments that might have accompanied a nineteenth-century presentation of Shakespeare, before creeping gentility set in. As purely visual delight, the chicken dances are the diametric opposite of the piece's ears-only conclusion.

In their quest to write a love scene as potent as Shakespeare's, Nature Theater lights upon perhaps the only theatrical love affair more profound than that of Juliet and her Romeo, that conducted between stage and auditorium, actors and spectators, artwork and experiencers. The piece's ending is a kind of two-part retelling of the play's romance, with the piece itself and its audience as the two lovers. First, after the two performers have finally found each other onstage, and shared a comically inadequate kiss, they begin to discuss if any modern love affair can (or should) equal the passion and sacrifice of Shakespeare's Veronese teens. The only answer they can come up with is the self-denying passion of actors striving for the love of spectators, sacrificing who they are to impersonate other people, or performing in projects they know are artistically bankrupt simply to reach the eyes of audiences. They fantasize about a piece that would simply be about actors admitting their need to be noticed, and beloved:

> BOBBY: We BOTH want to be loved!
> ANNE: Well, of course! We're both NEEDY!
> BOBBY: Yes. We're both needy! We both want to be loved! And we NEED the audience tonight!
> ANNE: Yes! (*pause*)
> BOBBY: To give—ALL THEY HAVE.
> ANNE: A paying audience![54]

Perhaps speaking for Nature Theater itself, they mischievously suggest what has so far only been implicit, that they are in competition with Shakespeare over "Who can do the—do a better love scene?"[55]

This is actually only half of the piece's "better" love scene, an overture left dangling in the air as the actors come out for their curtain call, receiving tokens of the kind of audience affection they were just discussing. The piece seems to be over. Then, the lights abruptly go out again, and in the inky blackness of the auditorium, we hear the voices of the piece's two performers reciting the "balcony" scene from Shakespeare's *Romeo and Juliet*, one of literature's most perfect renderings of erotic desire and expectation sublimated into poetry. There, in the dark, suggesting the "cover of night" under which Romeo sneaks into the Capulet orchard, and the hushed expectancy that attends the seconds before his first glimpse of Juliet at the window, we hear Shakespeare's words as if for the first time. Without seeing, we listen more intensely. Perhaps without fully realizing it, we have been yearning for the thing itself after all the cracked, misremembered, caricatured or otherwise partial renditions, all of them, even those that interpolate a half-remembered quotation or two, drained of Shakespeare's coruscating language.

Here is our half of the piece's consummating love scene, our own desire—our need—to hear the play's poetry. As with *Poetics*, the most important duet is that danced between performers and audience. All the everyday verbiage has primed us to hear the verse afresh, even as we know that our wandering minds can't retain the flash of poetry for longer than the fleeting instant it's experienced; that Nature Theater's piece, too, is already withering into the skeletal, anecdotal version memory will preserve; that, as with any erotic encounter, we are destined to forget the experiential details that made it truly a time apart except as sensory fragments; that with theatrical art as with perfect love, the beauty and the tragedy inhere in the unalterable fact that aesthetic experience is fleeting, irretrievably evanescent.

Perhaps the real tragedy of *Romeo and Juliet*, Nature Theater suggests, is that afterwards we can't perfectly recall what makes it so beautiful. The extreme fragility of the poetic instant, the speed of beauty, becomes a clarifying figure for the perishability of other kinds of experience, lost to the perceiver almost as soon as it's perceived, as soon as we try to find a form with which to retain it or objectify it. Like the too-brief period of happiness enjoyed by Shakespeare's doomed lovers, it is "too like the lightning, which doth cease to be / Ere one can say it lightens."[56]

As Worthen points out, this makes the piece, like the original, a story about loss and desire. But there are consolations. As in *Poetics*, a classical comparison has allowed us a clarifying glimpse at the serendipities of everyday creativity. It's a critical commonplace, of course, that Shakespeare's *Romeo and Juliet* begins as comedy, tantalizing with the withheld promise of matrimony, and ends as tragedy. And Nature Theater's version, too, appears to follow that trajectory, delighting us with gawky comedy before acquainting us with loss. But the piece's vision is perhaps better described as tragicomic. There are compensations to lighten our mourning for the already-evaporating moment of heightened communion with Shakespeare's words. The often wacky attempts of the speakers to compensate for the loss of Shakespeare, both cultural and mnemonic, have engineered some startling acts of ingenuity. They've created new versions of the story, made it a flexible container for new meanings.

We shouldn't forget that Nature Theater's piece is part of a diptych. It was devised at almost the same time that Copper and Liska were collaborating with Zachary Oberzan (from *No Dice*) on the chamber-thriller *Rambo Solo*, a one-man retelling of *First Blood*, incorporating both the original novel and the blockbuster Stallone film into a meditation on the obsessiveness of memory and the life-structuring power of artistic narrative.

If Nature Theater's *Romeo and Juliet* brought the everyday into a well-known story, *Rambo Solo* brought a similarly ubiquitous story into the everyday life of its performer, Zachary Oberzan, staging the way this particular fable, first encountered in childhood, has stalked his mind ever since. Both the novel and movie versions of *Rambo: First Blood* brought the Vietnam War back home—literally. In slightly different ways, both tell the story of a haunted vet, a finely calibrated fighting machine trained to slay with remorseless efficiency by the Green Berets, who runs afoul of local law enforcement while wandering the rural Pacific Northwest, and then proceeds to wage guerilla war against the benighted town, giving them a vivid taste of Vietcong tactics.

Rambo Solo brings Rambo's war home even more literally. It stages the reenactment of several prior reenactments of a retelling of the spliced stories of novel and film that performer Zachary Oberzan performed—over and over again—for Liska and Copper in his tiny studio apartment in Manhattan. His kitchen tap stands in for the rushing waterfall that Rambo catapults himself into; his vaulted bed becomes a mountain to climb; his kitchen stands in for a gas station. The many previous versions of the retellings are projected split-screen on monitors upstage, suggesting the vertiginous obsessiveness of Oberzan's repeated mulling-over of the Rambo story, rereading, rewatching, acting out bits of it in his apartment, juxtaposing mundane settings and humdrum life events with the nonstop action, and the superhuman abilities of Rambo.

Rambo Solo is premised on the sly proposition that the Rambo narrative, transposed to the right mind and infused with the right associations, could become as meaningful a fable, as profound a part of a personal mnemonic repertoire as *Romeo and Juliet*. The real question, for Nature Theater, is what we do with such experiences afterwards. How do they linger in our daily lives?

In this light, Nature Theater's diptych is as much about gain as it is about loss. Taken together, the pieces ask how the stories we've imbibed condition the stories we tell ourselves about ourselves. How much of everyday life is infused with borrowed gravity (or levity) by our experience of works of art, our adversities spiked with heroic zest by the recollection of Rambo's tribulations, our love affairs held up against the doomed Veronese example? The two pieces celebrate the brevity of both aesthetic and everyday experience, and the creative uses we find for its residue: the work of selecting and preserving fragments in memory, the creative possibilities for reanimating them. For Nature Theater, forgetting, too, can be a creative act.

This is where Nature Theater's next project, *The Life and Times*, began. The theatrical epic hymns the editorial virtuosity of memory on a grand scale. It celebrates the very partiality of the fragmented memories that constitute the self's claim to continuity: our common share of loss, our common desire to find them again. They're beautiful because they're broken, and they await our reassembly.

This Is Your Life: Nature Theater of Oklahoma's *The Life and Times*

Nature Theater of Oklahoma's most recent everyday project, *The Life and Times*, fuses the company's earlier preoccupations with the ingenuity of ordinary speech and the uses and difficulties of storytelling, as demonstrated in *No Dice*, with the interest in sifting ready-made stories through memory's faulty sieve evinced by *Rambo Solo* and *Romeo and Juliet*.[57] *The Life and Times* is an epic ten-part, partly sung-through retelling of the life story of frequent Nature Theater collaborator Kristin Worrall. She performed in *No Dice* as the mysterious keyboard-playing figure wearing sunglasses and a towering Marie Antoinette-style wig. Worrall extemporized an oral autobiography over sixteen hours of telephone calls to directors Copper and Liska. *Episode One*, which is more than three hours long, takes us from Worrall's birth to the beginnings of grade school. If the entire project can ever be performed at once, the giant cycle will likely span at least twenty-four hours, fitting the duration of an individual life (to date) into the duration of one of nature's irreducible cycles, that of night and day. (A marathon presentation of the first four parts, at New York's Public Theater, in January 2013, took about eleven hours, including breaks for meals—hot dogs, brownies—prepared and served by the cast.)

More than this, the piece is the record of many years in Nature Theater's artistic life. They've been at work on the project at least since 2009, and now, at the time of this writing in 2017, have recently premiered parts 7–9 in New York City after European showings last year. At this point, the entire project has consumed close to a decade. And life has been getting in the way of *The Life and Times*. As Kelly Copper recently told the critic Lawrence Switzky:

> It's exhausting. People have quit because now we are taking up too much of their biological lives, and they can't make it work for themselves anymore—the cost is too high. People want to have babies, people want to spend time with their families, get married, etc., take care of ailing parents—and to keep this going and keep the work funded requires us to be away much of the year, and they have to weigh that for themselves. Over the past two years in particular—we've worked to the point of physical exhaustion. People have ended up in the hospital (including Pavol last year [. . .]) and so we're

> engaging with this question right now, actually. We're trying to figure out—is it really something we can finish? Should we finish it?[58]

I'll concentrate here on *Episode One*, though. It set the pattern for the first four installments of the project, all of which are, in various ways, choral settings of Worrall's early memories, transforming particular experiences into allegorical drama: first according to musical genres suited to the life stage they embody, and then melodramatic forms suited to the volatile emotions of adolescence. In more recent episodes, Nature Theater has broken radically with this pattern: part 4.5 was an illuminated book—an illustrated *Kama Sutra* portraying the married sex life of Copper and Liska, as it relates the story of Worrall's first sexual encounter. Part 5 is a film, as are parts 6 through 9. As the company takes the project away from performance, it becomes less relevant to my interest here. To my mind, *Episode One* best illustrates the scale and the allegorical design of the project.

The first time I saw *Episode One* was in the gymnasium of a community center in the Bronx, in the winter of 2011. The company was holding a farewell open-rehearsal-style showing on the eve of a European tour. The setting was perfect, and was easy to imagine echoing with the shouts and laughter of children. The improvised auditorium, with its rows of temporary seating and old-fashioned wood-paneled proscenium stage, looked like a high school gym in Anytown, USA, tricked out for the performance of a school play, holiday concert, or community theater production. The spectators, mostly friends and acquaintances of the company, could easily have been the doting relatives assembled to watch the antics of a beloved child or the spirited performance of a dramatic aunt. Rendered even more endearingly amateurish in the absence of the professional trappings of sets, props, costumes, sound system, or lighting (they'd already been shipped), this atmosphere only amplified the bittersweet tang of the piece's reminiscing about childhood schooldays.

There is a strange poignancy, underlying all of *The Life and Times*, to the fact that this epic retelling of Worrall's life story dramatizes only one of many possible, contingent versions. Had Worrall been interviewed on different days, while in different moods, a different sort of narrative might have emerged. And, too, as Nature Theater toured this particular iteration, faithfully adhering to the contingent words of one contingent conversation, the subject herself was growing older, changing, perhaps unconsciously revising her preferred life story as new memories arose or the significance of old ones subtly altered. Certainly she was registering new impressions, thoughts, and sensations which may go unrecorded. I use the feminine pronoun tentatively here because although the biographical subject is a woman, in *Episode One*, and the next three, she is only temporarily embodied by female performers, and never by the same one for very long. Beginning with a solo song by a female singer, the piece passes her story back and forth between voices of both genders. The final performer we see onstage in *Episode One*, singing passionately, almost sobbing with operatically airborne emotion, about homesickness at a childhood sleepover, is male, and luxuriantly bearded.

What *Episode One* dramatizes, instead of a conventional narrative with stable characters and assigned dialogue, is the choreography of the originary conversation and with it, the ebb and flow of memory at work. New performers take over as a new scene is recalled, as the conversation abruptly changes directions, as new people are described for the first time, as new scenes are painted verbally, gaps in memory are stepped over, and leaps in time are achieved. As *Life and Times* progresses, these entrances and exits become wrenching in themselves. Fresh characters appear—childhood playmates, dimly recalled though beloved teachers—and are cherished for a time, then disappear into mnemonic oblivion. Where are they now, we wonder, thinking of the bit players in our own dramas.

As with earlier pieces like *No Dice,* dramatic conventions become handy metaphors for the way we experience big life events. On a basic level, the entirety of the project reminds us that memory itself is a theatrical process, the summoning and restaging in the mind's eye of vanished events, revising as we rehearse. Periodically, the action is interrupted by Worrall's bemused misgivings about talking so much about herself—"God, this must be so boring for you!"—or by the outside world breaking into the phone call. At one point, she asks some unknown interlocutors if they're "ready to go," and warns Liska or Copper that she "has to go pretty soon"—cueing, in Nature Theater's staging, a processional false exit by the entire company.

Similar to the high art/low art confusions propagated by *Romeo and Juliet* and the company's "ballet brut" *Poetics*, the overblown emotions of operatic form rub against the humdrum subject matter of swimming lessons and tea parties with grandma. Singing throwaway assiduously scored semi-words (the piece begins with a ringing "Um . . . So . . .") bedevils the distinctions between music and noise, sound and sense. The chaff of conversation is not only endowed with the weight of reenactment and re-utterance, but is elevated into song, the most exalted form of speech. The many different musical styles of the score, composed by longtime company member Robert M. Johanson, suggest the different moods of memory: jazz, blues, upbeat showstoppers, and stately arias. As Worrall's memories stabilize, so too do music and genre. In *Episode Two*, dealing with her preteen years, the music remains techno-inflected throughout, and the cast wears matching track suits and boogies as though at the junior high school dance Worrall describes. In parts 3 and 4, the memories are keyed to a melodramatic murder mystery setting.

A recurring, lyrical leitmotif in the score registers the first stirrings of aesthetic consciousness. "Oh my God, it was so beautiful" goes Worrall's refrain when these moments are recalled. Perhaps most important, none of these events are really tied to experiences of conventional artworks. Rather, the experiences, framed by memory, set apart, consummated, are themselves the artworks. She loves her friend's mother's wild curly hair, and the costume for her ballet recital. She recalls being overwhelmed by discovering a seething mass of insects leading their secret lives under a rock in the garden. This episode, significantly, also provides a first experience of the irrevocable speed and irretrievability of beauty. When she tries to find the buggy metropolis again, she can't.

So much of the run of quotidian experience is impersonal, simply befalling us or taking us unawares. Worrall didn't choose to notice the seething insects, couldn't have imagined that that particular chance event would remain with her for decades. It is in retrospection, Nature Theater suggests, in the consummation of the rearward glance, the summoning and restaging of a bygone swathe of experience, that perceptions become personal. Beauty is, in this sense, always in the past tense. Memory is akin to artmaking, and the ever-shifting object is oneself. The aesthetic space of the stage is, here, a synecdoche for the operation of memory's constant embellishment.

As *The Life and Times: Episode One* progresses, the scope of Worrall's memories expands from sensory impressions to the psycho-geography of childhood. We see sketched her mental maps of first her room, then the varied terrain of her house (rooms for children; rooms for parents; rooms inviolably hers; others remaining somehow alien), the yard, the neighborhood, school, the homes of playmates. We're privy to vivid recollections of taboos transgressed: the still-sharp shock of seeing her father naked, after walking in on him sitting on the toilet, his surprised yelp fresh in Worrall's mind despite intervening decades. We hear her recount incidents seminal to the development of an awareness of social class, as manifested in the material details of everyday life encountered on a visit to a friend's home—décor, appliances, neighborhoods, the peccadilloes and snobberies of her parents.

In the fully staged version of the piece, the company—six actors and several musicians, a few of whom occasionally migrate onstage—wears utilitarian outfits in drab hues, khaki for the actors, black for the orchestra; plain shirt-dresses for the women, Boy Scout-like quasi-military shirts and trousers for the men. Marked with an enigmatic red insignia, dressed up with red kerchiefs deployed in idiosyncratic ways, the only personal touch, the uniforms alternately suggest a Scout troop or a young-pioneer squad sponsored by the youth wing of a Communist party.

So does the choreography. When singing, the actors bop enthusiastically up and down in place, waggle jazz hands, stir imaginary pots, or chastely bump and grind with the unabashed exuberance of teenage drama queens in a high school musical or glee club somewhere in the American heartland. Between songs, they unite in geometric formations, adopting stark, repetitive sequences of poses, often involving a kitschy prop, such as a rubber ball or plastic ring, more reminiscent of the totalitarian rhythmic gymnastics of North Korean mass spectacles or the opening ceremonies of the Beijing Olympics. This central polarity between exuberant American individuality and the self-dissolving group ethos of socialist pageants, between impersonal adherence to choreographic diktats and shameless showboating, uniqueness and sameness, individuals and groups, becomes a versatile visual metaphor for the dynamics of memory, the dance of individual socialization, and the paradoxes of individual identity.

In *Life and Times*, the impersonality of the mass movement sequences (and the young-pioneer uniforms) is juxtaposed with the intensely personal nature of the story being told, which is, in turn, being rendered almost universal by its anonymity, and the curious transposability of key details. Our particular inventories of memories are perfectly unique, but many other people have memories not unlike them. Like a medieval morality play, allegorical generality is created by attention to shared inevitabilities of human life (at least in modern Western democracies). Most of us learn hard lessons living sociably at school, gain and shed playmates, awkwardly encounter adult life in fits and starts, and experience dramatic events that fade into unevenly recollected hills and valleys on life's graph. More than this, we all continually construct and revise a life story, and contingent self, based on repeated reimaginings of these receding memories. These memories are both the very substance of our selves and an unsteady foundation, shifting in meaning, fading into shadows, or subtly transforming themselves with time and use.

To borrow a formulation from Douglas Eklund, *The Life and Times* transforms the "irreducible specificity" of Worrall's spotty recollections "into a general accounting" for its spectators, all possessed of an equally slippery grasp of their own idiosyncratic histories.[59] The assumption is that any one of us, if called to account for our lives, could have said these things, or things like them, fumbling for words, dredging up and linking scattershot impressions fuzzed by time. The point is not the particulars of what is said, but the act of trying to say them, the record of extemporaneous conversational ingenuity and real-time mnemonic archaeology, the general relevance of human beings' common creativity. As though to illustrate this commonality, during the piece, the performers take expressive cues from the faces of their audience, mirroring their affective investments, creating an ephemeral record of the piece's progress through the minds of its audience.

The drab gray backdrop for the piece, a plain screen, is periodically splashed with vivid daubs of light in lurid, primary colors—yellow, blue, red, green. These chromatic flashes suggest the violent intensity and unmixed immediacy of a child's perceptions. Their interruption of the placid background suggests the sudden drama of incident overwhelming routine or memory triumphing over mnemonic oblivion, the sense of unprecedentedness that freezes experience as memory (or retroactively colors that experience with significance from recollection's remove).

Similarly, performers occasionally pop up from trapdoors concealed in the stage floor, their sudden entrances underlining the theatricality of a particular memory. A performer appears, be-caped, and be-fanged, leering with menace, to recapture childhood terror caused by the encounter between an overactive imagination and an ill-advised reading of *Dracula*. Another, clad in a plush rabbit outfit, complete with buckteeth, hops merrily around as singers rhapsodize the joys of Easter egg hunts. Sinister horror-film music swells around a singer's operatically anguished voice to suggest the fear and outrage prompted by the brutish behavior of a friend's domineering father, an early encounter with injustice. In one wrenching aria, Worrall recalls the terrible moment of exposure and shame when a callous boy revealed to the class that she had just wet her pants. She tries desperately to dissemble it, to no avail. Sung as a solo, the sequence briefly elevates childhood suffering to diva-ish heights. But the story marches on, propelled by memory's businesslike unsentimentality about old hurts and old pleasures, and these vividly recalled scenes quickly melt into the passing pageant.

As we listen to the memories shift in scope and mode from scattered sensory traces recalled from toddlerhood to more rounded sequences recalled as narrative, the staging subtly expands, dilating from solos to group configurations. Solitary songs swell into choruses to sing about the pleasures and pains of accommodating oneself to living with others, and contract again to evoke lonely moments or interior musings. Male company members join the piece at the moment Worrall becomes aware of boys, dabbling in developing crushes and learning to scorn nerdy outliers. The name of the narrator character shifts, even as the performers' possession of her proves transient. She is sometimes Julie, the name of the performer who begins the piece, and sometimes Katie. Worrall's solo autobiography gradually becomes a choral story and a communal experience, shared and affirmed by a temporary assembly suggesting humanity at large. United by the common time of theatrical performance, we simultaneously share Worrall's resurrected memories and relive our own, the auditorium abuzz with the murmur of a crowd remembering together.

We hear things Worrall has no doubt been told by others that nevertheless have become grafted onto her own memories. She was a quiet baby, and didn't cry a lot. She was breast-fed. These borrowed biographical details are juxtaposed with bright flashes of surviving sensory information. Her only recollections of the lost years of babyhood is getting bathed in the sink—the bubbles, the glinting silver of the basin—and getting changed on the washing machine by her father. She remembers her mother as a blur of motion, always engaged in some activity or other. The casually sketched tableau, set to yearning chords, of her strong, silent father sitting companionably in his armchair reading the paper, becomes an unutterably poignant meditation on the fierce power of paternal intimacy, and the sometimes unbearable recognition of its limits, an early intuition of the horizons of human subjectivity. How can someone be simultaneously near and so far, so entirely familiar yet ultimately unknowable? This same feeling is evoked in spectators by *Life and Times* itself. Although we have spent more than three hours learning this person's story, do we really feel closer to knowing her?

Two household memories provide vivid metaphors for the architecture and functioning of *Life and Times*. Worrall remembers a desk and a series of scrapbooks made by her mother, both crammed with youthful ephemera: drawings, report cards, photographs, the material detritus that ratifies and renews memory. We're reminded of the ways memory and emotions attach themselves to objects, the peculiar animism of recollection that transforms a childhood home into a cabinet of neglected wonders. *Life and Times* is itself like an animated scrapbook, a collage of personal history embellished with ornamental touches like costumes and music. Like a scrapbook, it is a new object that represents the past without being able to reproduce it. All the accumulated evidence in such a compendium is inevitably shadowed by what isn't there. The aesthetic decisions taken in the selection and arrangement of the material inevitably shape its interpretations. To borrow Diana Taylor's terms once again, the archive can't fully resuscitate the repertoire. (The homeliness of the scrapbook as folk-art object also suggests the deliberate amateurishness of the piece's high-school-musical staging.)

The present-moment rendering of the retrospective musings in boisterous song creates prosthetic flesh for skeletal memories, restoring something like the original fullness of experience while inevitably gesturing to its irrevocable loss. We're constantly reminded of the gaps, the fissures, the forgotten or poorly recollected people. The pointillist particularity of the memories Worrall has managed to keep only gestures to the vast swathes of time and experience forever lost to her (or any of us). *Life and Times*'s own duration and variety—at more than three hours, *Episode One* defies summary—compels spectators to become aware of how much of the piece itself they are already losing, even as they attempt to preserve moments of startling identification. We are forgetting Worrall's memories, and retaining a subjective selection of a few, in a kind of recapitulation of the mnemonic sifting that produced those memories in the first place. What we recall is twice-remembered; what we omit is twice-forgotten. *The Life and Times* celebrates the human facility for experiential arbitrage, even as it mourns the inevitable deprivations incurred by such cognitive transactions. In our daily perceptions, as at the theater, we are always trading present losses against the tantalizing promise of future meanings, observable only in retrospect. The story of Worrall's story, a smattering of brilliant specks accumulated against the wider dark of forgetting, is also the story of our own, an ordinary and impersonal autobiography.

Watching *Life and Times*, you are simultaneously following the unfurling of a stranger's life, keeping track of the performance in progress, and recklessly, almost inadvertently, sent spiraling back into your own past as some madeleine-moment onstage ignites dormant memories. And you can feel fairly sure that the many strangers sitting around you are similarly there and not there, sharing this public airing of a single life story, and following their own twisting, utterly individual but also strangely convergent paths backwards through life and time.

Of Marathons and Aliens

Faster and faster: watching succeeding episodes of *The Life and Times*, especially at one of the company's marathon performances, as I did, twice, in January 2013, is to experience this strange backwards-forwards movement through time and your own memory for much longer, at a dizzying intensity. More and more of Worrall's life is racing by, along with a corresponding volume of your own. Her memories are becoming more solid, more fitted to a sense of self expressed through narrative. The emergent drama of these later episodes is the appearance of semantic memory to replace the disjointed experiential shards of early life. Episode 2 matches the awkward fits and starts of pubescence to the tentative social dynamics of a school dance. Episodes 3 and 4 paired the heightened emotions of adolescence, the sharp peaks and deep valleys, with the suspense of a *Mousetrap*-style murder mystery, set at a parodic English country estate. Think low-budget Agatha Christie, filtered through *Masterpiece Theatre*, complete with tweedy costumes, and the flimsy painted sets and flimsier accents of a community theater production. As before, the narration is passed between performers, as much a communal ritual as a dramatized biography. As before, the conversational jetsam and verbal tics are savored and highlighted.

Just before midnight, though, as the long day of the marathon showing draws to a close, as spectators are fighting bleary-eyed fatigue, exhausted by the effort of many hours of concentrated attention and heightened experience, a strange group of figures begins to emerge. (Stranger, that is, than the chorus of faux-English-accented performers recounting the trespasses of Worrall's teenage years with the breathless tones of scandalized witnesses to a crime scene.) They're aliens, the extraterrestrial variety, with large blank eyes, almond-shaped heads, and iridescent bodysuits. They filter out from the wings, posing amid the characters already onstage, while a booming voice-over (it's Liska) begins to recite some of Worrall's testimony describing a teenage art project undertaken in a high school art class that she describes as a haven for misfits, during which she first began to think of herself as an artist. She made a diorama, an orderly, meaningful miniature world constructed from unlikely components through imaginative (and physical) labor: a food sculpture of an insect (noodles, a prune) resting on a basil leaf, poised on a bed of blue Jell-O. This, of course, is what Nature Theater has been doing all day, enlarging Worrall's teenage epiphany into a common consummation; constructing an artwork from ready-made materials that is almost as large as the life it transmutes. In Lawrence Switzky's lovely phrase, "The greatest product of their exhaustion may be our enlivening."[60]

We're left with a family portrait, as the aliens take up positions around the living room alongside the characters representing Worrall's remembered experiences. Memory is an alien realm, they seem to be telling us, for many reasons. We're not the people we were, so we can't really ever be sure if we remember experiences in a manner faithful to the intensity with which our stranger-selves understood them. As all the episodes of *Life and Times* have reminded us, our fragile self-stories are constructed on shifting ground, changing as we do, and every bright, sure shard of memory only indexes a deepening void.

But the aliens also represent artistic possibility. Because we're always going to be strange to others and to ourselves, our pasts not just another country, but another world, all autobiographical art is a kind of science fiction, more outlandish even than the fantastic imaginings of an Isaac Asimov or a George Lucas. Nature Theater's extravagant genre stagings are just the fit accompaniment to the ultimate strangeness of human consciousness, which successively blends opera, melodrama, tragedy, comedy, farce, every conceivable genre, depending on the day and the moment. But the marathon showings of *The Life and Times* also realize, on a grand scale, John Dewey's ideal of aesthetic consummation. Every life, Nature Theater suggests—Worrall's, each spectator's—is an emergent work of art, finding its own particular shape through the years. It's our task to see it as such and redeem bygone experience for art. Attending *The Life and Times*, you might catch a fleeting glimpse of the architecture of your own life.

The company recently completed parts 7–9 of *The Life and Times* as a series of films. But in a way, the cycle will never be finished—it never could be finished. Nature Theatre's theater of the everyday, like Kafka's, is too big, big as the world, and has to go uncompleted. Episode 4 was the last installment to take the form of a fully staged theatrical production. The marathon showings of episodes 1 through 6 in Germany, in the summer of 2013, were the last attempts (to date) to bring the whole series together. The more Nature Theater tries, in fact, the more we might think of everything they couldn't stage, everything they'll never stage: the rest of Worrall's life, speeding by unrecorded; the parts of her previous life she couldn't remember; the years of the company's life devoted to staging the pieces, on and on, ceaseless flux outracing fixity and form. The more omnivorous and encyclopedic the series becomes, the more it describes its limits, the more it gestures to that deepening void.

The titanic ambition of *The Life and Times*, its massive scope pointing to Nature Theater's even larger, unrealizable, and quixotic project of redeeming all of daily life's perished experience as art, returns us to where we began: the image of Karl Rossman gazing with awe at America's uncontainable splendor, trying to squeeze it all into the eye's overflowing frame, even as the speeding train carries him remorselessly away, deeper into the country's unknown recesses.

Coda

✦

Ghosts in the Machine

Noise, Presence, and the Archival Everyday

I conclude by discussing an actorless theater piece that relies almost entirely on the uncanny gaze of technology to achieve its illusions of immediacy, substituting mediated signs of everydayness for the physical presence of performers. In this way, it represents both a culmination of the theater of the everyday's tendency to amplify human perception with technology, and a response to a cultural situation in which the ubiquity of digital recording surrounds us with eerily preserved scraps of ordinary experience. It is also a discomfiting harbinger of future visions of the digital everyday.

The New York City Players' *Ads*, a performance piece without performers conceived and directed by Richard Maxwell, which premiered at the 2010 Under the Radar and Coil festivals in New York City, is a provocative inquest into the ineffable alchemy of live corporeal presence, and the manifold ways its digitally archived residue haunts the twenty-first-century everyday. The piece makes this most elusive of theater's fundamental forces visible by its absence, showing how noise has become the signifier of presence in a culture dedicated to digitally storing the everyday as never before, archiving the quotidian. Formerly perishable experience has a long afterlife now, and across social media we are continually hailed by recorded remnants of the ordinary lives of others. Presence is everywhere—everywhere, that is, but where we would most expect it to be.

Ads consists of a series of personal statements, delivered by the authors themselves, without rehearsal, on subjects of intimate importance. Maxwell asked friends and acquaintances from a wide variety of backgrounds, and a broad spectrum of ages and ethnicities—a few work in theater, but most don't—to compose a text, or, in some cases, to extemporize, about their individual matrices of beliefs. Maxwell videoed the monologues, and, in performance, they were projected across a complicated rig of mirrors and screens. The videos were the entire show, but they were so discomfitingly lifelike that at times it was easy to forget they were videos at all.

The unnerving result: hovering dimensional figures, neither present nor absent, live or recorded. The projections preserved accidental signs of everyday bodily presence usually edited out of more polished media images: nervous throat-clearing, stutters, fidgeting. Picking up where Method acting's media experiments left off, these mediated avatars aver their authenticity with the offhand signifiers of the uncanny everyday. These archived idiosyncrasies bring the performers uncannily closer, causing inadvertent surrender to sympathetic involvement with their likenesses, even as the reality of physical presence remained irretrievably absent. The "depth" of the performers' confessions jarred with the pixelated surfaces of their ghostly avatars. One speaker, an actor, describes encountering new audiences; another rues the flattening of personality in the age of Facebook. In our digital era, when new media strive to emulate the kinesthetic effects of bodily nearness—dance fads spread through YouTube restagings; Instagram videos archive social gatherings—Maxwell's experiment attempts to isolate the elusive thing-in-itself of corporeal encounter, by delivering every aspect of theatrical performance except live performers.

Throughout his career, Maxwell has shied away from conventional hallmarks of theatrical presence. The director is known for favoring a deader-than-deadpan style in which actors eschew passionate display or gestural flourishes, shrugging off their lines in an affectless monotone. His plays, too, often turn around the problem of feeling authentically in a cliché-ridden culture. How do we tap into wellsprings of real emotion when we're continually deluged with the culture industry's comestible units of prefabricated experience? How do we know when we do?

Maxwell mostly casts amateur performers, or performers capable of mimicking the gawky nerviness of nonactors, in his pieces, preferring untutored idiosyncrasies to the polished comfort of the professional. Like Stuart Sherman and Nature Theater of Oklahoma, he makes no attempt to shoehorn his performers into "characters." In *People without History* (2009), a recent piece set during an unnamed medieval war, one of the "knights" wore modern eyeglasses, and sported the same ponytail and beard he wears offstage. In *Ode to the Man Who Kneels* (2007), a Western, one actor's strong German accent went undisguised and unremarked-upon. As a result, there's always a gap between the figures onstage and the fiction they're intended to populate. An eccentric pause, a quirky gesture, an odd persona brought intact from daily life to the stage, these sorts of peculiarities create static—noise—in Maxwell's onstage worlds, interfering with the representational process. Several of the speakers in *Ads*, like the Maxwell muses Lakpa Bhutia and Bob Feldman, have performed this function in previous productions. In interviews Maxwell has described his writing method as "recording," preserving odd scraps of overheard dialogue, media culture detritus, or other conversational flotsam, and then collaging the scavengings into something resembling a plot and characters.[1] *Ads* extends Maxwell's affinity for the "ready-made" qualities of amateur performers, allowing them to speak for themselves without even the minimal mediation of his porous stage fictions.

At P.S.122, where *Ads* was first staged, the setting resembled a conventional, if minimalist, black-box theatrical arrangement. Upstage center, where the auditorium's sight lines converge, angled corridors of black masking frame a wooden crate, the soapbox for *Ads*'s public speakers, a sly allusion to its "Speakers' Corner" format. This makeshift podium is the only tangible object on *Ads*'s mostly immaterial stage. Once the piece begins, the projected performers seem to appear from behind the curtains as though coming from the wings, and audibly "step" onto the box, though in fact their recorded likenesses float insubstantially above it.

Ads updates a hoary piece of theatrical sleight of hand known as "Pepper's Ghost." The traditional version involves using a series of mirrors to catch and reflect the image of an offstage performer, creating a bodied but wispy figment onstage, suitable for representing restless spirits and other supernatural beings. Maxwell's version plays on both this theatrical inheritance and the strange properties of technologies of reproduction. As theorists of photography like Roland Barthes and Susan Sontag have noted, contemplating the uncanniness of images that preserve frozen likenesses of people now dead or simply transmogrified by age, photography, and moving pictures, too, traffic in ghosts. A photograph retains not just the optical trace of a fleeting moment ripped out of time, but its physical residue as well. The same light that struck the picture's subject also registered in the camera's lens. The image, as Barthes reminds us in *Camera Lucida*, is "literally an emanation of the referent. From a real body, which was there, proceed radiations which ultimately touch me, who am here."[2]

In *Gramophone, Film, Typewriter*, Friedrich Kittler points out that the genre of spirit photography, supposedly recording the unseen presence of spirits haunting quotidian life, appeared almost as soon as photographic portraiture did, creating a thriving parallel industry. Video, particularly the ready availability of digital video, multiplies this spectral sedimentation of vanished physical presence: the shadow of a voice striking the camera's microphone, the high-definition record of an offhand gesture or nervous fidgeting. As Kittler puts it: "The realm of the dead is as extensive as the storage and transmission capabilities of a given culture."[3]

In an age in which recording technologies capable of archiving formerly ephemeral aspects of everyday life continue to proliferate, we come across such revenants more than ever before. Status updates transfix a passing thought; a brief video posted online preserves some scattered moments of a social occasion; digital photographs pin down vanished moments from angles that clash with memory; locative technologies preserve our ordinary itineraries and health apps count our steps. We are fast becoming a haunted culture, surrounded by perished instants of quotidian life given archival longevity. *Ads*'s ghostly apparitions dramatize this ubiquitous hauntedness.

In *Ads*, fossil signs of the performers' physical presence haunt the moment of their digital resurrection: the thump as a new speaker "steps" onto or off the podium, the faint rustle of fingers drumming restlessly against a trouser hem, the catch in the voice of a performer stumbling over his or her words. Although only sophisticated recording devices and an excellent speaker system could carry such trivial details to eye and ear with jolting immediacy, the spectator can't help but forget these layers of mediation, responding with involuntary empathy to what seems to be tangible evidence of the speakers' earnestness, awkwardness, anxiousness, their dogged determination to say something meaningful for posterity. As with Marlon Brando's experimental line readings, what Barthes called the "grain of the voice," the physical textures preceding (and exceeding) signification, is picked up and amplified, made to sound and look impossibly close.[4] The percussive flutter of a nervous cough caught by the microphone and transmitted to our ears carries within it a ghostly residue of the unrepeatable instant when that voice first brushed across the apparatus, committing an offhand moment to digital permanence. In *Ads*, such uncanny fulfillments of interrupted instances of theatrical contact, the performers' stammering speech finally reaching human auditors, make the recorded bodies seem fulsomely present, even as such moments, once recognized as illusory, ultimately make them feel unreachably distant.

How is the patina of live presence in the theater the product of ingrained perceptual expectations, habits of watching, more than true nearness? Though valorized as the quintessential artistic medium of live encounter, much of traditional theatrical performance is built around concealing, mediating, or displacing such meetings, veiling performers' personalities with fictional roles, channeling moment-to-moment feeling into carefully rehearsed spontaneities. With *Ads,* Maxwell subtly asks in what ways his vaporous effigies are *more* present than performers in conventional theater. Most wear nondescript clothing of their own selection—jeans, T-shirts, business-casual khakis and button-downs. A few sport whimsical outfits that are clearly characteristic of their everyday self-presentations. Keith Connolly, one of only two performers to actually identify themselves by name, dresses like a poet-tramp in a rumpled suit, with a floppy hat shading his eyes and a long beard trailing down his shirtfront. Another speaker, declaring her lifelong allegiance to bohemianism, wears, naturally, a thrift store ensemble of solemn black. Their statements are unmediated by a fictive stage world, the mechanics of plot, or the pretense of inhabiting a character. They perform their own writing or improvise on the spot without concern for usual performance considerations like "good" acting (measured by whatever standard, traditional or progressive, mimetic or ironic) or audience approval. To borrow a distinction from Lionel Trilling, their performances come across as authentic, composed without concern for theatrical or social conventions, rather than simply sincere.[5] Absent everydayness somehow substitutes for present fictiveness in producing such an effect.

Similarly, the apparently unedited nature of the video images disarms the modes of skeptical resistance inculcated by habitual film spectatorship. We see each performer in an unwavering head-on, life-size, full-body shot that preserves the figural integrity of each body—no deforming close-ups or disorienting pans, no obscure angles or distorting effects. Non-purposive gestures, empty pauses, and inadvertent shifting in place are kept intact. The videos preserve and resurrect evanescent moments of personal expression without implicating them in the inevitable repetitions and codifications of rehearsal and performance, or, for that matter, of multiple takes in film. We are seeing and hearing these performances the way they looked and sounded the first and only time they were delivered. Added to this is *Ads*'s mode of exhibition. The videos can't be seen except in a theatrical context, and the composition of the program varies. During the piece's New York presentation, Maxwell adjusted the running order from night to night. Not all the testimonials were seen on a given evening, and so each "performance" was subtly different from the last, never to be duplicated. Video participated in a kind of theatrical liveness. Each unique iteration of the event was destined for disappearance.

The slightly stuffy and formal "public speaking" attitudes adopted by many performers—the pathos of their struggles to appear authoritative, dynamic, fluent—only bring them closer, as we sympathize with their sometimes stilted but always ardent desire to communicate through layers of technological mediation to imagined future audiences. The speakers' visible nervousness, or simply their obvious awareness that they are speaking both for, and to, prospective spectators, creates fleeting instants in which you believe you are being directly spoken to. The images seem to make eye contact, to address themselves directly to the audience watching the projections. Though the speakers are not actually performing in the here and now, their delayed intention to speak to a gathering of people like us is being fulfilled, despite the hiatus between recording and projection. A broken circuit is being mended by our attention.

As *Ads* suggests, in both form and content, this kind of communication, interrupted by layers of technology, disjointed in time and space, is endemic today. Looked at this way, *Ads*'s substitution of mediated signs of physical presence for the real thing is actually a form of realism: a mixed realism, for the age of augmented and otherwise admixed reality. So many of the means by which we seem to encounter each other in daily life—social networking sites, email, cellphones—attempt to embed "live" immediacy within their own particular, noisy forms of insistence (constant updates, instantaneous message exchanges).

But Maxwell also inserts interruptions that disrupt the delusive proximity of his apparitions: once or twice in the piece, figures lurch disconcertingly in place, wrenched forward in archival time by a deliberately choppy video edit. As the eye drifts over the projections, the grainy texture of the images—the enlarged pixels look like clouds of circulating particles on the verge of dissipation—occasionally reminds the viewer of the simulacra's digital origins. Such estranging moments cause spectators to become acutely aware of the other living bodies all around, the manifold ways in which the presence of the stranger seated next to you differs from that of the insubstantial figure onstage.

The subjects of the monologues are often weirdly resonant with their disembodied presentation, haunted by the trace of person-to-person connection. One speaker rhapsodizes the family dinner as a bastion of warm communal feeling threatened by internet social networks and electronic gizmos like smartphones that scatter attention, presence, and communication across vast expanses of time and space. Another, Wooster group mainstay and downtown icon Kate Valk, improvises on the jittery anticipation experienced by an actor about to confront a new audience and embark on an unrepeatable performance shaped by all the pressures of theatrical encounter. Musing on today's overindoctrinated parents, one performer delivers the kind of practical, folksy advice usually proffered on the spot by family friends and older relatives (to quell squabbling over who gets the biggest piece of cake, simply let one sibling slice and the other choose). Several speakers pointedly assert the ultimate privacy of their personal beliefs and indeed, their identities, maintaining that the self is that which we conceal from view, our most intimately vital thoughts are those that can't ever be adequately expressed. A few others describe the supreme importance of music to their lives, the art form most resistant to verbal definition, whose effects are most difficult to quantify, not unlike the indescribable *something* that electrifies memorable theatrical performances.

Each segment of *Ads* is like a Facebook profile turned inside out. On the site, rote or narrowly subversive answers to set biographical questions—favorite books, movies, and music, academic and work histories—supplemented with albums of photographs candid and posed and the aggregating record of correspondence and commentary created by one's wall and posts, add up to a composite public self, a collection of attitudes supposedly pointing to a unique individual. Although there are questions about both political and spiritual life—the "religion" box—the profile form tends to foster brief glib or banal statements, not serious self-examination. The performers in *Ads* present themselves not in terms of entertainment preferences or scholastic pedigrees but rather with their animating principles, however inchoate, inarticulate, or autodidactic. If the Facebook profile displays mostly surfaces, the human being as bundle of digestible data, the testimonials in *Ads* evince only depth. Here, we have just the deeply personal, idiosyncratic beliefs without any of the detail that might give these figures ground. Without their names, occupations, and origins, the performers are curiously contextless. We hear about their systems of ethics but can't know how these ideas are shaped by their daily lives.

Which brings up the question of the piece's title. Why *Ads*? Influenced by Naomi Klein's *No Logo*, which is about the insidious colonization of personal identity by corporate branding, Maxwell has said he decided to create a forum for decidedly noncommercial statements about the self. As he puts it, "the human body is seen as the final frontier for advertising."[6] Instead of commodity culture transforming the live body into a simulacrum of purchased and performed traits, life becoming lifestyle, he would stage the opposite: recorded images becoming somehow live. In *Performing Consumers*, Maurya Wickstrom uses Michael Taussig's notion of the "really made up" to describe the process whereby consumers "embody the resonances of the brand as feelings, sensations, and even memories . . . We loan the brand's character the phenomenological resources of our bodies. We play out its fictions, making them appear in three dimensions, as if they were real."[7] *Ads* hijacks our ingrained capacity to confer liveness on such immaterial fictions, turning our attention back on itself.

In his brief 1928 essay "These Surfaces for Rent," Walter Benjamin, confronted with the everyday shock tactics of modern advertising bombarding the gaze of the strolling pedestrian, comes to the unsettling conclusion that its obtrusive images and violent rhetoric actually represent the best hope of returning vitiated realities to themselves, restoring auratic luster to objects depreciated by endless reproduction:

> "Matter-of-factness" is finally dispatched, and in the face of the huge images spread across the walls of houses, where toothpaste and cosmetics lie handy for giants, sentimentality is restored to health and liberated in American style, just as people whom nothing moves or touches any longer are taught to cry again by films.[8]

Maxwell's advertisements, staging presence-in-absence and absence-in-presence, accomplish a similar trick. In parsing the gap between the almost-bodies, the near-proximity, of *Ads*'s simulacra and the imagined fullness of a tangible physical encounter, Maxwell's spectators are confronted with a more forceful iteration of theatrical presence—one more "live" than most theatrical performances. In this ghostly theater, everyday noise points the way back to music.

Looked at from the vantage point of 2017, Maxwell's piece anticipated many of the developments in mixed reality—the blending of digital representations and everyday actualities—that are fast becoming deeply ingrained in our daily lives. The wildly popular game Pokemon Go layers digital fantasias on prosaic geographies, making quotidian scenes into romping grounds for monsters, while also recording the feats of virtual capture and combat that take place in these impromptu arenas. Fitbits and health apps track the number of steps we take, and other vital signs, without knowing where we were strolling and what we saw along the way. Location settings suggest our routes while tracking our trajectories. Emojis aggregate and standardize transitory moods. We check in, self-locate, tag photos, look for our friends. These more recent self-monitoring practices join more venerable ones like Facebook sharing, Instagram posting, tweeting, and so on. The various archives that result from all this tabulation are at once deeply personal and deeply generic. One Fitbit tally looks very much like another, though those indexed strolls must have been scenes of private rumination.

The *Wire* magazine writers Gary Wolf and Kevin Kelly have termed this phenomenon the "quantified self,"[9] and this picture of identity is an inherently transmedial phenomenon: the aggregate of different data representations across many different platforms and devices; the living nexus of performance and archive. The quantified self exists at the scriptive intersection of app and body, mind and digital archive. New lived habits can be dictated by app notifications, memories reshuffled by photo feeds. In the mixed reality of contemporary life, tangible and digital blend together, in a dance of actuality and virtuality. Taken together, these practices add up not just to the quantification of the self, but to the creation of virtual bodies, ghostly doubles, like those that populate Maxwell's piece. But these surrogates can haunt our daily lives, shaping our future destinies. To this list, we can also add the imponderably huge archives once created by bulk data collection programs—the sedimented record of billions of conversations.

Social media's more benign practices of self-surveillance have arisen in tandem with cascading revelations about the ubiquity of government monitoring programs. In 2013, Edward Snowden's disclosures about the extent and scope of U.S. domestic surveillance programs brought a somewhat esoteric concept into widespread everyday parlance: metadata. A formerly innocuous technical term—referring to data that gives information about other data—had become the byword for government overreach. Among the data collected wholesale by security agencies were logs listing phone numbers, call times, and call durations. (Email addresses and time stamps were gathered, too.) For the National Security Agency, it seemed, the medium had become the message: how, for how long, and between what interlocutors communication was taking place was as important as what was being said. An accurate, if attenuated, portrait of whole networks of relations could be drawn without knowing a single word that had been exchanged. The conceptions of identity and intention implied by mass surveillance depend on a quasi-metaphysical logic: tracking a fleeting avatar across clusters of contacts, reading motive into medium. The actual aims and intentions of surveillance subjects—their thoughts, feelings, and beliefs—are ghosts in the apparatus.

Richard Maxwell, *Ad*'s author, couldn't have known about Snowden, but he did see, clearly, the emergent reality of the quantified self. We could think of *Ads*'s recorded fidgets and murmurs as the inverse of the tallied steps preserved by a Fitbit. Although like those tallied walks they're a record of the body's habitus, this data doesn't aggregate, predict, or illustrate. This is useless data, and deliberately so. It's noise. It doesn't signify anything useful, anything, that is, except the urge to communicate ineffable experience. Let's call this infradata. By that, I mean all the messy surplus of experience, affect, and speech that can't—and won't—be quantified. Maxwell deliberately stages the unquantified (and unquantifiable) self. *Ads* at once archived the "selves" of its participants, preserving their testimony as data, and frustrated any attempt to consider it as such an archive—the monologues can't easily be seen again, and aren't always available in the same sequence. *Ads*'s full-body images tantalize us with the possibility of seeing the "whole" person. And they offer us a mode of theatrical spectatorship more perfectly objectifying than the usual version. We're free to gaze at these figures without the risk that they'll look back, without the (small) danger that they'll notice the way we're looking at them. In this light, theatrical spectatorship is being stretched into something more like classical surveillance—our viewing position is even more remote than our close proximity to the figures would suggest, our safety seemingly more absolute.

But the piece is also acting on us in the way a good app does: it's compelling us to react to its digital figments as if they're actually there, to change our own thoughts, feelings, assumptions—our infradata—based on theirs. We're absorbing them into consciousness, and perhaps changing our future behaviors based on the experience. *Ads* is an app for re-engineering spectatorial assumptions, reminding us that proliferating self-representations only gesture to larger absences, that no archive is complete, that all promises of total self-knowledge are also invitations to hubris. Its transmedial meditations gesture to the still-elusive thing-in-itself of identity, always fleeing our reach. No medium is equal to our messages. The self remains unquantifiable, more than the sum of its statistics.

The NSA's immense dragnets are strangely evocative of Nature Theater of Oklahoma's expansive records of telephone eavesdropping, realized on a grander scale, or Lee Strasberg's extensive trove of self-surveillant recordings. In the digital age, it's not only the artists who aspire to see everything again, or who imagine that unforeseen meanings are encoded in everyday things. In the second decade of the twenty-first century, the cosmic murmur imagined by Thornton Wilder and revisited by Nature Theater of Oklahoma is now whispering in the air, and humming in server banks, as data-clouds archive passing words, thoughts, and gestures in rows of invisibly bright binary code. The iron cage grows more expansive as more and more of our daily lives is quantified, weighed, and measured, made searchable and recallable, archived and exhibited. We perform for ourselves, and for others, across many kinds of intangible stages, with the knowledge that we're being watched by spectators we choose—and many that we don't.

The emergent digital age presents us with a vision of quotidian experience and quotidian consciousness at once more reified and stable (archived, searchable) and more dispersed (spread out among platforms, apps, and databases) than ever before.

As a consequence, one of the quintessential affects of day-to-day life now is surfeit. We are always navigating a too-muchness: too many messages, notifications, images, facts, too many layers, to fully grasp. What are we to do with all these fragments, all these pieces, all this incompletion? But this vision of modern life as fragmented, assailing us with inassimilable noise, is nothing new.

Perhaps everything moves faster now, though the sense of modernity as moving too fast is hardly a new feeling. In my introduction, I mentioned John Dewey's hope that art could heal the fragmented perceptual fields of modern life, the frantic sense that no single experience has a chance to complete itself before another begins, that coherence can never emerge because there's always a new interruption: "What is called experience is so dispersed and miscellaneous as hardly to deserve the name."[10] The technologies have changed, as have contemporary life's characteristic forms of noisiness. But our awareness of everyday life as rife with distraction, the thwarting of attention with interruptions, or dispersal, or miscellaneousness, or ambiguity, would have been familiar to Dewey, too.

But Dewey's diagnosis didn't correspond to an imperative to retreat from modern life, or to a wish that a return to some cleaner, more profound form of experience was desirable, or even possible. Instead, he meant that art's serendipitous vantages, its unexpected perspectives and foci, could help us find new ways to gather the scattered fragments of the everyday. Art's consummating experiences could point us to the apprehension of new, necessarily temporary, unities, allowing us to see more clearly some of the small phenomena that pass us by all the time.

It has been the argument of this book that the artists of the American theater of the everyday have seen the theater as a place to realize Dewey's aspiration to forms of art that refine experience in this manner. They have organized new modes of seeing around the smallest shards of fleeting everyday experience, from Thornton Wilder's vagrant glances, to the Method's uncanny mumbles, to Stuart Sherman's restive things, to Nature Theater of Oklahoma's murmurs of consciousness, to Richard Maxwell's archived tokens of elapsed physical presence. The efforts of the artists considered here remind us that every piece of archived everyday experience awaits reconsideration, that the smallest thing, lifted from its place in a database or in our daily inventories, can be a source of reenchantment.

By all indications, we are now poised on the brink of a massive epistemological shift. A new age of automation beckons, with alluring promises and as-yet unimaginable consequences. Future advances in machine learning and artificial intelligence will mean that we conduct more and more of our day-to-day lives in collaboration with the uncanny gaze of technology. Self-driving cars and medical advice bots augur a future in which machine-perceived realities and human realities will overlap, in collusion and collision. But this still doesn't mean that the iron cage will finally succeed in enveloping everyday reality with perfect rationality.

The uncanny gaze of technology will continue to reveal new and surprising wonders lurking in previously unknown and unseen places. And the theater of the everyday reminds us that enchantment lies in those areas of ordinary experience that are still unnamed and unknown, that the smallest thing can prompt unforeseen insights. The difference beyond difference awaits us in the places we haven't glimpsed yet. And theater, a perceptual laboratory, the place where representation meets experience, the threshold zone where art encounters life, where composed objecthood is challenged by fallible materiality, can still give us a vital second look at what we never see for the first time.

NOTES

Introduction

1. Thornton Wilder, *Collected Plays & Writings on Theater,* ed. J. D. McClatchy (New York: Library of America, 2007), 203.

2. Ibid., 207.

3. Maurice Blanchot, "Everyday Speech," *Yale French Studies*, no. 73, "Everyday Life" (1987): 14.

4. Fernand Braudel, *The Structures of Everyday Life, Vol. 1*, trans. Siân Reynolds (New York: Harper and Row, 1981), 24.

5. Ludwig Wittgenstein, *Culture and Value* (Cambridge: Blackwell, 1998), 6e.

6. Rita Felski, introduction to "Everyday Life," special issue, *New Literary History* 33, no. 4 (2002): 607.

7. Arthur Danto, *The Transfiguration of the Commonplace: A Philosophy of Art* (Cambridge, Mass.: Harvard University Press, 1981), 2–3.

8. Solange Guénon, "Cinematographic Image, Democracy, and the 'Splendor of the Insignificant': Interview with Jacques Rancière," *Sites: The Journal of Contemporary Francophone Studies* 4, no. 2 (fall 2000): 249–58, at 253.

9. Arthur Miller, "Tragedy and the Common Man," in *Dramatic Theory and Criticism: Greeks to Grotowski*, ed. Bernard F. Dukore (Boston: Thomson Heinle, 1974), 894.

10. Ibid., 895.

11. Fredric Jameson, *The Antinomies of Realism* (London: Verso, 2013), 20.

12. See, for example, Patrick Healy's *New York Times* ArtsBeat blog piece on the subject: "'The Flick' Prompts an Explanation from Playwrights Horizons," March 25, 2013.

13. Peter Schjeldahl, *Let's See: Writings on Art from "The New Yorker"* (New York: Thames and Hudson, 2008), 153. Schjeldahl, writing about Thomas Struth's photographs, says that "Struth suggests photography is not a way to possess reality but a way to be possessed by it."

14. Lisi Schoenbach, *Pragmatic Modernism* (Oxford: Oxford University Press, 2012), 1–19.

15. James Harding, *The Ghosts of the Avant-Garde(s): Exorcising Experimental Theater and Performance* (Ann Arbor: University of Michigan Press, 2013), 62–63, 68–69.

16. Erich Auerbach, "On the Serious Imitation of the Everyday," in *Madame Bovary: A Norton Critical Edition,* ed. Margaret Cohen (New York: W. W. Norton, 2005), 434.

17. Jameson, *Antinomies of Realism*, 142–43.

18. Max Weber, "The Vocation of Science," in *The Essential Weber,* ed. Sam Whimster (London: Routledge, 2004), 282.

19. Jane Bennett, *The Enchantment of Modern Life* (Princeton, N.J.: Princeton University Press, 2001), 62.

20. Henri Lefebvre, *Critique of Everyday Life, Volume I* (London: Verso, 2008), 13–14.

21. Viktor Shklovsky, "Art as Technique," in *The Critical Tradition,* ed. David H. Richter (New York: Bedford/St. Martin's, 1997), 778.

22. Jameson, *Antinomies of Realism*, 29–31. For Amy Holzapafel, too, this uneasy interplay between subjective and objective impulses is the key to understanding theatrical realism. In her pathbreaking reappraisal of nineteenth-century playwrights like Ibsen, Strindberg, and Hauptmann, she argues that by the end of the century, realism, far from being a naive mode of mirror-like reflection, had become "a process of making visible the act of seeing." See her *Art, Vision, and Nineteenth-Century Realism: Acts of Seeing* (New York: Routledge, 2014), 186.

23. I am inspired here by the eloquent rationale laid out by Joshua Landy and Michael Saler for their superb collection of philosophical essays, *The Re-Enchantment of the World: Secular Magic in a Rational Age* (Stanford, Calif.: Stanford University Press, 2009). In their introduction, they argue that "there are, in the modern age, *fully secular and deliberate* strategies for re-enchantment . . . offering fully secular subjects an affirmation of existence that does not come at the cost of naïvete, irrationalism, or hypocrisy" (2; their emphasis).

24. Boris Groys, *Art Power* (Cambridge, Mass.: MIT Press, 2008), 36.

25. Ibid., 36.

26. Danto, *Transfiguration of the Commonplace*, 5.

27. See Kristin Ross, *Fast Cars and Clean Bodies: Decolonization and the Reordering of French Culture* (Cambridge, Mass.: MIT Press, 1996); and Ben Highmore, *Everyday Life and Cultural Theory* (London: Routledge, 2001).

28. Lefebvre, *Critique of Everyday Life*, 13–24.

29. Felski, introduction to "Everyday Life," 609.

30. Qtd. in ibid., 609.

31. Ibid., 610.

32. Michel de Certeau, *The Practice of Everyday Life*, trans. Steven Rendall (Berkeley: University of California Press, 1988), xviv.

33. Alan Read, *Theatre and Everyday Life: An Ethics of Performance* (New York: Routledge, 1993), 137.

34. De Certeau, *Practice of Everyday Life*, xx.

35. Liesl Olson, *Modernism and the Ordinary* (Oxford: Oxford University Press, 2009), 15.

36. Felski, introduction to "Everyday Life," 612.

37. Peter Burger, *The Theory of the Avant-Garde*, trans. Michael Shane (Minneapolis: University of Minnesota Press, 1984).

38. Toril Moi, *Ibsen and the Birth of Modernism: Art, Theater, Philosophy* (Oxford: Oxford University Press, 2006), especially 1–14 and 15–37.

39. Hans-Thies Lehmann, *Postdramatic Theatre,* trans. Karen Jurs-Munby (New York: Routledge, 2006), 43.

40. Stanley Cavell, *In Quest of the Ordinary: Lines of Skepticism and Romanticism* (Chicago: University of Chicago Press, 1994), especially 8–25.

41. George J. Leonard, *Into the Light of Things: The Art of the Commonplace from Wordsworth to John Cage* (Chicago: University of Chicago Press, 1994), 13–14.

42. John Dewey, *Art as Experience* (New York: Perigree, 2005), 49. See also the chapter on "Experience, Nature, and Art" in Dewey's *Experience and Nature* (New York: Dover, 1958), 354–94.

43. Ben Highmore, *Ordinary Lives* (London: Routledge, 2011), 38–40.

44. Harding, *Ghosts of the Avant-Garde(s)*, 68.

45. Dewey, *Art as Experience*, 42.

46. Martin Jay, *Songs of Experience: Modern American and European Variations on a Universal Theme* (Berkeley: University of California Press, 2006), 163.

47. Dewey, *Art as Experience*, 45.

48. Dewey, *Experience and Nature*, 167. I first encountered this statement in Martin Jay's *Songs of Experience.*

49. Jay, *Songs of Experience*, 295.

50. Ibid., 295–96.

51. See Harding, *Ghosts of the Avant-Garde(s)*, 19–20.

52. Harding coins the term "hybrid vanguardism" to characterize the more flexible ambitions of American experimentalists.

53. In employing this term, I of course rely on the thinking of Jacques Rancière, particularly his *Dissensus: On Politics and Aesthetics* (London: Continuum, 2010).

54. Michael Warner, *Publics and Counterpublics* (New York: Zone Books, 2005), 87.

55. Jonathan Katz, "John Cage's Queer Silence: or, How to Avoid Making Matters Worse," *GLQ: A Journal of Lesbian and Gay Studies* 5, no. 2 (1999): 231–52, at 248.

56. Jose Esteban Muñoz, *Cruising Utopia: The Then and There of Queer Futurity* (New York: New York University Press, 2009), 185–89.

57. Sacvan Bercovitch, "The Rites of Assent: Rhetoric, Ritual and the Ideology of American Consensus," in *The American Self: Myth, Ideology and Popular Culture*, ed. Sam Girgus (Albuquerque: University of New Mexico Press, 1980), 19–45.

58. Rebecca Schneider, *Performing Remains: Art and War in Times of Theatrical Re-Enactment* (London: Routledge, 2011), 12–26.

59. I'm influenced here by Walter Benjamin and Friedrich Kittler's examinations of the interrelation between modern media and modern knowledge, especially Benjamin's *The Work of Art in the Age of Its Technological Reproducibility and Other Writings on Media* (Cambridge, Mass.: Belknap Press, Harvard University, 2008); and Kittler's *Gramophone, Film, Typewriter*, trans. Geoffrey Winthrop-Young and Michael Wutz (Stanford, Calif.: Stanford University Press, 1999).

60. Benjamin, *The Work of Art in the Age of Its Technological Reproducibility*, 37.

61. See Juan A. Suárez's excellent discussion of the concept in the introduction to his *Pop Modernism: Noise and the Reinvention of the Everyday* (Urbana: University of Illinois Press, 2007), 1–19.

62. Kittler, *Gramophone, Film, Typewriter,* xxxix.

63. William James, *Essays in Radical Empiricism* (Lincoln: University of Nebraska Press, 1996), 23. I'm indebted to Martin Jay's *Songs of Experience* for bringing this book to my attention.

64. James, *Essays in Radical Empiricism*, 93–94.

65. Philip Auslander, *Liveness: Performance in a Mediatized Culture*, 2nd ed. (New York: Routledge, 2008).

66. In this, I have been profoundly influenced by Suárez's marvelous *Pop Modernism*. He links the increasing noisiness of American everyday life to the evolution of new cultural forms dedicated to transfiguring that noisiness. I gratefully acknowledge the debt here.

67. Bennett, *Enchantment of Modern Life*, 7.

68. John Cage, Michael Kirby, and Richard Schechner, "An Interview with John Cage," *The Tulane Drama Review* 10, no. 2 (winter 1965): 53–54.

69. Branka Arsic, *On Leaving: A Reading in Emerson* (Cambridge, Mass.: Harvard University Press, 2010).

70. As articulated in Cage's *Silence: Lectures and Writings* (Middletown, Conn.: Wesleyan University Press, 1973).

71. Benjamin, *The Work of Art in the Age of Its Technological Reproducibility*, 37.

72. Lehmann, *Postdramatic Theatre*.

73. Sally Banes, *Greenwich Village 1963: Avant-Garde Performance and the Effervescent Body* (Durham, N.C.: Duke University Press, 1993), 122–23.

74. See Marc Robinson, *The American Play: 1787–2000* (New Haven, Conn.: Yale University Press, 2009), 1–24.

75. Ben Highmore, "Bitter After Taste: Affect, Food and Social Aesthetics," in *The Affect Theory Reader,* ed. Melissa Gregg and Gregory J. Seigworth (Durham, N.C.: Duke University Press, 2010), 124.

Chapter 1

1. Ronald Gallup, ed., *The Journals of Thornton Wilder 1939–1961* (New Haven, Conn.: Yale University Press, 1985), 45.

2. Penelope Niven, *Thornton Wilder: A Life* (New York: HarperCollins, 2012), 369.

3. David Castronovo, *Thornton Wilder* (New York: Ungar, 1986), 1.

4. I'm far from the first to note the affinities between these early works and *Our Town*. Tappan Wilder calls *Our Town* the "dramatic child" of the three early plays in his afterword to the 2003 edition of *Our Town* (New York: Harper Perennial), 221.

5. See Edward M. Burns and Ulla E. Dydo with William Rice, eds., *The Letters of Gertrude Stein and Thornton Wilder* (New Haven, Conn.: Yale University Press, 1996), 68.

6. See Tappan Wilder's afterword to the 2003 edition of *Our Town*, 221. Also see Burns and Dydo, *Letters of Gertrude Stein*, 373.

7. Ann Douglas, *Terrible Honesty: Mongrel Manhattan in the 1920s* (New York: Farrar, Straus and Giroux, 1995), 179.

8. Thornton Wilder, *Collected Plays & Writings on Theater,* 657.

9. Ibid., 207.

10. Lincoln Konkle, *Thornton Wilder and the Puritan Narrative Tradition* (Columbia: University of Missouri Press, 2006), 107.

11. Ibid., 122.

12. Amos Niven Wilder, *Thornton Wilder and His Public* (Philadelphia: Fortress, 1980), 38–39.

13. Paul Lifton, *"Vast Encyclopedia": The Theatre of Thornton Wilder* (Westport, Conn.: Greenwood, 1995), 21–22.

14. Christopher J. Wheatley, *Thornton Wilder & Amos Wilder: Writing Religion in Twentieth Century America* (Notre Dame, Ind.: Notre Dame University Press, 2011), 116–23.

15. Ibid., 123.

16. Robinson, *American Play,* 200–201.

17. Jackson Bryer, ed., *Conversations with Thornton Wilder* (Jackson: University Press of Mississippi, 1992), 68.

18. Arsic, *On Leaving*, 3.

19. See Wilder's essay "Toward an American Language" in *American Characteristics* (New York: Harper and Row, 1979), 3–34.

20. Isabel Wilder, "Foreword," in *American Characteristics,* xiii.

21. Qtd. in Arsic, *On Leaving*, 87.

22. Thornton Wilder, *Collected Plays & Writings on Theater*, 686.

23. Qtd. in Arsic, *On Leaving*, 10.

24. Ibid., 87–88.

25. Thornton Wilder, *American Characteristics*, 5–6.

26. Cavell, *In Quest of the Ordinary,* 8–25.

27. Gallup, ed., *Journals of Thornton Wilder*, 207.

28. Dewey, *Art as Experience*, 49.

29. Thornton Wilder, *American Characteristics*, 16.

30. Ibid., 694.

31. In his valuable essay on Wilder's "American loneliness," Timothy Youker analyzes Wilder's notion of "houses of thought" in terms of his "desire to use the cooperative work of representation and performance to cure the existential loneliness that was fundamental to his own exceptionalist definition of American character." See Timothy Youker, "'His Own House of Thought': Thornton Wilder's 'American Loneliness' and the Consolation of Theater," *The Journal of American Drama and Theatre* 24, no. 2 (spring 2012): 89–108, at 89.

32. At the beginning of *Our Town*'s third act, the stage directions stipulate that "ten or twelve ordinary chairs" representing the graves "have been placed in three openly spaced rows facing the audience." Thornton Wilder, *Collected Plays & Writings on Theater*, 195.

33. Ibid., 95.

34. Ibid., 77.

35. Ibid., 139.

36. Dwight Macdonald, *Against the American Grain* (New York: Da Capo, 1983), 43–44.

37. Ibid., 43–44.

38. Amos Niven Wilder, *Thornton Wilder and His Public*, 27.

39. Bryer, ed., *Conversations with Thornton Wilder.*

40. Reprinted in Thornton Wilder, *American Characteristics*, 65–74.

41. Bryer, ed., *Conversations with Thornton Wilder*, 157.
42. Ibid., 102.
43. Ibid., 108.
44. Robinson, *American Play*, 207–8.
45. For examples: Thornton Wilder, *Collected Plays & Writings on Theater*, 96, 99, 190, and many other places besides.
46. Bryer, ed., *Conversations with Thornton Wilder*, 102.
47. Thornton Wilder, *Collected Plays & Writings on Theater*, 682–85.
48. Thornton Wilder, *American Characteristics*, 7.
49. Ibid., 7–8.
50. Thornton Wilder, *Collected Plays & Writings on Theater*, 688.
51. Peter Brooks, *Realist Vision* (New Haven, Conn.: Yale University Press, 2005), 1.
52. Ibid., 3.
53. Bert O. States, *Great Reckonings in Little Rooms: On the Phenomenology of Theater* (Berkeley: University of California Press, 1987), 68.
54. "Plays without Scenery Give New York Theatre-Goers a New Dramatic Thrill," *Life Magazine*, February 28, 1938.
55. Thornton Wilder, *Collected Plays & Writings on Theater*, 195.
56. Amos Niven Wilder, *Thornton Wilder and His Public*, 56.
57. Travis Bogard notes these details to a different interpretive purpose in his "The Comedy of Thornton Wilder," in *The Modern American Theatre,* ed. Alvin B. Kernan (Englewood Cliffs, N.J.: Prentice-Hall, 1967), 52–53, 61–62.
58. Arsic, *On Leaving*, 55.
59. Ibid., 71.
60. Ibid.
61. Ibid., 69.
62. Thornton Wilder, *Collected Plays & Writings on Theater*, 686.
63. Peter Szondi, *The Theory of the Modern Drama* (Minneapolis: University of Minnesota Press, 1987), 91.
64. Stephen Kern, *The Culture of Time and Space, 1880–1918* (Cambridge, Mass.: Harvard University Press, 2003).
65. In his preface to *Our Town*, Wilder phrases this split concern with private and public time like this: "What is the relation between the countless 'unimportant' details of our daily life, on the one hand, and the great perspectives of time, social history, and current religious ideas, on the other?" *Collected Plays & Writings on Theater*, 657.
66. Jameson, *Antinomies of Realism*, 29–31.
67. Thornton Wilder, *Collected Plays & Writings on Theater*, 175.
68. Ibid., 194.
69. Ibid., 209.
70. Ibid., 170–72.
71. Ibid., 71.
72. Ibid., 684.
73. In Robin G. Wilder and Jackson R. Bryer, eds., *The Selected Letters of Thornton Wilder* (New York: Harper Perennial, 2008), 571.
74. Ibid., 71.
75. Thornton Wilder, *Collected Plays & Writings on Theater*, 657.

76. Ibid., 72.
77. Michael Fried, *Art and Objecthood: Essays and Reviews* (Chicago: University of Chicago Press, 1998), 148.
78. Ibid., 157.
79. Thornton Wilder, *Collected Plays & Writings on Theater,* 108.
80. Wilder and Bryer, *Selected Letters of Thornton Wilder*, 508.
81. Robinson, *American Play*, 202.
82. Bryer, ed., *Conversations with Thornton Wilder*, 23.
83. Ibid., 19–20.
84. Burns and Dydo with Rice, eds., *Letters of Gertrude Stein and Thornton Wilder*, 68.
85. Qtd. in Szondi, *Theory of the Modern Drama*, 91.
86. Thornton Wilder, *Collected Plays & Writings on Theater*, 61.
87. Siobhan Phillips, "The Daily Living of Robert Frost," *PMLA* 123, no. 3 (2008): 598.
88. Thornton Wilder, *Collected Plays & Writings on Theater*, 62.
89. Robinson, *American Play*, 202.
90. Thornton Wilder, *Collected Plays & Writings on Theater*, 61.
91. Qtd. in Jeffrey S. Cramer, ed., *I to Myself: An Annotated Selection from the Journal of Henry D. Thoreau* (New Haven, Conn.: Yale University Press, 2012), 3. I'm deeply grateful to Marc Robinson for bringing this telling piece of homage to my attention.
92. Ibid., 3.
93. Thornton Wilder, *Collected Plays & Writings on Theater*, 61.
94. Ibid., 655.
95. Ibid., 61.
96. Ibid., 77.
97. Sources listing this date are too numerous to count, ranging from popular histories, to memoirs, to collections of Puritan songs and stories. It is still reproduced in works of popular American history.
98. Thornton Wilder, *Collected Plays & Writings on Theater*, 95–96.
99. Ibid.
100. Ibid., 686–87.
101. Ibid., 103.
102. Ibid., 100–103.
103. Ibid., 97.
104. Ibid., 104.
105. Ibid., 106.
106. Ibid., 106–7.
107. Ibid., 99.
108. Ibid., 102.
109. Ibid.
110. Ibid., 101.
111. Ibid., 102–3.
112. Ibid., 100.
113. Ibid., 101.
114. *Pullman Car Hiawatha*'s railcar setting recalls other important train images from the period: most of all, the talkative Pullman train whose "monotonous

rumble" concludes Henry James's *The American Scene*, trumpeting "See what I'm making of all this—see what I'm making, what I'm making." (I'm indebted to Bill Brown's *A Sense of Things* for bringing the passage to my attention. See Brown, *A Sense of Things: The Object Matter of American Literature* [Chicago: University of Chicago Press, 2003], 177–78.) But it also calls to mind the locomotive that carries Kafka's Karl Rossman, transfixed by awe, deeper into the unknown American sublime at the end of *Amerika*; and the scene of the narrator's observation, at the end of *The Great Gatsby*—a book Wilder knew and loved—that he feels most like an American while in motion, seeing the country in blurred swatches from the window of a speeding train. It's worth making at least a passing comparison with Witkiewicz's 1923 play *The Crazy Locomotive* as well, since it was roughly coincident, but markedly different in import. Witkiewicz figures modernity as a train accelerating off its rails, no longer in the control of either passengers or conductor; Wilder simply sees constant momentum as the predicament of the human mind, whether we realize it or not.

115. Thornton Wilder, *Collected Plays & Writings on Theater*, 102.

116. Arsic, *On Leaving*, 55.

117. Thornton Wilder, *Collected Plays & Writings on Theater*, 129–31.

118. Qtd. in Niven, *Thornton Wilder: A Life*, 349.

119. Thornton Wilder, *Collected Plays & Writings on Theater*, 141.

120. Ibid.

121. Ibid., 136–37.

122. Ibid., 134.

123. Ibid., 140.

124. Ibid., 135.

125. Ibid., 139.

126. Ibid., 142.

127. Arsic, *On Leaving*, 3.

128. Ibid., 3.

129. Highmore, "Bitter After Taste," 122.

130. Thornton Wilder, *Collected Plays & Writings on Theater,* 151–53.

131. Ibid., 192–93.

132. Joseph R. Roach. "The Great Hole of History: Liturgical Silence in Beckett, Osofisan, and Parks," *The South Atlantic Quarterly* 100, no. 1 (2001): 307–17.

133. Thornton Wilder, *Collected Plays & Writings on Theater*, 203–4.

134. Ibid., 149.

135. Ibid., 152, 153, 156–57.

136. Roland Barthes, "The Reality Effect," in Roland Barthes, *The Rustle of Language*, trans. Richard Howard (Berkeley: University of California Press, 1989), 141–48.

137. Thornton Wilder, *Collected Plays & Writings on Theater*, 162.

138. Ibid., 686.

139. Arthur Miller, "The Family in Modern Drama," in *The Theater Essays of Arthur Miller*, ed. Robert A. Martin and Steve Centola (New York: Da Capo, 1996), 79.

140. Thornton Wilder, *Collected Plays & Writings on Theater*, 659.

141. Ibid., 165.

142. Thornton Wilder, *American Characteristics*, 148.

Chapter 2

An abridged version of this chapter was previously published as "Mediating the Method," in *Theatre Survey* 56, no. 3 (September 2015): 291–313.

1. Cage, *Silence: Lectures and Writings*, 3.

2. Richard Blum, *American Film Acting: The Stanislavski Heritage* (Ann Arbor: University of Michigan Research Press, 1984), xvi.

3. For an evocative account of the Town Hall concert and its place in John Cage's body of work, see David Grubbs, *Records Ruin the Landscape: John Cage, the Sixties, and Sound Recording* (Durham, N.C.: Duke University Press, 2014).

4. Robert Brustein, "America's New Culture Hero: Feelings without Words," *Commentary* 25 (February 1958): 123–29.

5. Ibid., 123.

6. For recent considerations of these and other questions raised by the Method and its legacy, see David Krasner, ed., *Method Acting Reconsidered: Theory, Practice, Future* (New York: St. Martin's, 2000); Rosemary Malague, *An Actress Prepares: Women and "the Method"* (New York: Routledge, 2012); and Shonni Enelow, *Method Acting and Its Discontents* (Evanston, Ill.: Northwestern University Press, 2015).

7. Benjamin, *The Work of Art in the Age of Its Technological Reproducibility*, 37.

8. Kittler, *Gramophone, Film, Typewriter*, 23–24.

9. Cage predicted this new mode of music-making in his 1937 essay-manifesto "The Future of Music: Credo," reprinted in Cage, *Silence: Lectures and Writings*, 3–6.

10. Juan A. Suárez, *Pop Modernism: Noise and the Reinvention of the Everyday* (Urbana: University of Illinois Press, 2007), 8.

11. Ibid., 8–9.

12. Ibid., 9.

13. Ludwig Wittgenstein, *Culture and Value*, trans. Peter Winch (Chicago: University of Chicago Press, 1980), 4e. I first encountered this enormously suggestive fragment in Michael Fried, *Why Photography Matters as Art as Never Before* (New Haven, Conn.: Yale University Press, 2008).

14. Robert H. Hethmon, ed., *Strasberg at the Actors Studio: Tape-Recorded Sessions* (New York: Viking, 1965), 118. Cited hereafter directly in the text with parenthetical text references.

15. See Strasberg's discussion of these exercises in *A Dream of Passion: The Development of the Method* (New York: Plume, 1988). *Strasberg at the Actors Studio* contains several pages of evocative photographs of students performing the exercises in the classroom.

16. Marianne Conroy, "Acting Out: Method Acting, the National Culture, and the Middlebrow Disposition in Cold War America," *Criticism* 35, no. 2 (1993): 239–63, at 249.

17. Harold Clurman, introduction to Robert Lewis, *Method—or Madness?* (New York: Samuel French, 1958), xi–xiii, at xi.

18. Lewis, *Method—or Madness?* 5.

19. Ibid. Lewis also admits (jokingly?) that he can't prove it's really Salvini on the record. ("It better be—I paid the guy enough for it.")

20. Ibid., 11.

21. Gordon Rogoff, "Lee Strasberg: Burning Ice," *Tulane Drama Review* 9, no. 2 (1964): 131–54, at 141.

22. Ibid., 140.

23. Malague, *An Actress Prepares*, especially 30, 33–34.

24. Enelow, *Method Acting and Its Discontents*, 43.

25. Ibid., 26–27.

26. Lewis, *Method—or Madness?* 109.

27. See Harold Clurman, "Actors in Style—and Style in Actors," *New York Times Magazine*, December 7, 1952, 26–27, 34, 36, 38, at 38.

28. Michael Redgrave quoted in Conroy, "Acting Out," 247.

29. Howard Taubman, "A Tender *Three Sisters*," *New York Times*, June 23, 1964.

30. Ibid.

31. Conroy, "Acting Out," 253.

32. Elia Kazan, *Kazan on Directing* (New York: Vintage, 2009), 57. Also see Brenda Murphy, *Tennessee Williams and Elia Kazan: A Collaboration in the Theatre* (New York: Cambridge University Press, 1992), 53–54.

33. Conroy, "Acting Out," 255–56.

34. Laura Marks, "Video Haptics and Erotics," *Screen* 39, no. 4 (1998): 331–48, at 331.

35. Kazan, *Kazan on Directing*, 157.

36. Paige McGinley, "Reconsidering the 'American Style': Black Performers and Black Music in *Streetcar* and *Cat*," *Theatre Journal* 68, no. 1 (March 2016): 1–15, at 3.

37. George Crandell, "Misrepresentation and Miscegenation: Reading the Racialized Discourse of Tennessee Williams's *A Streetcar Named Desire*," *Modern Drama* 40, no. 3 (fall 1997): 337–46.

38. Brustein, "America's New Culture Hero," 7.

39. Suárez, *Pop Modernism*, 10.

40. In Richard Kostelanetz, ed., *John Cage* (New York: Praeger, 1970), 115.

Chapter 3

The epigraphs are from "Stuart Sherman, Journals—Loose Sheets," Stuart Sherman Papers, series III, box I, folder 26, Downtown Collection, Fales Library, New York University, n.p.

1. John Matturi makes a similar observation in a different context in his excellent essay on Sherman's drawings, John Matturi, "Legible Worlds: The Early Drawings of Stuart Sherman," in *Beginningless Thought/Endless Seeing: The Works of Stuart Sherman* (New York: 80SWE, 2009), 79.

2. Yolanda Hawkins, "Quotidian Performance" in *Beginningless Thought/Endless Seeing: The Works of Stuart Sherman*, 31.

3. Trudy Scott, "Stuart Sherman's Singular Spectacles," *The Drama Review* 23, no. 1, "Autoperformance" issue (March 1979): 77.

4. Ibid.

5. Stuart Sherman, "Misc. Notes and Poetry—Loose Sheets and Notebook," Stuart Sherman Papers, series III, box I, folder 28, Downtown Collection, Fales Library, New York University, n.p.

6. Here, and throughout this chapter, I refer to the video recordings of Sherman's pieces held with his papers at New York University's Fales Library and in the digitized collections at Electronic Arts Intermix, the New York performance and video art archive.

7. Brooks McNamara, "Stuart Sherman's Third Spectacle," *The Drama Review* 20, no. 2, "American Theatre" issue (June 1976): 54.

8. Qtd. in catalog insert, *Beginningless Thought/Endless Seeing*, n.p.

9. Ibid., n.p.

10. Ibid., n.p.

11. The drawing is reproduced in *Beginningless Thought/Endless Seeing*, 64–65.

12. Matturi, "Legible Worlds," 79.

13. Scott, "Stuart Sherman's Singular Spectacles," 69.

14. Matturi, "Legible Worlds," 78.

15. Qtd. in catalog insert, *Beginningless Thought/Endless Seeing*, n.p.

16. Stuart Sherman, "Journals—Loose Sheets," Stuart Sherman Papers, series III, box I, folder 26, Downtown Collection, Fales Library, New York University, n.p.

17. Philip Fisher, *Wonder, the Rainbow, and the Aesthetics of Rare Experiences* (Cambridge, Mass.: Harvard University Press, 1998), 20–21.

18. McNamara, "Stuart Sherman's Third Spectacle," 48.

19. Ibid., 54.

20. Ibid., 54–55.

21. Berenice Reynaud has also made this communion comparison, though to opposite ends—using the analogy to suggest that Sherman's "manner" during a performance is "withdrawn in his concentration" and that his "fleeting eye-contact negates the existence of his audience." She also suggests that this policy of deliberate understatement "evokes no sense of pleasure, none of the evident delight one might see in an actor or musician." I must disagree: where she sees withdrawal, I see quiet irony, and gentle solicitude. Sherman is alive to his audience's presence in manifold ways, the most profound being his self-effacing desire to present fertile material for their contemplation without obtruding his own pre-interpretations. See her essay "Stuart Sherman: Object Ritual," trans. Thomas Repensek, *October* 8 (spring 1979): 66–67.

22. See the introduction to Sofer's *The Stage Life of Props* (Ann Arbor: University of Michigan Press, 2003), 1–30.

23. Sherman, "Misc. Notes and Poetry—Loose Sheets and Notebook."

24. Stuart Sherman, "Reviews by Stuart Sherman," Stuart Sherman Papers, series III, box I, folder 31, Downtown Collection, Fales Library, New York University, n.p.

25. Jennifer Anna Gosetti-Ferencei, *The Ecstatic Quotidian: Phenomenological Sightings in Art and Literature* (Philadelphia: University of Pennsylvania Press, 2007), 1.

26. Arnold Aronson, *American Avant-Garde Theatre* (New York: Routledge, 2000), 173–74.

27. Babette Mangolte, "Stuart Sherman: Performer and Performance Artist," in *Beginningless Thought/Endless Seeing*, 19–20.

28. Bonnie Marranca, *The Theatre of Images* (New York: PAJ Books, 2005).
29. Sherman, “Misc. Notes and Poetry—Loose Sheets and Notebook.”
30. Bert O. States, *Great Reckonings in Little Rooms: On the Phenomenology of Theater* (Berkeley: University of California Press, 1985), 65.
31. Bill Brown, “Thing Theory,” *Critical Inquiry* 28 (2001): 3–4. See also Brown’s *A Sense of Things: The Object Matter of American Literature* (Chicago: University of Chicago Press, 2003).
32. Robin Bernstein, “Dances with Things: Material Culture and the Performance of Race,” *Social Text* 101, 27, no. 4 (winter 2009): 67–94.
33. Brown, “Thing Theory,” 4.
34. Sherman, “Journals—Loose Sheets,” n.p.
35. My discussion here is inspired by Barbara Johnson’s brilliant meditation on these figures in her book *Persons and Things* (Cambridge, Mass.: Harvard University Press, 2008), 3–23.
36. Reynaud, “Stuart Sherman: Object Ritual,” 60.
37. Ibid., 58.
38. Ibid., 63.
39. Ibid., 72.
40. Ibid., 61.
41. Ibid., 60.
42. Ibid.
43. Jay Hoberman, “‘Like Canyons and Rivers’: Performance for Its Own Sake,” in Jay Sanders and Hoberman’s catalog for the Whitney Museum exhibition *Rituals of Rented Island* (New Haven, Conn.: Whitney Museum/ Yale University Press, 2013), 16.
44. Brown, *A Sense of Things*, 178.
45. Ibid., 185.
46. Ibid., 187.
47. Reynaud, “Stuart Sherman: Object Ritual,” 67–68.
48. Ibid., 69.
49. Ibid., 73.
50. Qtd. in catalog insert, *Beginningless Thought/Endless Seeing*, n.p.
51. Michael Taussig, “Physiognomic Aspects of Visual Worlds,” *Visual Anthropology Review* 8, no. 1 (spring 1992): 15–28.
52. Gosetti-Ferencei, *Ecstatic Quotidian*, 165.
53. Maurice Merleau-Ponty, *Sense and Nonsense*, trans. Hubert L. Dreyfus and Patricia A. Dreyfus (Evanston, Ill.: Northwestern University Press, 1964), 64.
54. Qtd. in Sherman, “Journals—Loose Sheets,” n.p.
55. Gosetti-Ferencei, *Ecstatic Quotidian*, 32.
56. Ibid., 27–28; my italics.
57. Martin Heidegger, “The Thing,” in *Poetry Language Thought*, trans. Albert Hofstadter (New York: Harper and Row, 1971).
58. Stefan Brecht, *Queer Theatre* (London: Methuen, 1986).
59. Sherman, “Misc. Notes and Poetry—Loose Sheets and Notebook.”
60. See Jill Johnston’s vivid account of the piece in the *Village Voice*, May 21, 1964, 12. I first encountered Johnston’s review in Sally Banes’s peerless *Terpsichore in Sneakers: Postmodern Dance* (Middletown, Conn.: Wesleyan University Press, 1987), 134–35.

61. Martha Rosler, "Semiotics of the Kitchen," available at http://ubu.com/lm/rosler_semiotics.html.

62. I'm grateful to Miriam Felton-Dansky for alerting me to the affinities between Rosler and Sherman, and for her incisive reading of Rosler's piece, which I draw on here. See her article "Anonymous Is a Woman: The New Politics of Identification in *Magical* and *Untitled Feminist Show*," *Theatre Journal* 67, no. 2 (May 2015): 253–71, at 258–60.

63. Gaston Bachelard, *The Poetics of Space,* trans. Maria Jolas (Boston: Beacon, 1994), 154–55.

64. Fisher, *Wonder, the Rainbow*, 20–21.

65. Jacques Rancière, *The Politics of Aesthetics: The Distribution of the Sensible* (New York: Continuum, 2004), 1.

Chapter 4

1. Franz Kafka, *Amerika*, trans. Willa Muir and Edwin Muir (New York: Schocken, 1996), 272.

2. Ibid., 279.

3. Blanchot, "Everyday Speech," 14.

4. Kafka, *Amerika*, 273–77.

5. Ibid., 298.

6. Young Jean Lee, "Nature Theater of Oklahoma," *Bomb* 108 (summer 2009): 89.

7. Unless otherwise noted, all quotations from Copper and Liska come from my interview with them at their apartment on St. Mark's Place in New York City on June 22, 2009.

8. Lee, "Nature Theater of Oklahoma," 89.

9. Karinne Keithley, "Uncreative Writing: Nature Theater of Oklahoma's *Romeo and Juliet*," *Theater* 40, no. 2 (2010): 72.

10. In an email she sent me some time after I initially drafted this chapter, about the published version of the chapter's section about *The Life and Times*, Kelly Copper mentions in passing that John Dewey is one of Nature Theater's biggest influences.

11. Blanchot, "Everyday Speech," 14.

12. Diana Taylor, *The Archive and the Repertoire: Performing Cultural Memory in the Americas* (Durham, N.C.: Duke University Press, 2003), 19.

13. I'm indebted to Joseph Roach for this formulation. See his editorial "Kinesis: The New Mimesis" in *Theater* 40, no. 1 (2010): 1–2, at 2.

14. Walt Whitman, *The Portable Walt Whitman* (New York: Penguin, 2003), 558.

15. Qtd. in Banes, *Greenwich Village 1963*, 119.

16. Kelly Copper and Amber Reed, "Getting Cosmic with Kelly Copper," *The Brooklyn Rail*, December 2006, 8.

17. See W. B. Worthen, "Intoxicating Rhythms: Shakespeare, Literature, and Performance: Nature Theater of Oklahoma, Romeo and Juliet," in his *Shakespeare Performance Studies* (New York: Cambridge University Press, 2014), 66–67.

18. Siobhan Phillips, *The Poetics of the Everyday: Creative Repetition in Modern American Verse* (New York: Columbia University Press, 2009), 204.

19. Ibid., 204–5.

20. To call this an "aesthetics of fun," as Rachel Anderson-Rabern does in a recent article on the company's work, is perhaps to overemphasize surface gratifications at the expense of fully considering the rigorous artistic program that lies underneath. It's vital to recognize the ambiguous, anxious, and subtle thinking coursing beneath this theater's considerable charm. See Anderson-Rabern, "The Nature Theater of Oklahoma's Aesthetics of Fun," *TDR: The Drama Review* 54, no. 4 (winter 2010): 81–98.

21. In this and following sections, my analyses of Nature Theater's pieces are based primarily on firsthand viewing of the pieces in performance, supplemented by consulting video recordings provided by the company. Where noted, I quote from the published versions of the scripts.

22. Portions of this section of the chapter were previously published as "Dancing to the Cosmic Murmur: John Cage, Richard Foreman, and Nature Theater of Oklahoma's *No Dice*," *TheatreForum* 34 (winter 2009): 92–98.

23. Nature Theater of Oklahoma, *No Dice* (New York: 53rd State, 2007), 68.

24. Ibid., 71.

25. Ibid., 79–80.

26. Ibid., 81–82.

27. Ibid., 98.

28. Ibid., 147.

29. Ibid., 3.

30. In his recent book *Passionate Amateurs* (Ann Arbor: University of Michigan Press, 2013), Nicholas Ridout makes a similar point, arguing that "what is to be redeemed, in and through the production and performance of *No Dice*, is precisely the (life)time spent on all those other jobs, some of which seem to have involved little more than the passing of time through the mere occupation of space" (130).

31. Qtd. in Sarah Benson, "Working Downtown," *PAJ: Performing Arts Journal* 83 (2006): 45.

32. Campbell Robertson, "Theater Team Makes an Ally of Random Circumstance," *New York Times*, January 3, 2008, 1.

33. Amber Reed, Introduction to Nature Theater, *No Dice*, 2.

34. Robertson, "Theater Team," 2.

35. Nature Theater, *No Dice*, 148.

36. Ibid., 149.

37. Richard Schechner, *Performance Theory* (New York: Routledge, 2003), 28.

38. Nature Theater, *No Dice*, 28.

39. Ibid., 33.

40. Michael Kirby and Richard Schechner, "An Interview with John Cage," in *The Drama Review: Thirty Years of Commentary on the Avant-Garde*, ed. Brooks McNamara and Jill Dolan (Ann Arbor: University of Michigan Press, 1986), 84.

41. Qtd. in Benson, "Working Downtown," 60.

42. Thornton Wilder, *Collected Plays & Writings on Theater*, 686.

43. Nature Theater, *No Dice*, 151.

44. Ibid., 152.

45. Kelly Copper, email to the author.

46. W. B. Worthen, in his fascinating essay on the piece, implicating it in recent debates about the relative primacy of literature and theater in shaping our

conception of Shakespeare the author, also links Nature Theater's investigations to Levine's argument. But Worthen's emphasis is different: he ingeniously links the piece to traditions of Shakespeare education in the United States, and to vernacular "translations" of Shakespeare like *No Fear Shakespeare.* I focus here on the piece's place in Nature Theater's larger body of work: its investigation of the everyday use value of well-known stories—whether of high or low art origins—and the creative substitutions that compensate for the inevitable loss endemic to our encounters with the absent original. See Worthen, "Intoxicating Rhythms," 30–79.

47. Lawrence Levine, *Highbrow/Lowbrow: The Emergence of Cultural Hierarchy in America* (Cambridge, Mass.: Harvard University Press, 1986), 11–82.

48. Nature Theater of Oklahoma, "*Nature Theater of Oklahoma's Romeo and Juliet*," *Theater* 40, no. 2 (winter 2010): 76.

49. George Hunka, "The Booking of the Play," *Theater* 40, no. 2 (winter 2010): 23.

50. Nature Theater, "*Nature Theater of Oklahoma's Romeo and Juliet*," 83.

51. Ibid., 77.

52. Ibid., 91.

53. Worthen, "Intoxicating Rhythms," 53.

54. Nature Theater, "*Nature Theater of Oklahoma's Romeo and Juliet*," 109.

55. Ibid., 112.

56. William Shakespeare, *Romeo and Juliet*, in *The Oxford Shakespeare: The Complete Works*, ed. Stanley Wells and Gary Taylor (Oxford: Oxford University Press, 2005), 2.1.161–62.

57. A version of part of this section was previously published as "This Is Your Life: Nature Theater of Oklahoma's The Life and Times, One Episode In," in *PAJ: Performing Arts Journal* 102 (2012): 63–70.

58. Lawrence Switzky, "Marathon Theatre as Affective Labour: Productive Exhaustion in the *Godot Cycle* and *Life and Times,*" *Canadian Theatre Review* 162 (spring 2015): 29.

59. Douglas Eklund, *The Pictures Generation: 1974–1984* (New York: Metropolitan Museum of Art, 2009), 56.

60. Switzky, "Marathon Theatre," 30.

Coda

A version of this section was previously published as "Maxwell's Ghosts: The New York City Players' Ads," *PAJ: Performing Arts Journal* 98 (2011): 44–50.

1. Jesse McKinley, "Playwright's Trademark Is Deadpan. Now He Wants to Tweak It," *The New York Times*, January 18, 2006.

2. Roland Barthes, *Camera Lucida* (New York: Hill and Wang, 1981), 80.

3. Kittler, *Gramophone, Film, Typewriter*, 13.

4. Roland Barthes, *Image Music Text* (New York: Hill and Wang, 1977), 157.

5. Lionel Trilling, *Sincerity and Authenticity* (Cambridge, Mass.: Harvard University Press, 1972).

6. Richard Maxwell, "Ads: Artist's Preface," *Theater* 40, no. 3 (winter 2010): 68.

7. Maurya Wickstrom, *Performing Consumers: Global Capital and Its Theatrical Seductions* (New York: Routledge, 2006), 2.

8. Benjamin, *The Work of Art in the Age of Its Technological Reproducibility*, 173.

9. See, for example, Gary Wolf's *Wired* essay "Know Thyself: Tracking Every Facet of Life from Sleep to Mood to Pain, 24/7/365," June 22, 2009.

10. Dewey, *Art as Experience*, 45.

BIBLIOGRAPHY

Anderson-Rabern, Rachel. "The Nature Theater of Oklahoma's Aesthetics of Fun." *TDR: The Drama Review* 54, no. 4 (winter 2010): 81–98.

Aronson, Arnold. *American Avant-Garde Theatre*. New York: Routledge, 2000.

Arsic, Branka. *On Leaving: A Reading in Emerson*. Cambridge, Mass.: Harvard University Press, 2010.

Auerbach, Erich. "On the Serious Imitation of the Everyday." In *Madame Bovary: A Norton Critical Edition*, ed. Margaret Cohen, 423–48. New York: W. W. Norton, 2005.

Auslander, Philip. *Liveness: Performance in a Mediatized Culture*. 2nd ed. New York: Routledge, 2008.

Bachelard, Gaston. *The Poetics of Space*. Trans. Maria Jolas. Boston: Beacon, 1994.

Banes, Sally. *Democracy's Body: Judson Dance Theater, 1962–1964*. Durham, N.C.: Duke University Press, 1993.

———. *Greenwich Village 1963: Avant-Garde Performance and the Effervescent Body*. Durham, N.C.: Duke University Press, 1993.

———. *Terpsichore in Sneakers: Postmodern Dance*. Middletown, Conn.: Wesleyan University Press, 1987.

Barthes, Roland. *Camera Lucida*. New York: Hill and Wang, 1981.

———. *Image, Music, Text*. New York: Hill and Wang, 1977.

———. "The Reality Effect." In *The Rustle of Language*, trans. Richard Howard, 141–48. Berkeley: University of California Press, 1989.

Benjamin, Walter. *The Work of Art in the Age of Its Technological Reproducibility and Other Writings on Media*. Cambridge, Mass.: Belknap Press, Harvard University, 2008.

Bennett, Jane. *The Enchantment of Modern Life*. Princeton, N.J.: Princeton University Press, 2001.

Benson, Sarah. "Working Downtown." *PAJ: Performing Arts Journal* 83 (2006): 42–60.

Bercovitch, Sacvan. "The Rites of Assent: Rhetoric, Ritual and the Ideology of American Consensus." In *The American Self: Myth, Ideology and Popular Culture*, ed. Sam Girgus, 19–45. Albuquerque: University of New Mexico Press, 1980.

Berger, Jonathan, ed. *Nothing Up My Sleeve: An Exhibition Based on the Work of Stuart Sherman*. New York: Participant/Regency Arts, 2010.

Bernstein, Robin. "Dances with Things: Material Culture and the Performance of Race." *Social Text* 101, vol. 27, no. 4 (winter 2009): 67–94.

Blanchot, Maurice. "Everyday Speech." *Yale French Studies*, no. 73, "Everyday Life" (1987): 12–20.

Blum, Richard. *American Film Acting: The Stanislavski Heritage*. Ann Arbor: University of Michigan Research Press, 1984.

Bogard, Travis. "The Comedy of Thornton Wilder." In *The Modern American Theatre,* ed. Alvin B. Kernan, 51–63. Englewood Cliffs, N.J.: Prentice-Hall, 1967.

Braudel, Fernand. *The Structures of Everyday Life, Vol. 1*. Trans. Siân Reynolds. New York: Harper and Row, 1981.

Brecht, Stefan. *Queer Theatre*. London: Methuen, 1986.

Brooks, Peter. *Realist Vision*. New Haven, Conn.: Yale University Press, 2005.

Brown, Bill. *A Sense of Things: The Object Matter of American Literature*. Chicago: University of Chicago Press, 2003.

———, ed. *Things*. Chicago: University of Chicago Press, 2004.

Brustein, Robert. "America's New Culture Hero: Feelings without Words." *Commentary* 25 (February 1958): 123–29.

Bryer, Jackson R., ed. *Conversations with Thornton Wilder*. Jackson: University Press of Mississippi, 1992.

Burger, Peter. *The Theory of the Avant-Garde*. Trans. Michael Shane. Minneapolis: University of Minnesota Press, 1984.

Burns, Edward M., and Ulla E. Dydo, with William Rice, eds. *The Letters of Gertrude Stein and Thornton Wilder*. New Haven, Conn.: Yale University Press, 1996.

Cage, John. *Silence: Lectures and Writings*. Middletown, Conn.: Wesleyan University Press, 1973.

Cage, John, Michael Kirby, and Richard Schechner. "An Interview with John Cage." *The Tulane Drama Review* 10, no. 2 (winter 1965): 50–72.

Castronovo, David. *Thornton Wilder*. New York: Ungar, 1986.

Cavell, Stanley. *In Quest of the Ordinary: Lines of Skepticism and Romanticism*. Chicago: University of Chicago Press, 1994.

Clurman, Harold. "Actors in Style—and Style in Acting." *New York Times Magazine*, December 7, 1952, 38.

———. Introduction to Robert Lewis, *Method—or Madness?* xi–xiii. New York: Samuel French, 1958.

Conroy, Marianne. "Acting Out: Method Acting, the National Culture, and the Middlebrow Disposition in Cold War America." *Criticism* 35, no. 2 (1993): 239–52.

Copper, Kelly, and Amber Reed. "Getting Cosmic with Kelly Copper." *The Brooklyn Rail*, December 2006.

Cramer, Jeffery S., ed. *I to Myself: An Annotated Selection from the Journal of Henry D. Thoreau*. New Haven, Conn.: Yale University Press, 2012.

Crandell, George. "Misrepresentation and Miscegenation: Reading the Racialized Discourse of Tennessee Williams's *A Streetcar Named Desire*." *Modern Drama* 40, no. 3 (fall 1997): 337–46.

Crary, Jonathan. *Techniques of the Observer: Vision and Modernity in the Nineteenth Century*. Boston: MIT Press, 1992.

Danto, Arthur. *The Transfiguration of the Commonplace*. Cambridge, Mass.: Harvard University Press, 1981.

Debord, Guy. "Perspectives for Conscious Alterations in Everyday Life." In *The Everyday Life Reader*, ed. Ben Highmore, 237–46. London: Routledge, 2002.

De Certeau, Michel. *The Practice of Everyday Life*. Trans. Steven Rendall. Berkeley: University of California Press, 1988.

Dewey, John. *Art as Experience*. New York: Perigree, 2005.

———. *Experience and Nature*. New York: Dover, 1958.

Douglas, Ann. *Terrible Honesty: Mongrel Manhattan in the 1920s*. New York: Farrar, Straus and Giroux, 1995.

Eklund, Douglas. *The Pictures Generation: 1974–1984*. New York: Metropolitan Museum of Art, 2009.

Emerson, Ralph Waldo. *Emerson: Essays and Lectures*, ed. Joel Porte. New York: Library of America, 1983.

Enelow, Shonni. *Method Acting and Its Discontents: On American Psychodrama*. Evanston, Ill.: Northwestern University Press, 2015.

Felski, Rita. Introduction to "Everyday Life," special issue, *New Literary History* 33, no. 4 (2002), 607–22.

Fisher, Philip. *Wonder, the Rainbow, and the Aesthetics of Rare Experiences*. Cambridge, Mass.: Harvard University Press, 1998.

Fried, Michael. *Art and Objecthood: Essays and Reviews*. Chicago: University of Chicago Press, 1998.

———. *Why Photography Matters as Art as Never Before*. New Haven, Conn.: Yale University Press, 2008.

Gallagher-Ross, Jacob. "Dancing to the Cosmic Murmur: John Cage, Richard Foreman, and Nature Theater of Oklahoma's *No Dice*." *TheatreForum* 34 (winter 2009): 92–98.

———. "Maxwell's Ghosts: The New York City Players' *Ads*." *PAJ: Performing Arts Journal* 98 (2011): 44–50.

———. "Mediating the Method." *Theatre Survey* 56, no. 3 (2015): 291–313.

———. "This Is Your Life: Nature Theater of Oklahoma's *The Life and Times*, One Episode In." *PAJ: Performing Arts Journal* 102 (2012): 63–70.

Gallup, Ronald, ed. *The Journals of Thornton Wilder 1939–1961*. New Haven, Conn.: Yale University Press, 1985.

Gann, Kyle. *No Such Thing as Silence: John Cage's 4'33"*. New Haven, Conn.: Yale University Press, 2010.

Gosetti-Ferencei, Jennifer Anna. *The Ecstatic Quotidian: Phenomenological Sightings in Art and Literature*. Philadelphia: University of Pennsylvania Press, 2007.

Greenberg, Clement. *The Collected Essays and Criticism, Volume Four: Modernism with a Vengeance, 1957–1969*. Chicago: University of Chicago Press, 1993.

Groys, Boris. *Art Power*. Cambridge, Mass.: MIT Press, 2008.

Grubbs, David. *Records Ruin the Landscape: John Cage, the Sixties, and Sound Recording*. Durham, N.C.: Duke University Press, 2014.

Guénon, Solange. "Cinematographic Image, Democracy, and the 'Splendor of the Insignificant': Interview with Jacques Rancière." *Sites: The Journal of Contemporary Francophone Studies* 4, no. 2 (fall 2000): 249–58.

Harding, James. *The Ghosts of the Avant-Garde(s): Exorcising Experimental Theater and Performance*. Ann Arbor: University of Michigan Press, 2013.

Hawkins, Yolanda. "Quotidian Performance." In *Beginningless Thought/Endless Seeing: The Works of Stuart Sherman*, 30–40. New York: 80SWE, 2009.

Heidegger, Martin. "The Thing." In *Poetry Language Thought*, trans. Albert Hofstadter. New York: Harper and Row, 1971.

Heller, Agnes. *Everyday Life*. London: Routledge, 1984.

Hethmon, Robert, ed. *Strasberg at the Actors Studio: Tape Recorded Sessions*. New York: Viking, 1965.

Highmore, Ben. "Bitter After Taste: Affect, Food and Social Aesthetics." In *The Affect Theory Reader*, ed. Melissa Gregg and Gregory J. Seigworth, 118–37. Durham, N.C.: Duke University Press, 2010.

———. *Everyday Life and Cultural Theory*. New York: Routledge, 2001.

———. *The Everyday Life Reader*. New York: Routledge, 2001.

———. *Ordinary Lives*. London: Routledge, 2011.

Holzapfel, Amy. *Art, Vision, and Nineteenth-Century Realism: Acts of Seeing*. New York: Routledge, 2014.

Hunka, George. "The Booking of the Play." *Theater* 40, no. 2 (winter 2010): 19–31.

James, William. *Essays in Radical Empiricism*. Lincoln: University of Nebraska Press, 1996.

Jameson, Fredric. *The Antinomies of Realism*. London: Verso, 2013.

Jay, Martin. *Songs of Experience: Modern American and European Variations on a Universal Theme*. Berkeley: University of California Press, 2006.

Johnson, Barbara. *Persons and Things*. Cambridge, Mass.: Harvard University Press, 2008.

Johnstone, Stephen, ed. *The Everyday (Documents in Contemporary Art)*. Boston: MIT Press, 2008.

Kafka, Franz. *Amerika*. Trans. Willa Muir and Edwin Muir. New York: Schocken, 1996.

Kaprow, Allan. *Essays on the Blurring of Art and Life*. Berkeley: University of California Press, 2003.

Katz, Jonathan. "John Cage's Queer Silence: or, How to Avoid Making Matters Worse." *GLQ: A Journal of Lesbian and Gay Studies* 5, no. 2 (1999): 231–52.

Kazan, Elia. *Kazan on Directing*. New York: Vintage, 2009.

Keithley, Karinne. "Uncreative Writing: Nature Theater of Oklahoma's *Romeo and Juliet*." *Theater* 40, no. 2 (winter 2010): 67–73.

Kern, Stephen. *The Culture of Time and Space, 1880–1918*. Cambridge, Mass.: Harvard University Press, 2003.

Kirby, Michael, and Richard Schechner. "An Interview with John Cage." *The Drama Review: Thirty Years of Commentary on the Avant-Garde*, ed. Brooks McNamara and Jill Dolan, 79–99. Ann Arbor: University of Michigan Press, 1986.

Kittler, Friedrich A. *Gramophone, Film, Typewriter*. Trans. Geoffrey Winthrop-Young and Michael Wutz. Stanford, Calif.: Stanford University Press, 1999.

Konkle, Lincoln. *Thornton Wilder and the Puritan Narrative Tradition*. Columbia: University of Missouri Press, 2006.

Kostelanetz, Richard, ed. *John Cage*. New York: Praeger, 1970.

Krasner, David. *Method Acting Reconsidered: Theory, Practice, Future*. New York: St. Martin's, 2000.

Lambert-Beatty, Carrie. *Being Watched: Yvonne Rainer and the 1960s*. Cambridge, Mass.: MIT Press, 2008.

Landy, Joshua, and Michael Saler, eds. *The Re-Enchantment of the World: Secular Magic in a Rational Age*. Stanford, Calif.: Stanford University Press, 2009.

Lee, Young Jean. "Nature Theater of Oklahoma." *BOMB* 108 (summer 2009): 88–94.

LeFebvre, Henri. *Critique of Everyday Life, Volume I*. London: Verso, 2008.

———. *Everyday Life in the Modern World*. New York: Transaction, 1984.

Lehmann, Hans-Thies. *Postdramatic Theatre*. Trans. Karen Jurs-Munby. New York: Routledge, 2006.

Leonard, George J. *Into the Light of Things: The Art of the Commonplace from Wordsworth to John Cage*. Chicago: University of Chicago Press, 1994.

Levine, Lawrence. *Highbrow/Lowbrow: The Emergence of Cultural Hierarchy in America*. Cambridge, Mass.: Harvard University Press, 1986.

Lewis, Robert. *Method—or Madness?* New York: Samuel French, 1958.

Lifton, Paul. *"Vast Encyclopedia": The Theatre of Thornton Wilder*. Westport, Conn.: Greenwood, 1995.

Macdonald, Dwight. *Against the American Grain*. New York: Da Capo, 1983.

Malague, Rosemary. *An Actress Prepares: Women and "the Method."* New York: Routledge, 2012.

Mangolte, Babette. "Stuart Sherman: Performer and Performance Artist." In *Beginningless Thought/Endless Seeing: The Works of Stuart Sherman*, 18–22. New York: 80SWE, 2009.

Marks, Laura. "Video Haptics and Erotics." *Screen* 39, no. 4 (winter 1998): 331–48.

Marranca, Bonnie. *The Theatre of Images*. New York: PAJ Books, 2005.

Matturi, John. "Legible Worlds: The Early Drawings of Stuart Sherman." In *Beginningless Thought/Endless Seeing: The Works of Stuart Sherman*, 78–95. New York: 80SWE, 2009.

Maxwell, Richard. "Ads: Artist's Preface." *Theater* 40, no. 3 (summer 2010): 68–69.

McGinley, Paige. "Reconsidering the "American Style": Black Performers and Black Music in *Streetcar* and *Cat*." *Theatre Journal* 68, no. 1 (March 2016): 1–15.

McKinley, Jesse. "Playwright's Trademark Is Deadpan: Now He Wants to Tweak It." *The New York Times*, January 18, 2006.

McNamara, Brooks. "Stuart Sherman's Third Spectacle." *The Drama Review* 20, no. 2, "American Theatre" issue (June 1976): 47–55.

Merleau-Ponty, Maurice. *Sense and Nonsense*. Trans. Hubert L. Dreyfus and Patricia A. Dreyfus. Evanston, Ill.: Northwestern University Press, 1964.

Miller, Arthur. "The Family in Modern Drama." In *The Theater Essays of Arthur Miller*, ed. Robert A. Martin and Steve Centola, 69–84. New York: Da Capo, 1996.

———. "Tragedy and the Common Man." In *Dramatic Theory and Criticism: Greeks to Grotowski*, ed. Bernard F. Dukore, 894–97. Boston: Thomson Heinle, 1974.

Moi, Toril. *Ibsen and the Birth of Modernism: Art, Theater, Philosophy*. Oxford: Oxford University Press, 2006.

Muñoz, Jose Esteban. *Cruising Utopia: The Then and There of Queer Futurity*. New York: New York University Press, 2009.

Murphy, Brenda. *Tennessee Williams and Elia Kazan: A Collaboration in the Theatre.* New York: Cambridge University Press, 1992.
Nature Theater of Oklahoma. *Life and Times, Episode One.* New York: 53rd State, 2011.
———. *Life and Times, Episode Two.* New York: 53rd State, 2013.
———. *Life and Times, Episodes Three and Four.* New York: 53rd State, 2013.
———. "*Nature Theater of Oklahoma's Romeo and Juliet.*" *Theater* 40, no. 2 (winter 2010): 74–113.
———. *No Dice.* New York: 53rd State, 2007.
Niven, Penelope. *Thornton Wilder: A Life.* New York: HarperCollins, 2012.
Olson, Liesl. *Modernism and the Ordinary.* Oxford: Oxford University Press, 2009.
Perloff, Marjorie. *The Poetics of Indeterminacy: Rimbaud to Cage.* Evanston, Ill.: Northwestern University Press, 1981.
Phillips, Siobhan. "The Daily Living of Robert Frost." *PMLA* 123, no. 3 (2008): 598–613.
———. *The Poetics of the Everyday: Creative Repetition in Modern American Verse.* New York: Columbia University Press, 2009.
Puchner, Martin. *Stage Fright: Modernism, Anti-Theatricality, and Drama.* Baltimore: Johns Hopkins University Press, 2002.
Rancière, Jacques. *Dissensus: On Politics and Aesthetics.* London: Continuum, 2010.
———. *The Politics of Aesthetics: The Distribution of the Sensible.* New York: Continuum, 2004.
Randall, Bryony. *Modernism, Daily Time, and Everyday Life.* New York: Cambridge University Press, 2007.
Read, Alan. *Theatre and Everyday Life: An Ethics of Performance.* New York: Routledge, 1993.
Reynaud, Berenice. "Stuart Sherman: Object Ritual." Trans. Thomas Repensek. *October* 8 (spring 1979): 58–74.
Ridout, Nicholas. *Passionate Amateurs.* Ann Arbor: University of Michigan Press, 2013.
Roach, Joseph R. "The Great Hole of History: Liturgical Silence in Beckett, Osofisan, and Parks." *The South Atlantic Quarterly* 100, no. 1 (2001): 307–17.
———. "Kinesis: The New Mimesis." *Theater* 40, no. 1 (2010): 1–2.
Robertson, Campbell. "Theater Team Makes an Ally of Random Circumstance." *The New York Times*, January 3, 2008.
Robinson, Marc. *The American Play: 1787–2000.* New Haven, Conn.: Yale University Press, 2009.
Rogoff, Gordon. "Lee Strasberg: Burning Ice." *The Tulane Drama Review* 9, no. 2 (winter 1964): 139–51.
Ross, Kristin. *Fast Cars and Clean Bodies: Decolonization and the Reordering of French Culture.* Cambridge, Mass.: MIT Press, 1996.
Sanders, Jay, and J. Hoberman, eds. *Rituals of Rented Island.* New Haven, Conn.: Whitney Museum/Yale University Press, 2013.
Sayre, Henry M. *The Object of Performance: The American Avant-Garde since 1970.* Chicago: University of Chicago Press, 1989.
Schechner, Richard. *Performance Theory.* New York: Routledge, 2003.

Schjeldahl, Peter. *Let's See: Writings on Art from "The New Yorker."* New York: Thames and Hudson, 208.

Schneider, Rebecca. *Performing Remains: Art and War in Times of Theatrical Re-Enactment.* London: Routledge, 2011.

Schoenbach, Lisi. *Pragmatic Modernism.* Oxford: Oxford University Press, 2012.

Scott, Trudy. "Stuart Sherman's Singular Spectacles." *The Drama Review* 23, no. 1, "Autoperformance" issue (March 1979): 69–78.

Shakespeare, William. *The Oxford Shakespeare: The Complete Works.* Ed. Stanley Wells and Gary Taylor. Oxford: Oxford University Press, 2005.

Sherman, Stuart. "Journals—Loose Sheets." Stuart Sherman Papers, series III, box I, folder 26, Downtown Collection, Fales Library, New York University, n.p.

———. "Misc. Notes and Poetry—Loose Sheets and Notebook." Stuart Sherman Papers, series III, box I, folder 28, Downtown Collection, Fales Library, New York University, n.p.

———. "Reviews by Stuart Sherman." Stuart Sherman Papers, series III, box I, folder 31, Downtown Collection, Fales Library, New York University, n.p.

Shklovsky, Viktor. "Art as Technique." In *The Critical Tradition*, ed. David H. Richter, 778. New York: Bedford/St. Martin's, 1997.

Sofer, Andrew. *The Stage Life of Props.* Ann Arbor: University of Michigan Press, 2003.

States, Bert O. *Great Reckonings in Little Rooms: On the Phenomenology of Theater.* Berkeley: University of California Press, 1985.

Stewart, Kathleen. *Ordinary Affects.* Durham, N.C.: Duke University Press, 2007.

Strasberg, Lee. *A Dream of Passion.* New York: Plume, 1985.

———. *The Lee Strasberg Notes.* New York: Routledge, 2010.

Suárez, Juan A. *Pop Modernism: Noise and the Reinvention of the Everyday.* Urbana: University of Illinois Press, 2007.

Switzky, Lawrence. "Marathon Theatre as Affective Labour: Productive Exhaustion in the *Godot Cycle* and *Life and Times.*" *Canadian Theatre Review* 162 (spring 2015): 26–30.

Szondi, Peter. *The Theory of the Modern Drama.* Minneapolis: University of Minnesota Press, 1987.

Taubman, Howard. "A Tender *Three Sisters.*" *The New York Times,* June 23, 1964.

Taussig, Michael. "Physiognomic Aspects of Visual Worlds." *Visual Anthropology Review* 8, no. 1 (spring 1992): 15–28.

Taylor, Diana. *The Archive and the Repertoire: Performing Cultural Memory in the Americas.* Durham, N.C.: Duke University Press, 2003.

Trilling, Lionel. *Sincerity and Authenticity.* Cambridge, Mass.: Harvard University Press, 1972.

Warner, Michael. *Publics and Counterpublics.* New York: Zone Books, 2005.

Weber, Max. *The Essential Weber.* Ed. Sam Whimster. London: Routledge, 2004.

———. "The Vocation of Science." In *The Essential Weber,* ed. Sam Whimster, 270–87. London: Routledge, 2004.

Weinberg, Barbara H., ed. *American Stories: Paintings of Everyday Life, 1765–1915.* New York: Metropolitan Museum of Art, 2009.

Wheatley, Christopher J. *Thornton Wilder & Amos Wilder: Writing Religion in Twentieth Century America.* Notre Dame, Ind.: Notre Dame University Press, 2011.

Whitman, Walt. *Poetry and Prose*. Ed. Justin Kaplan. New York: Library of America, 1982.

———. *The Portable Walt Whitman*. New York: Penguin, 2003.

Wickstrom, Maurya. *Performing Consumers: Global Capital and Its Theatrical Seductions*. New York: Routledge, 2006.

Wilder, Amos Niven. *Thornton Wilder and His Public*. Philadelphia: Fortress, 1980.

Wilder, Robin G., and Jackson R. Bryer, eds. *The Selected Letters of Thornton Wilder*. New York: Harper Perennial, 2009.

Wilder, Tappan. "Afterword to *Our Town: A Play in Three Acts*," by Thornton Wilder, 113–72. New York: HarperCollins, 2003.

Wilder, Thornton. *American Characteristics and Other Essays*. New York: Harper and Row, 1979.

———. *Collected Plays & Writings on Theater*. Ed. J. D. McClatchy. New York: Library of America, 2007.

Williams, Raymond. *Drama from Ibsen to Brecht*. New York: Oxford University Press, 1969.

Wittgenstein, Ludwig. *Culture and Value*. Cambridge: Blackwell, 1998.

Wolf, Gary. "Know Thyself: Tracking Every Facet of Life from Sleep to Mood to Pain, 24/7/365." *Wired*, June 22, 2009.

Worthen, W. B. *Shakespeare Performance Studies*. New York: Cambridge University Press, 2014.

Yeazell, Ruth. *Art of the Everyday: Dutch Painting and the Realist Novel*. Princeton, N.J.: Princeton University Press, 2008.

Youker, Timothy. "'His Own House of Thought': Thornton Wilder's 'American Loneliness' and the Consolation of Theater." *The Journal of American Drama and Theatre* 24, no. 2 (spring 2012): 89–108.

INDEX

Actors Studio, 75–76, 80, 81–82, 84, 89. *See also* Method acting
Adler, Stella, 75, 96
affect, 12, 71, 78; affective memory, 75, 83–84; affective recall, 86, 87; affect studies, 13
"America" concept, 25–26, 152
Anderson-Rabern, Rachel, 218n20
Aronson, Arnold, 120
Arsic, Branka, 19, 30, 41–42, 50, 64, 68
art and life distinction, 6, 7, 8, 17–24, 30, 33, 35, 43; Cavell on, 19, 42, 45; Dewey on, 155; Method acting and, 82–83; Nature Theater of Oklahoma and, 147, 148, 151, 152–53, 159–60, 175; Wilder and, 72. *See also* experience and art
Ashbery, John, 159, 163
audiences. *See* spectatorship
Auerbach, Erich, 10
Auslander, Philip, 28
avant-gardism, 5, 6, 7–8, 10, 15, 16–19, 22, 29–30, 32–33, 54, 75

Bachelard, Gaston, 17, 143
Baker, Annie, 6
Baker, Benjamin, 9
Banes, Sally, 32–33
Barthes, Roland, 52, 71, 195, 196
Belasco, David, 9
Benjamin, Walter: on advertising, 199; on film, 30, 199; on "optical unconscious," 26, 78, 86
Bennett, Jane, 11, 13, 28
Bercovitch, Sacvan, 25
Bernstein, Robin, 122–23
Bhutia, Lakpa, 194
Blanchot, Maurice, 4, 7, 17; on the everyday, 148, 155
Blum, Richard, 75
Brando, Marlon, 3, 77, 78–79, 82, 84, 91, 95–103, 196
Braudel, Fernand, 4, 14
Brecht, Bertolt, 15, 35, 40
Brecht, Stefan, 107, 120, 140
Brooks, Peter, 48–49
Brown, Bill, 122, 123, 128
Brustein, Robert, 76–77, 78, 93, 94, 96, 98, 100–101
Burger, Peter, 18, 22

Cage, John, 17, 19, 29, 56, 97, 103, 128, 148, 153; *4' 33"*, 5, 54; on film, 103; influence on Nature Theater of Oklahoma, 34, 151, 167, 173–75; noise and, 24, 75–76, 157–58
Castronovo, David, 37
Cavell, Stanley, 19, 42, 45
Certeau, Michel de, 16–17
Cézanne, Paul, 134
Chekhov, Anton, 91, 95, 121
Childs, Lucinda, 141
Clurman, Harold, 84, 94
Connolly, Keith, 196
Conroy, Marianne, 83, 96, 98
Copper, Kelly, 147, 150–54, 158, 167, 175; *The Life and Times* and, 184–85; in *No Dice*, 170–71; *Romeo and Juliet* and, 178, 180. *See also* Nature Theater of Oklahoma
Crandell, George, 100

Danto, Arthur, 5, 14
Davidovitch, Jaime, 116
Dean, James, 77, 83, 84, 100
Debord, Guy, 14–16, 20
defamiliarization. *See* estrangement
democratization of art, 8–9, 22–23, 45, 64, 125

Dewey, John, 11, 19, 23, 25, 27, 202; on consummation, 20–21, 31, 43, 155, 192, 202; Wilder and, 41, 43, 45, 53
Dickinson, Emily, 50, 55
digital culture and social media, 35, 193–95, 198–202
disenchantment and re-enchantment, 10–13, 28–29, 206n23; Nature Theater of Oklahoma and, 148; Sherman and, 128, 134
Douglas, Ann, 38
dramatic conventions, 5–6, 33, 63; Nature Theater's use of, 153–54, 156, 186
Duchamp, Marcel, 5, 14, 17, 151

Eklund, Douglas, 188
Eliot, T. S., 45
Emerson, Ralph Waldo, 19–20, 30, 50–51, 68; Nature Theater and, 20, 152; Wilder and, 41–42
Enelow, Shonni, 93
estrangement (defamiliarization), 12, 15, 24; of language, 67; Sherman and, 106
everyday, the: Blanchot on, 148, 155; Cage on, 174; definitions of, 3–5, 10, 12; density of, 48; dramatic use of, 6–10, 11, 12–14, 17, 18, 22, 24, 29, 32; Emerson on, 41, 152; French theory on, 14–17; Gosetti-Ferencei on, 119, 135; negative views of, 5–6, 10; noise and, 79; queerness and, 24–25; in theater history, 9–10, 29; "unconscious" of, 26; Weber on, 10–11; Wittgenstein on, 4, 7, 80, 87. *See also under featured artists*
experience and art, 11–12, 17, 18, 27–28, 45; Dewey's *Art as Experience*, 20–21, 43; experiential purity, 53–54

Feldman, Bob, 194
Felski, Rita, 4, 15–17
Felton-Dansky, Miriam, 217n62
film, 75–76, 79, 96–103, 197; Cage on, 103
Fisher, Philip, 114, 144
Fitzgerald, F. Scott, 212n114
Foreman, Richard, 120, 123; influence on Nature Theater, 167–69, 171–73, 175, 177
Foucault, Michel, 16
Fried, Michael, 54

Garfield, John, 77
gazing vs. glancing, 51
gender: the everyday and, 9; Method acting and, 78, 92, 98; in Rosler's *Semiotics of the Kitchen*, 141; in Sherman's *Eleventh Spectacle*, 140–41
Glaspell, Susan, 9
Gosetti-Ferencei, Jennifer Anna, 118, 133–34, 135
Gridley, Anne, 171, 180
Groys, Boris, 13, 176

Happenings, 20, 32–33
Harding, James, 7–8, 21, 207n52
Harrell, Trajal, 9
Hawkins, Yolanda, 116
Hegel, Georg Wilhelm Friedrich, 18
Heidegger, Martin, 136–37, 144
Hethmon, Robert H., 88–89, 91–92
Highmore, Ben, 14, 20, 35, 68
Hoberman, Jay, 128
Holzapafel, Amy, 206n22
Hunka, George, 178–79
Hurston, Zora Neale, 9

James, William, 19, 27; Wilder and, 41, 53
Jameson, Fredric, 6, 10, 12, 52, 71
Jay, Martin, 21–22
Johanson, Robert M., 180, 186
Judson Dance Theater, 13, 30, 33–34, 151, 166

Kafka, Franz, 28; *Amerika*, 147, 148, 149–50, 160, 192, 212n114
Kaprow, Allan, 20
Katz, Jonathan, 24
Kazan, Elia, 30, 76, 77, 93, 96–102
Keithley, Karinne, 152
Kelly, Kevin, 200
Kern, Stephen, 52
Kirby, Michael, 29
kitsch, 13, 127, 172
Kittler, Friedrich, 27, 78–79, 195

Klein, Naomi, 199
Konkle, Lincoln, 39

Lambert-Beatty, Carrie, 33
Landy, Joshua, 206n23
Lee, Young Jean, 150–51
Lefebvre, Henri, 11–12, 14–16
Lehmann, Hans–Thies, 18
Leigh, Vivien, 98, 99
Leonard, George, 19–20
Levine, Lawrence, 177
Lévi-Strauss, Claude, 135
Lewis, Robert, 76, 84, 94–95
Lifton, Paul, 39
Liška, Pavol, 24, 147, 150–53, 156, 167, 173, 175; in *The Life and Times*, 185; in *No Dice*, 171, 176; in *Romeo and Juliet*, 180. *See also* Nature Theater of Oklahoma
Living Theatre, 6
Ludlam, Charles, 120

Macdonald, Dwight, 44–45, 47
Magritte, René, 144
Malague, Rosemary, 93
Mangolte, Babette, 120
Manheim, Kate, 120, 121, 123
Marks, Laura, 98
Marranca, Bonnie, 120
Matturi, John, 112, 113
Maxwell, Richard, *Ads*, 35, 193–202
McGinley, Paige, 100
McNamara, Brooks, 110, 116, 120, 126
mediated performance, 28, 30; Method acting and, 77–78, 79, 82, 95, 97, 99
Merleau-Ponty, Maurice, 134–35
Method acting, 3, 23, 34, 75–103, 194; hypothetical actor description, 77; "noise" (mumbling, slurring, sobbing) in, 9, 13, 26–27, 29–30, 32, 76, 79, 84, 9, 93, 95, 96–97, 101; recording technology and, 27, 30, 32, 79, 82, 84–92, 94, 96. *See also* art and life distinction; gender; race; Strasberg, Lee
Miller, Arthur, 6, 72
modernism, 21, 23, 27, 29–30, 45; Method acting and, 83; noise and, 79; objects and, 128; "pragmatic," 7–8; Wilder and, 31, 38, 50, 65
Moi, Toril, 18
Moissi, Alexansder, 84
Muñoz, Jose Esteban, 25

naturalism, 18, 30, 46–48
Nature Theater of Oklahoma, 3–4, 13, 23–24, 26–27, 30, 32, 34, 56, 147–92; acting style, 150, 159, 172; casts, 147–48; Dewey and, 155, 217n10; Emerson and, 20, 152; the everyday and, 121, 148, 151, 152–55, 175; "noise" (mumbling, stuttering, fumbling) and, 27, 147, 156, 163, 186; recording technology and, 148–49, 156–59, 172, 201. *See also* art and life distinction; spectatorship
  PRODUCTIONS: *Empire!*, 157; *The Life and Times*, 72, 151, 152, 154, 158, 184–92; *No Dice*, 148, 151, 154, 167–77, 184, 186, 218n30; *Poetics: a ballet brut*, 148, 151, 154, 160–67, 173, 178, 182, 186; *Rambo Solo*, 151, 154, 183–84; *Romeo and Juliet*, 148, 151, 152, 154, 157, 158, 177–83, 186
Newman, John Henry, 64
Newman, Paul, 77
New York City Players, 193
Niven, Penelope, 37
noise, 24–26, 28; Cage's use of, 24, 75, 76, 157–58; new media and, 78; queerness and, 24–25; in *A Streetcar Named Desire*, 96–100, 102; Wilder's use of, 59. *See also under* Method acting; Nature Theater of Oklahoma

Oberzan, Zachary, 183
Odets, Clifford, 85, 88, 97
Olson, Liesl, 16
O'Neill, Eugene, 6, 29, 63
On the Waterfront (film), 96, 102
oral histories, 157

Parks, Suzan-Lori, 8
Paxton, Steve, 166
"Pepper's Ghost," 195
Perloff, Marjorie, 152–53
Phillips, Siobhan, 57, 159, 163
photography theory, 195
Pirandello, Luigi, 41
Presley, Elvis, 100–101

queerness, 24–25, 140. *See also* noise; Sherman, Stuart

race: the everyday and, 9, 101; Method acting and, 9, 78, 100–101; in *A Streetcar Named Desire*, 100–101
Rainer, Yvonne, 33, 166
Rambo franchise, 183
Rancière, Jacques, 5, 35, 145–46, 207n53
Rauschenberg, Robert, 34, 115, 128
Read, Allan, 16
ready-made and found objects, 5, 10, 12, 13–14, 19, 56, 75, 128; Copper and, 158; dada and, 151; Heidegger's "ready-at-hand," 136–37; Maxwell and, 194–95
realism, 5–6, 7, 23, 29, 52–54; the everyday vs., 48–49, 71–72; Holzapafel on, 206n22; Jameson on, 10, 12, 52; Method acting and, 75; Sherman and, 120–22, 123; Wilder and, 47–48, 55, 63, 120
recording and reproduction technology, 26–29, 30, 73, 75–76, 78–79, 82, 100–103, 195. *See also under* Method acting; Nature Theater of Oklahoma
Redgrave, Michael, 95
Reed, Amber, 158
Reynaud, Berenice, 126–31, 215n21
Ridout, Nicholas, 218n30
Rimini Protokoll, 157
Roach, Joseph, 70
Robinson, Marc, 34, 39–40, 46, 55, 57
Rogoff, Gordon, 90
Rosler, Martha, 141
Ross, Kristin, 14

Saler, Michael, 206n23
Salvini, Tommaso, 84, 213n19
Schechner, Richard, 29, 173
Schjeldahl, Peter, 7
Schneider, Rebecca, 26
Schoenbach, Lisi, 7
Scott, Trudy, 108, 112, 120, 126
Shakespeare, William, 92; *Nature Theater of Oklahoma's Romeo and Juliet*, 157, 177–82, 218n46
Sherman, Stuart, 3, 7, 9, 13, 25–27, 32, 56, 105–46; acting career, 120; communion and, 117, 125, 132, 134, 144, 215n21; critical response to, 108, 110, 112, 116, 120, 126–31; cutouts and silhouettes in, 144–45; drawings, 112–13; Emerson and, 20; the everyday and, 105–6, 108, 112, 116, 120, 121, 130, 139, 144; images and, 34, 111; miniscule in, 142–43; object manipulations, 106, 107–10, 111, 115, 117, 121–23, 127, 129–30, 135, 136–37, 146; pacing in, 108–9, 110; posthumous fame, 119–20; queerness and, 24–25, 140–41; *Quotidian Review*, 106; sculptures and installations, 115; Wilder and, 120–21; writings, 118, 119, 131. *See also under* realism; spectatorship
  SPECTACLES: 23, 24, 29–30, 30–31, 105–7, 110–11, 116–17, 126, 128, 132–33, 145–46; *Chekhov Spectacle*, 121; *First Spectacle*, 115–16, 119, 120, 123–24; *Second*, 107, 120, 121–22, 123; *Seventh*, 113–14; *Eighth*, 106–7; *Eleventh*, 108, 128–30, 132–33, 140–41; *Twelfth*, 109–10, 119, 144–45; *Fifteenth*, 107, 118, 124–25, 135–36, 137–39, 142–43; eighteenth (*Queer Spectacle*), 140
Shklovsky, Viktor, 12
Smith, Anna Deavere, 157
Smith, Jack, 172
Snowden, Edward, 200
social media. *See* digital culture
Sofer, Andrew, 117
Song of Hiawatha, The (Longfellow), 61
Sontag, Susan, 195
spectatorship, 34–35, 201; Method acting and, 81–82; Nature Theater and, 153–54, 155, 158–59, 164, 169–70, 175, 181–82; Sherman and, 108–9, 113–14, 117, 121, 215n21; Wilder and, 40, 44–45, 49–50, 52–53, 56, 64, 68, 73, 164
Stanislavski, Konstanin, 75, 96
States, Bert, 49, 121, 122
Stein, Gertrude, 38, 53, 56, 153, 167
Stieglitz, Alfred, 94

Strasberg, Lee, 3, 30, 75, 76, 78–95, 97, 99; on acting, 85, 88, 91; *A Dream of Passion*, 93; Emerson and, 20; everyday speech in, 23, 24, 56; pedagogical tools of, 82, 92, 94; "private-moment" exercise, 80–81; *Strasberg at the Actors Studio*, 83–88, 90–92, 93, 95, 98. *See also* Method acting
Streetcar Named Desire, A (play and film), 6, 77, 93, 95–102
Strindberg, August, 48
Suárez, Juan A., 79, 101, 208n66
Switzky, Lawrence, 184
Szondi, Peter, 18, 52, 57

Tandy, Jessica, 98
Taubman, Howard, 95
Taussig, Michael, 133, 134, 199
Taylor, Diana, 34, 72, 155–56, 190
teleology, 15, 20
theatricality, 16, 52, 54, 99, 112, 123, 127
Thoreau, Henry David, 19, 30, 42, 45; Wilder and, 41, 42, 57–58
time: changing perceptions of, 52; personal vs. historical, 56, 73, 210n65
Trilling, Lionel, 196
Trojan Women, The (Euripides), 55

Valk, Kate, 198
Vega, Lope de, 37

Wallach, Eli, 77
Warhol, Andy, 5, 19, 20, 34, 128, 157
Warner, Michael, 22–23
Weber, Max, 10–11; iron cage trope, 11, 13, 29, 201–2
Wheatley, Christopher, 39
Whitehead, Alfred North, 53
Whitman, Walt, 157
Wickstrom, Maurya, 199
Wilder, Amos, 39, 45, 50
Wilder, Isabel, 41
Wilder, Thornton, 9, 13, 25, 27–28, 29–32, 37–73, 146, 298n31; authorial comments on *Our Town*, 38, 53, 55–56, 60, 70, 72, 176; autobiographical elements in plays, 50; bare stages in, 38, 47, 49–51, 54, 55, 71; departure and motion in, 26,38–44, 46, 47, 49–50, 56, 58, 69–70, 73, 211n114; Emerson and, 20; the everyday in, 3, 4, 34, 38–49, 56–58, 64, 71–73; influences on, 40–41; innovations of, 40–41; lists in, 60–61; normative, nostalgic assumptions about, 38–39, 44–45, 56, 69, 70; queerness and, 24–25; seeing in, 51, 61, 65, 66, 202; Stage Manager figure in, 38, 46–47, 54–55, 59, 61, 62–63, 64, 65, 66, 69–71; time in, 52–53, 56–57, 64, 69–70, 210n65. *See also* art and life distinction; realism; spectatorship
  WORKS: *American Characteristics*, 40, 42, 43, 48, 61; *The Happy Journey to Trenton and Camden*, 38, 46, 49–50, 54, 56, 64–68; *The Long Christmas Dinner*, 38, 46, 49–50, 56–59, 70, 73; *Our Town*, 23, 30, 35, 42, 45, 46, 49, 60, 65, 69–73; *Pullman Car Hiawatha*, 23, 38, 46, 49–50, 54–55, 56, 59–64, 68, 71, 211n114
Williams, Raymond, 23, 35
Williams, Tennessee. *See A Streetcar Named Desire*
Wilson, Robert, 8–9, 120
Witkiewicz, Stanisław Ignacy, 212n114
Wittgenstein, Ludwig, 4, 7, 80, 81, 87, 144
Wolf, Gary, 200
Worrall, Kristin, 184–92
Worthen, W. B., 180, 182, 218n46

Yates, Frances, 119
Youker, Timothy, 209n31